D1559550

Democracy and the Political Unconscious

New Directions in Critical Theory

AMY ALLEN, GENERAL EDITOR

New Directions in Critical Theory presents outstanding classic and contemporary texts in the tradition of critical social theory, broadly construed. The series aims to renew and advance the program of critical social theory, with a particular focus on theorizing contemporary struggles around gender, race, sexuality, class, and globalization and their complex interconnections.

Narrating Evil: A Postmetaphysical Theory of Reflective Judgment, MARÍA PÍA LARA

The Politics of Our Selves: Power, Autonomy, and Gender in Contemporary Critical Theory, AMY ALLEN

The Force of the Example: Explorations in the Paradigm of Judgment, ALESSANDRO FERRARA

DEMOCRACY AND THE
POLITICAL UNCONSCIOUS

Noëlle McAfee

Columbia University Press   New York

Columbia University Press

Publishers Since 1893

New York   Chichester, West Sussex

Copyright © 2008 Columbia University Press

Library of Congress Cataloging-in-Publication Data

McAfee, Noëlle, 1960–

Democracy and the political unconscious / Noëlle McAfee.

p.   cm. — (New directions in critical theory)

Includes bibliographical references and index.

ISBN 978-0-231-13880-2 (cloth : alk. paper)

1. Democratization. 2. Democracy. 3. Political science—Philosophy.

4. Political psychology. 5. Critical theory. 6. Feminism—Political aspects.

I. Title. II. Series.

JC423.M38334   2008

321.8—dc22   2007025259

Columbia University Press books are printed on permanent
and durable acid-free paper.
This book was printed on paper with recycled content.

Printed in the United States of America

Designed by Audrey Smith

c 10 9 8 7 6 5 4 3 2 1

CONTENTS

ACKNOWLEDGMENTS

I have several debts to acknowledge. This book took shape with the support of my editor at Columbia University Press, Wendy Lochner, the kind of editor one dreams of: smart, ethical, creative, supportive, available, an ally, a friend, and a wonderful dinner companion. For helping get this book in better shape, I am grateful to Cynthia Willett and Vincent Colapietro, especially for their careful reading of drafts of the manuscript and suggestions for how to improve it. Also, for helping see this book into press, I thank other editors at Columbia University Press, including Christine Mortlock for overseeing logistics and Leslie Kriesel for her superb editing.

John Stuhr has been a great friend and colleague in thinking about how American pragmatism and continental philosophy intersect with contemporary political problems. Kelly Oliver not only guided me through a dissertation a decade ago but also continues to stimulate my thinking about psychoanalysis and politics. Her work on sublimation especially nurtured this book. My sensibilities about democracy were shaped through twenty years of conversations with my dear friend, David Mathews, the president of the Charles F. Kettering Foundation, as well as other Kettering colleagues, namely Bob Kingston and John Dedrick. Also through Kettering and its larger circles, I have learned much from other thinkers who care deeply about democracy, including David Brown, Harry Boyte, the late Cole Campbell, Rich Harwood, Alison Kadlec, Peter Levine, Scott Peters, Harold Saunders, Randa Slim, Claire Snyder, Maxine Thomas, and Debi Witte. This project got started thanks to a Joseph P. Healey Endowment Research Grant from the University of Massachusetts Lowell, which provided funding for a visit to the International Center for Transitional Justice, where I benefited from initial advice from Pablo de Greiff. I thank my colleagues in the philosophy departments at the University of Massachusetts Lowell and George Mason University for their support and ideas for this project, especially Debra Bergoffen, Rose Cherubin, Wayne Froman, Martin de Nys, Robert Innis, Daniel Rothbart, and P. Christopher Smith. I also thank Katherine Arens who, a decade ago at my doctoral dissertation defense, made some comments about Kristeva and public space and Elaine Scarry's work, ideas that I did nothing with at the time but that must have been at work subconsciously when I embarked on this projection. I think this book is something like what she had in mind. I am also grateful to Fredric Jameson for his guidance when I was at Duke and for the ideas sparked by the title of his book, *The Political Unconscious.*

Patricia Aufderheide and the Ford Foundation provided a time for me at American University to work on public media and democracy. Through that venue I also came to know and learn from Barbara Abrash, Orlando Bagwell, Robert Lavelle, Martin Lucas, Rebecca Mackinnon, Karen Menichelli, and Ellen Schneider. Sharon Meagher shares my passion for public philosophy. I also thank the Society for the Advancement of American Philosophy, the Society for Phenomenology and Existential Philosophy, the Western Political Science Association, the Seminar in the Human Sciences at George Washington University, and the Institute for Philosophy and Public Policy at the University of Maryland for opportunities to present earlier versions of this work. I also thank my dear friends, Linda Hesh, Leslie Milofsky, Beth Myler, Ann Carr, Paige Totaro, Vero Autphenne, and Kelly Valceanu, and my family, Erin, Paul, and Marika McAfee and Eliza, Guthrie, and David Armstrong, for helping me fathom what is at stake in the subject of this book.

I have been working out the ending of this book for the past few years, with much of it published as separate articles. Part of chapter 5 was first published in the Kettering Foundation's journal, *Connections*, and another part first appeared in *Revolt, Affect, Collectivity: The Unstable Boundaries of Kristeva's Polis,* edited by Tina Chanter and Ewa Plonowska Ziarek (Albany: The State University of New York Press, 2005). A portion of chapter 7 was published in the *Journal of Speculative Philosophy* 19, no. 2. Chapter 8 first appeared in *Philosophy and Social Criticism* 30, no. 2 (2004): 139–157. Chapter 9 first appeared in the *Journal of Speculative Philosophy* 18, no. 1, and an earlier version of chapter 10 first appeared in the *Kettering Review* 24, no. 1 (Spring 2006): 58–68.

The first part of this book sets up the challenge to which all these later chapters respond. I am grateful for the opportunity to pull this material together into a larger argument and, I hope, a persuasive case for why in times of trouble we need to talk.

Democracy and the Political Unconscious

Introduction

The Sociosymbolic Public Sphere

This book aims to make sense of a pathology unleashed on September 11, 2001—a pathology that had certainly been at work for millennia but now became a more overt threat to peoples around the world. Bizarrely, one of the weapons this pathology wielded was "democracy," not the real thing but an ersatz form in the guise of "democratization," a process of repetition that is anything but democratic. For "their" sake, we invade a people's homeland and root out enemies of democracy, people who "hate our freedoms." The events of September 11 have many old and tangled roots, but one of the more recent ones was the end of the Cold War, when instead of two superpowers that put a hold on internecine ethnic tensions we had one superpower that maintained its position by "being the bully on the block," in the words of Colin Powell, even if that meant taking sides in, and hence adding fuel to, ethnic and religious conflicts, with the purported aim of democratization. Instead of pausing after 9/11 to try to untangle the roots of the conflict, to use the real tools of true democracy—public talk and collective decision making and bridge building—the United States set in motion an endless war on terror, a repetition compulsion that unveiled other repetition compulsions. Note this one, as reported by the BBC, of Saddam Hussein's last moments:

> Dressed in a white shirt and dark suit and overcoat, he was handcuffed with his hands in front of him and carried a copy of the Koran in his hands, which he asked to be given to a friend.
>
> A judge then read out the death sentence.
>
> Judge Haddad described what happened next:
>
> "One of the guards present asked Saddam Hussein whether he was afraid of dying.

Saddam's reply was that 'I spent my whole life fighting the infidels and the intruders,' and another guard asked him: 'Why did you destroy Iraq and destroy us? You starved us and you allowed the Americans to occupy us.'

His reply was, 'I destroyed the invaders and the Persians and I destroyed the enemies of Iraq . . . and I turned Iraq from poverty into wealth.' "

Who were these "Persians" he "destroyed"? The Iranians? The Kurds? The majority Shi'ite population? Was he, had he been, conflating the Arab Shi'ite majority of Iraq with "the Persians," meaning with Shi'ite Iran? Which destruction was he referring to? The one of ten years earlier? Twenty years earlier? Or centuries earlier, resulting in Sunni dominance over Shi'ite Islam in the Arab world? In Saddam Hussein's last moments, if not for decades before, under siege, time was collapsing upon itself.

In his 1997 book *Bloodlines: From Ethnic Pride to Ethnic Terrorism*, Vamik Volkan describes this phenomenon of time collapse.

Under normal conditions, with the passage of time, individuals mourn losses—of people, land, prestige—associated with past traumatic events and work through feelings of fear, helplessness, and humiliation. Mourning and working through the effects of an injury signify the gradual acceptance that a change has occurred. The "lost" elements—a parent, a country—no longer exist in the present reality; they can no longer satisfy one's wishes. (Volkan 1997)

Volkan notes that in situations where people who were once enemies finally meet, there is a time collapse, the stinging sensation in which something that occurred generations or even centuries earlier is immediately felt. Describing meetings arranged in the 1980s between Arabs and Israelis, Volkan writes: "The traumatic events . . . sounded as though they had occurred only the day before. The feelings about them were so fresh it was clear that genuine mourning for the losses associated with these events had not taken place. Furthermore, representatives of opposing groups acted as if they themselves had witnessed such events, even though some had taken place before they were born."

"This is an example of time collapse," Volkan writes, "in which the interpretations, fantasies and feelings about a past shared trauma commingle with those pertaining to a current situation. Under the influence of a time collapse, people may intellectually separate the past from the present one, but emotionally the two events are merged" (Volkan 1997:34–35).

I recognized this phenomenon immediately. My mother is Greek, and I grew up hearing about centuries of subjugation by the Turks during the Ottoman Empire. My mother's land, Crete, freed itself in the nineteenth century, but the wounds were still not healed a century later when I was a college student. In my early twenties I hadn't yet read Foucault or Nietzsche or any postmodern theory that would give me pause about the discipline of "history," but I was already acutely aware that there was always more than one story about what had occurred in the past, even about what occurred five minutes ago. So I decided to take a course on the Ottoman Empire. The class met around a small conference table in the library of a beautiful old building on the University of Texas campus. Across from me during that first session was a demure young woman with thick, wavy brown hair. We all introduced ourselves, and she introduced herself as Turkish. This was the first Turk I had ever met in my life. And immediately, without any conscious bidding or will, I was filled with dread and horror that here, just two feet from me, sat my enemy. The feeling was cognitively shocking. What was I thinking? But it overwhelmed me nonetheless. I was, now I know, experiencing a time collapse. I had been walking around all these years carrying the trauma of my ancestors, a trauma never worked through, a trauma that afflicted me even though I had never experienced it first hand.

The psychoanalyst Christopher Bollas describes the psychic effect of trauma as unconscious imprisonment (Bollas 1995:5). During normal psychic processes, in our dreams and throughout the day, "hundreds of psychically intense experiences . . . conjure ideas from an inner medley of body experience, unconscious memories, and instinctual response" (4). The mind takes these and condenses them into an idea that in turn is disseminatively scattered and fragmented in other activities and ideas. Bollas calls this "the rhythm of unconscious mental activity" and sees it as the source of unconscious creativity and play and a "separate sense" that we often call intuition, which helps us pick up on what is going on in the world and in the people around us. But the experience of trauma jams up this ability. The mind gets stuck and fixates, like that of the "obsessive-compulsive patient who upon entering a supermarket is not only prey to inner commands that he remove, let us say, all the tins of asparagus from the shelf but also victim of the demand that in fact he do so" (5). This person is imprisoned by previous trauma and instinctual experience. "People who live inside the structure of a pathology rather than as comparatively free spirits will have altogether different 'separate senses.' Their intuitions will arise out of defective knowledge of the terms of their own fate, and although they may become exquisitely sensitive to certain structures in life, their intuition will express and often echo the traumas imposed upon them" (5).

What psychic structures has our country triggered in Iraq? The Sunni/ Baathist antipathy to Shï'ism, to the majority of Iraq, is now grimly exploding. The ancient Arab strand of Shï'ism is being conflated with the Iranian "threat." The holy lands of Iraq, dear to all Muslims, are now contested territory for Islam itself. Iran has an interest in it. Arab Shï'ite culture, including the majority of the Iraqi people, has an interest in it. Sunnis have an interest in it. And here it all goes, time collapsing upon itself. This world of ours has much mourning to undergo.

∎∎

This book explores how we can undertake the work of mourning and how we might approach the project of democracy, which for some peoples involves recovering from brutality and for others, who already live in supposed democracies, involves rejecting the kind of complacency that leaves all public matters to public officials. For those reeling from trauma (whether the Sunnis in Iraq or Americans after 9/11), this work of mourning will not be accomplished through war. War is just an "acting out" of trauma, not a way to work through it. War—especially war that is decidedly not in self-defense—is a repetition compulsion. And often what is perceived as "self-defense" is an instantiation of time collapse. I cannot begin to fathom the overdetermined status of the war in Iraq, how many traumas are overlaid on other traumas. But I can perceive this much: in the fifteenth century the West began to colonize the Americas just as the Ottomans conquered Eastern Europe. My dear (in time-collapse time) city of Constantinopoli was conquered by Turks who renamed it Istanbul (the shorthand Turkish way for saying "to the City," *i-stin-mpoli*—Constantinople was "the city," *tin poli*—of that day, as New York City is "the city" of our day). The Battle of Kosovo gets replayed hundreds of years later after the disintegration of Yugoslavia. These schisms and traumas and wounds over centuries, between brothers (in Islam), between cousins (in Serbia), between peoples (Europe, Americas, Arab, Persian, East, West), even "peoples of the book," are endlessly reenacted so long as we do not meet with each other, so long as we do not sit two feet across a table from each other and try to fathom what our peoples have undergone.

OUTLINE OF THE BOOK

In this book I draw on the powerful ideas of psychoanalysis, semiotics, and critical theory to chart a course for democratic transformation in a world sorely lacking democratic practice. I focus on the effects of oppression, terror, and brutality and on the democratic potential of deliberative dialogue and other public testimonies, such as those presented to South Africa's Truth and Reconciliation Commission. I see the public sphere as a discursive space, that is, as a space that can be fruitfully examined according to the logic of various interpretive schema including psychoanalysis, semiotics, systems theory, and critical theory. In the first four chapters, I show how this public sphere is often formed by attempting to repress or abject what is deemed foreign or strange, leading toward the danger—and current reality—of an endless war on terror. The remaining chapters point toward possible "talking cures" as ways toward becoming democratic, especially the discursive practices in truth commissions and deliberative forums, where members of a political community are able to claim their title as citizen and help set their community's direction.[1]

A central task of the first four chapters is to understand the ways the political identity of a people is formed, malformed, or sundered. Does a political community form because of perceived commonalities and connections—or because of a need to circle the wagons and keep perceived threats at bay? To the extent that it is formed by excluding what is other, as many poststructuralists tend to understand identity, it develops a precarious understanding of identity that is easily threatened and undermined, leading to symptoms of xenophobia, nationalism, and violence. This is bad for the body politic, but it is downright evil for those who are excluded or silenced.

I explain these malformations by drawing on psychoanalytic theory and semiotics. Freud focused primarily on the development of individuals (ontogenesis), but in his later works he started to think about how his theory might also apply to the development of peoples (phylogenesis). Is it possible, he wondered, that, just as a person might become neurotic, so also might a society? Freud asked that question on the eve of World War II. Certainly now we know the answer is yes, not only because of the scars of the Holocaust but also because of the recurrence of other genocides and traumas. Now we might ask to what extent these horrors are aberrations, or whether there is something in the very nature of our thinking about "the social contract" that leads to an illogic of annihilating what is deemed foreign or strange. Is our approach to a social contract founded on original traumas, whether of repression, oppression, abjection, or annihilation? Might there be—are there not already—other ways in which community takes place?

The early chapters address humanity's misadventures in constructing political identity, the ways political identity is malformed. When identity is formed by an exclusion of what is other—by a closing of the ranks of "we" against foreign and strange elements—then a dangerous process is set in motion. Political identity becomes founded on homogeneity; difference and diversity of religions, worldviews, and orientations become matters ripe for annihilation. Those who are denied agency are denied the ability to transform inchoate affects and energy into meaningful articulations; that is, they are excluded from shaping the discursive public sphere. They cannot "find themselves" there, which is the worst kind of alienation. Becoming a subject involves becoming one who makes meaning publicly.

As chapter 3 discusses, those seeking political change target the discursive sphere itself because it is the arena in which political identity and purpose are formed and charted. It is itself the subject of political action, both a site for political contest and a contested site. When we begin thinking of the public sphere as a discursive space, politics, civil and otherwise, takes on a new aspect. Political actions become less about particular policies and parties; their object seems to be the public sphere itself—ultimately to silence the critical, vibrant, democratic public sphere and put in its place one in which questioning is silenced.

Chapter 4 turns to the logic that has driven the United States since 9/11. Countries that imagine or perceive themselves to be in danger—traumatized countries—too often try to protect themselves by inflicting trauma on others. They also clamp down on perceived internal threats. The vigilant search for homeland security begins to tighten a noose on the homeland's own lifeblood, its own discursive public sphere, reining in dissent even as it dispatches forces abroad to eliminate perceived threats without. The traumatized state becomes a traumatizer, enacting and reenacting the repressions and oppressions that created its own political identity.

If in the public sphere there is life and movement, talk and contestation, politics can proceed constructively. When politics goes well, it aims to imagine new, more humane possibilities and directions for the public sphere that is its home. But when it goes badly, it tends to annihilate this very arena that is politics' home. Absent an open and vibrant discursive public space, politics has no place to occur. In its stead arises totalitarian administration of power. When power overruns politics, the public sphere becomes the ultimate casualty. Both international and civil wars aim to destroy public space, as they do individuals and governments. Wars and other political brutalities target the public space of discussion and association. They do so by severing people's ability or willingness to engage in it as well as the receptiveness of others in the community to those who have been cut off. An attack on the public sphere is simultaneously an attack on people's self-understanding and title as citizens, as beings worth heeding or entitled to steer public action.

Identity has at least two aspects, just as a single diamond can have many facets: one's "title" as citizen is integral to one's self-understanding as a being worth heeding, as having subjectivity, having a place in the world. These "personal," "social," and "political" dimensions are all facets of one process, subjectivity.

Beginning with chapter 5, the book considers ways a traumatized or traumatizing country might transform itself. These ways could be considered a "talking cure," playing off the psychoanalytic notion that to keep from continuously repeating, acting out, or reenacting trauma, the subject needs to work through its troubles. In Freud's view, working through repression and neurosis could best be done by talking. Freud's French heir, Jacques Lacan, was suspicious of any aim for a cure, by talk or any other means; hence I put "talking cure" in scare quotes. Yet even Lacan saw a value in talk. He famously modified Freud's theory of the psyche with the observation that the unconscious is structured like a language. Drawing on the insights of formalists and linguists, Lacan began to see how the unconscious worked according to a kind of linguistic logic, in which a "slip of the tongue" might reveal an inner repression via the linguistic structure of metaphor or metonymy. There might not be a "cure" for a precarious psyche, but by talking with an analyst there certainly was a hope for rapprochement, however tenuous, between the forces within via working through the conflict, by talking with an analyst, of whatever ailed the person. The psyche may never be cured—it is always a precarious negotiation of forces—but via *parole* or talk, one may find a way to some kind of conciliation.

Could a similar process work for the public sphere? If it too is structured like a language, as an arena of disparate forces (and here I am indebted to Julia Kristeva's conception of the semiotic and symbolic aspects of signification), as seen in street demonstrations clamped down upon by the forces of law and order, then perhaps talk will have a role in public attempts to work through the kinds of trauma and repression discussed in the first part of the book. Hence I take up various attempts at public talking cures—criminal tribunals, truth and reconciliation commissions, deliberative public forums, and even the blogosphere. All the while, the backdrop is one in which a political community is thought of otherwise than through the model of the social contract, where antecedently formed individuals decide, or don't, to enter into community. Rather, subjectivity is thoroughly social; denying one side leads to a collapse of the other.

In this part of the book I draw on empirical observations of these public forums, and in them I find much hope, especially in those that forego vengeance or retribution in favor of reconciliation and deliberation. Though criminal tribunals may well have a place in addressing past wrongs—and in helping a country admit the magnitude of its crimes—they are often another instance of acting out rather than working through trauma. Alone they will not help a country work through its traumas; focusing solely on the wrongdoers does little to reweave the social fabric. For a public sphere to arise, public talk needs to occur throughout the society. In a traumatized country this may require the aid of a truth commission that affords an opportunity for survivors to reclaim a public voice.

As chapter 5 addresses, a central task in recovering from political trauma and war is for members of a political community to reclaim their title as citizens and, in the process, to re-create the public sphere. The most effective way to do so is through public deliberation or public testimony, such as those that occur in truth and reconciliation commissions. In this kind of political discourse, the distinctions between what is properly private and what is public begin to disintegrate. By speaking in public of the devastating crimes committed, often clandestinely, that robbed victims of their humanity, these speakers begin to restore their own and their nation's soul, especially its public space and public being. What is healed is the psychic space or mental geography in which an individual is oriented in a world with others. When people testify in public to the wrongs they have endured, they are, in the process, reclaiming their title as someone to be heeded; when the public hears and responds to these testimonies, they performatively acknowledge the speaker as a subject worth heeding and themselves as a public space of common action and discourse.

In chapters 6 through 9, I discuss what I mean by "deliberative democracy," with chapter 7 considering it through feminist theory. Chapters 9 and 10 focus on a task that any country with democratic aspirations and self-understanding should engage in: public deliberation on matters of common concern. In these chapters I develop an alternative to the usual conceptions of deliberative democracy, different even from the groundbreaking work of Iris Marion Young. Instead of a model for reaching agreement, of which Young was rightly critical, I lay out a model of deliberation as integration. I point to many actually existing networks of integrative deliberation, though they themselves do not call it that, and show how they exemplify many insights from hermeneutics, pragmatism, psychoanalysis, and poststructuralism. By the end I hope that the story of trauma laid out at the beginning of the book can find its next chapter in the story of deliberation as a way of working through our troubles and finding ways to proceed forward.

There is a certain posture needed for a country to transform itself and to set or continue on a democratic course, one where members of a political community lean toward each other, rather than digging in their heels and leaning back. This is the posture we find in public deliberations, from the New England town meeting to the televised national deliberative public opinion polls. For real transformation to occur, there needs to be an inclination to be open to others and to change.

What are the conditions for the possibility of such a posture and inclination? One major condition seems to be the presence and work of mediating institutions, which I discuss in chapter 10. Another condition, discussed in the final chapter, is the availability of media that allow people to claim membership in the human sociosymbolic world. The picture I lay out here is not just the musings of a political philosopher; it is also based on observing real people throughout the world building new democratic lives in their communities. It would be naïve to be sanguine about the possibility of democratic change, especially given the evils this past century has seen. But one vital condition for such change seems to be an ability to imagine coherently such a possibility. That is a role of political theory. And so I put this book forward with hope that it be not just a topographical mapping of an idea but a postulation that might have positive political force.

CHAPTER 1

The Political Unconscious

Nations are not the same as individual psyches, but both can be described as "subjects," albeit of different orders.

—Judith Butler (2004:41)

Sublimation allows the subject to put into signification the trauma of separation from the community to become an individual, a being who means. And through this articulation of the affect of transgression, the individual speaks to and though the community as one who belongs.

—Kelly Oliver, from "Forgiveness and Subjectivity" (286)

I began writing this book on the day of the Madrid bombings of 2004, when it seemed that the clash of civilizations between East and West was suffering a repetition compulsion, with each side promising to annihilate the other and both sides vowing to kill rather than ever talk. Why not talk? I wondered. Why this thought that talking with perpetrators was a kind of caving in, a submission, a negotiation (as in, "we do not negotiate with terrorists")? Why the terrible apprehension about engaging the other? What was going on, to put it boldly, in the world's political unconscious? How might we get out of this seemingly endless cycle of traumas and repetitions, this endless war on terror? Putting these questions in this way, as addressed to national and even global psyches, calls for an answer that is bold, even preposterous. It calls for mapping out and conceptualizing the subterranean repressions, longings, and misconceptions of a political unconscious. At the same time it calls for teasing out the potential within the political unconscious for democratic transformations.

SUBLIMATION AND THE PUBLIC SPHERE

In reflecting on the wreckage of 9/11—of bodies, souls, and buildings, and the dysfunction of traditional philosophy—I want to play out an extended metaphor, though without embracing it too thoroughly or stringently. The metaphor is that of the world as a body politic, a libidinal and signifying body (even if fragmented and decentered) with a political unconscious. This is a body that can be recognized through the discourse of psychoanalysis, an entity with a conscious mind or ego operating according to a socio-symbolic structure, according to laws of meaning, exchange, "reasonableness," order, what Freud termed secondary processes. Below this mind are the presymbolic structures of affect, desire, libidinal energy, narcissism, twisted cathexes, and repression, where meaning has not yet become symbolic, either because of repression (both the kind that forecloses expression and the kind that tries to drive back underground something "forbidden"), what Kelly Oliver calls the colonization of psychic space, or because it is still being worked out and worked through in inchoate presymbolic structures, what Freud called primary processes.

To play out the metaphor, I will start by outlining a theory of human development that I think is most compelling; then I will discuss sublimation as the process by which the public sphere is born. I will describe how the underside of the public sphere is the political unconscious, regardless of the scale being considered (local, national, international) or the point of departure. There is no one, single political unconscious. The political unconscious is not a thing waiting to be identified; it is not a natural entity. It is an *effect* of processes: failures to sublimate well, desires unarticulated, voices kept silent, repressions reenacted without acknowledgment of their origins. The political unconscious is a contingent effect of power relations and harms that have not been tended to. Now, some might worry that my theory equates the social body and the disenfranchised with primary processes and the unconscious. But it is not my theory that is making that equation—it is the political state of affairs and relationships that have disenfranchised some and driven their desires underground and politically unconscious. The theory offered here charts a way to understand and undo this.

Even with this book's global focus, its point of departure is quite local, locating the origins of the political unconscious in the motivations and longings of individuals. This is not to say that "the individual" is anterior to the social or that it is an uncomplicated and transparent unit understandable outside of context. The "individual" is always born in a social context, constituted through that context's prescriptions, shaped in the to and fro of human connection. But let me bracket these difficulties for just a moment, to make the larger point that here I will show how the public sphere is always already made by and tethered to—is, in effect, an effect of—desiring, living, passionate people.

RETHINKING HUMAN DEVELOPMENT

I connect these passionate people with the global body politic through a particular conception of human development. This conception differs sharply from the classical or conventional account, which holds that human beings begin as relatively helpless and dependent and eventually mature (it is hoped) into independent, autonomous, rational agents, beings who can, using their reason, know what is right and good and choose how to act accordingly.[1] This conventional view, even in its less conventional forms (e.g., Habermas's), sees development progressing from dependence to independence, from gullibility to autonomy. Once psychologically and morally matured, an individual should be independent and autonomous.

Drawing on a considerable amount of scholarship and research, I mark another trajectory: from speechlessness to participation. An infant is one, as the Latin origin of the term holds, who lacks speech (*in* for not and *fans* for speaking). There is little terribly surprising in this notion. Researchers and parents can see that in the latter part of the first year of life, an infant can understand a great deal of what is said; but it cannot verbalize what it knows in response. It understands the meanings of words but cannot yet physically utter them. It babbles and coos or cries and screams, emitting what Julia Kristeva calls "echolalias," signaling needs and desires (wittingly or not). But these are clumsy and imperfect means of conveying what in particular the child might want. Some parents now teach their eight-month-old children a rudimentary sign language in order to ease the evident frustration that babies experience as they want to articulate some desire or need but cannot manage to do so.

Our culture generally stops calling someone an infant by the time she or he is about twelve months old, a period in which the child is beginning to grab hold of objects and stand on its own feet, as well as articulating sounds to identify objects: "dada," "mama," "cat," "ball." By then we call it a toddler, indicating that the ability to walk, to teeter away from mother and father, is the significant feature of this phase of development. But is this locomotion, this independence, the most salient feature of the end of infancy? A baby becomes a toddler at about a year, we say, as he or she begins to move independently around the room. But the second year of life is also marked by an explosion of speech. As a child approaches the second birthday, she or he is beginning to rattle nonstop. Rather than the terrible frustration of speechlessness, the child experiences glee at being able to express what it wants. Desire becomes channeled through language into articulations that can circulate in the larger human world.

The psychoanalytic views of Freud, Lacan, and Kristeva help explain the importance of the child's move into language. As bodily, living, desiring beings, we are brimming with impulses, energy, and drives. These energies cannot remain static; they must move. In infancy these feelings often circulate back onto the self, in a process Freud called primary narcissism. Speech allows for a different movement of desire. With speech we can ask for what we want. What do we ultimately want? A mother's love, her undying, thoroughly focused rapture back onto us. Maybe we want to be folded back into her? Well, this we certainly cannot have, so we go looking for substitutes. We use speech to ask for this, that, and the other, hoping that something will satisfy us. But nothing ever fully does, so we go on speaking, asking. That's the sort of picture that Lacan offers.

Kristeva, following Freud, moves in a slightly different direction. Affects, channeled through language, help us create literary works, whose meaning is always partly constituted through these affective (or what she calls semiotic) dimensions.[2] As symbol-using beings, we make meaning, part of which is the meaning of our own desire. Where in Lacan's view there is never really any satisfaction, in the theories of both Freud and Kristeva there is the possibility of happiness through channeling desire into cultural creations. This is the process of sublimation, as I will discuss by drawing on and developing the political implications of Kelly Oliver's theory. Through language, we can turn private desire into public meaning. In a sense, we use language and other forms of expression to locate ourselves outside ourselves, to find ourselves in a public sphere of meaning.

To preface this discussion, let me quote Oliver on the meaning of sublimation so as to clarify the positive sense in which I use this term:

Subjectivity develops through sublimation, through elevating bodily drives and their affective representations to a new level of meaning and signification. In addition, sublimation always and only takes place in relation to others and the Other that is the meaning into which each individual is born. Sublimation in the constitution of subjectivity is analogous to sublimation in chemistry, which is defined as the conver-

sion of a solid substance by means of heat into a vapor, which reso-
lidifies upon cooling. Sublimation transforms bodily drives and affects
that seem solid and intractable into a dynamic vapor that liberates the
drives and affects from repression (specifically, the repression inherent
in oppression) and discharges them into signifying systems that then
resolidify them. (Oliver 2004:xx)

Consider the contrary: the worst kind of alienation is the situation in
which one is prevented from sublimating, when one cannot make public
one's own wants, when the public world seems oblivious and impervious
to one's concerns. Alienation can occur at many levels: not being able to
speak, not being given an opportunity to speak, and not being heard or
heeded. One suffers as much from not being heard as from not being
able to speak. In contrast, public happiness occurs when one can see one's
own desires writ somewhere in a public world of meaning, when instead
of being speechless, one belongs and participates in a public world, when
others take up and affirm one's expressions.

So here are the two pictures of human development: the conventional
view sees development as a process of moving from dependence to independence; the view I am articulating sees it quite differently—as a move
from speechlessness to participation.[3] Either could be used to explain
an infant's behavior when it cries because of some need. The first view
focuses on the infant's helplessness, something that will be relieved when
it gets some assistance, ultimately when it becomes an autonomous adult.
The second focuses on the infant's speechlessness, something that will be
alleviated when it can put its desires into words.

Consider another situation: the child develops and learns to use a
favorite word, "no." The first view sees a glimmer of independence and
autonomy, the second a glimmer of articulation of desire. But the explana-
tory strength of the first view weakens as the child grows and moves into
a social world. What drives us to belong, to take part in the world, to have
friends, feel important, write, garden, create? Something urges us on,
compels us to join the social realm. The first view does not account for
this well. When the *telos* of a human being is seen as autonomy, it seems
that the relationship between an individual and a social world would be
contentious, or at least that the individual somehow is antecedent to that
world and decides whether or not to enter, whether to *exchange* something
private for something public.

The view I am proposing does not necessarily hold that human beings have any sort of *telos*, any natural or essential tendency to want to be social animals. It does look like a kind of Aristotelian or Arendtian notion that human beings are political animals. But I would say that we (Aristotle, Arendt, and I) hold this view because of the contingent fact that human beings are biological organisms that have the physical and mental capacity to speak. It is not that we are necessarily political animals, but that we happen to have desires that seek satisfaction, and we happen to have the tool of speech. Hence we seek out a public world with others.

To the extent that individuals have cause to seek out and create together a public world of meaning—entered through all kinds of communicative structures, spaces, and venues—this public world is never a realm separate from individuals. It is always already an effect of desiring human beings' collective evocations. The public world is a space in which human beings' multiple evocations, their desires writ large, crisscross and interconnect. Our public articulations always have a semiotic force; in fact, the semiotic realm of drive, impulse, energy is what propels us to find channels—media—to make impressions and participate in a world with others. So this book's aim to understand the political unconscious of this global public sphere may not be far-reaching after all. While we might read that the morning paper contains simply and objectively "all the news that's fit to print," someone somewhere (an editor, perhaps, at *The New York Times*) chose a piece of "news" as fit to print for some particular human purpose. Some value drove him or her, them, us, to seek out some information and publish it in the world. There is always an interest, conscious or not, seeding the public realm. We have always something at stake, some motivations that propel our articulations.

As a realm of seemingly autonomous signs, the public world may appear separate from the affects and interests of human beings, but the reality is otherwise. The public sphere is the perceived effect of the affects and interests of all who gain entrée there. It is also the skewed product of silencing some, of rendering speechless and deeming meaningless vast sectors of the world's people, creating in effect a political unconscious. To locate that political unconscious, we need to look at the semiotic dynamics of the public sphere.

THE MANY POLITICS OF THE PUBLIC SPHERE

By "public sphere" I mean the space that publics create as they use semiotic modes to participate with others, to coordinate action and produce outcomes; a space in which public uses of semiotic structures, discursive and otherwise, construct meaning, identity, purpose, and political direction. By "public" I mean what John Dewey meant in *The Public and Its Problems*: an array of people who are related vis-à-vis some common interests or concerns. "The public consists of all those who are affected by the indirect consequences of transactions to such an extent that it is deemed necessary to have those consequences systematically cared for" (Dewey 1954). Members of a public need not share the same views on these things, but they find themselves to be a public when they see that they are affected by the same things. For example, the people of South Texas share the same air, air that is being polluted by factories across the border. South Texans may disagree among themselves about the nature of the problem or what to do, but they are a public insofar as they are find themselves together being affected by a shared set of problems.

In my view, the discursive public sphere can be found in civil society, in the array of civil associations and joint actions that occur somewhere between the realm of formal government and the private, supposedly individual realm of households. But this public sphere itself is not an entity. As Habermas once said, wherever two or more people gather to discuss matters of common concern, there is the public sphere. In this sense, it is not a place but an occurrence, a process, an event, something that arises when people try in the presence of others to make sense of and reorient their common world. To paraphrase Gertrude Stein, there is no *there* there of the public world. Instead, there is only a who, a gathering of people communicating one on one or by satellite, over fiber optic lines, or through newspapers; in the cross-currents of the letters to the editor pages and lunchtime conversation; in a sidewalk demonstration or in the televised plea of a hostage. Without people engaged in talking, writing, expressing, demonstrating, signifying, performing in a world with and for others, there would be no public sphere. It is not that a space would be waiting and empty, it would no longer exist, for it is nothing other than these events of conversation and expression.

This is where democracy takes place. It is in this public realm that public meaning and purpose are created, ultimately the meaning and purposes that steer a political community. A true democracy begins early and deep, in the ability of all members of the polity to feel themselves members of a common public space who have a hand in shaping the contours of that space. It does not focus on the apparatus of voting or protesting, though these may have their place. Democracy happens in the assembly and the town meeting, not in the private space of a voting booth. A democracy is not an agglomeration of free individuals as much as it a way for a *demos* to take place. Democracy needs a public that can develop judgment and set direction about things common. Members of a truly democratic society are able to express themselves—that is, to sublimate successfully their longings and aspirations—and to see their expressions circulating in this public realm. Where oppressive societies alienate members from membership in a common world with others, a democratic society should be able to create pathways for citizens to talk with each other, coordinate their aspirations, and help fashion and shape their public world. In a discursive public sphere at its best, citizens can create meaning and set direction that lead to policies under which all can flourish. Sometimes this will happen through the kind of communicative action that Habermas describes; but meaning and purpose will also arise in the ways that the public sphere's semiotic, signifying processes structure experience and create identity. Ideally, a discursive public sphere can fashion a robustly democratic world.

I'd even say that short of such opportunities to affectively shape the public sphere, democracy cannot take place. Most democratic theorists focus on the apparatus of voting and governance. Freedom of expression is seen as a right, but not necessarily as a central condition for the possibility of democracy. Even the term "freedom of expression" fails to capture the force of what expression is: it is not merely an ability to say what is on one's mind once one has made up one's mind. Sublimation is the condition for the possibility of having what is recognizably a mind and of being a member of a human, and not merely animal, existence. To be human (something that other higher animals might be able to be) is to be a member of a sociosymbolic world, able to move beyond narcissism and silence, to imagine moral as well as liberatory possibilities that might exceed the here and now. With the term "sociosymbolic world or order," I mean the realm of a society's language, signs, customs, structures, and laws.[4] To be human is to be able to performatively help create in the sociosymbolic world what we think of as humanity.

No doubt something like this reasoning led to Aristotle's famous claim that humans are *zoon politicon*, often translated as political animals, though *zoon* could more aptly be defined as living being. Because they have the gift of speech, they are able to traffic with others, to be part of a *polis*. What sets human beings above other animals, in Aristotle's view, is the use of speech in a common world with others.

But the public sphere is also a semiotic space in which society's anxiet-ies, sentiments, opinions, and prejudices appear. It may be the product of many years of some groups being deemed human and others not. Not all artistic sublimations are liberatory: the art of blackface was an expression, but one founded on denying the ability of others to express themselves as dignified members of a public sphere. A public sphere may be twisted and thwarted by years of freedom for some at the expense of the free-dom of others. When there are distortions or traumas at work, when the effects of these maladies become icons that circulate in the semiotic public sphere, the results can be brutal. The icons provide the basis for oppres-sive regimes whose public and foreign policies reenact the traumas that initiated their own brutality.

Such destructive turns call for powerful analyses and interventions, far more powerful than are offered by liberal political theory. This theory does provide useful ways of thinking about the political public sphere in the modern era, but alone it does little to account for political develop-ments that *exceed* or transgress it, that are, by the lights of liberal theory, manifestly irrational. The model of human development and of the public sphere laid out above calls for another kind of political theorizing.

THE LIMITS OF LIBERAL THEORY POST–9/11

For some time, beginning well before 9/11, I have worried about how a polit-ical theory can make sense of the growing global schism between those of radically different worldviews. Is it possible for people with few, if any areas of agreement on fundamental questions to find a way to live together peace-fully? Can political solutions be found when what counts as properly politi-cal is itself in question? If the political is defined so narrowly that it makes no room for addressing differences that fall outside any overlapping con-sensus among all the parties, the only alternative seems to be to use force to settle differences or achieve goals, or to throw our hands up in despair. This was a bad enough problem before 9/11, with extremists targeting abortion clinics and federal buildings, but after 9/11 it is downright remiss to have such a narrow conception of politics. It overlooks the ways "unreasonable" processes can be at work, even in seemingly well-ordered societies.

The Western liberal conception of the political, running from Kant to Rawls and Habermas, calls on people to think rationally for themselves, to be swayed only by the unforced force of the better argument, not by any seemingly irrational means. This tradition's definition of reason excludes religious revelation as a legitimate authority in deciding political questions. People, and peoples (in the sense of the people of a society), should only be subject to their own rational will, not the will of a god or a king or some other exterior power. For me to say, "God said we should do such-and-such," does not provide any compelling reason for someone of a different faith, or of no faith at all, to go along.

Western liberal philosophy depends heavily on reason and reasons. According to the Western tradition, reason is what I use to gauge the reasons you offer me, and vice versa. Reasons are like common coins that circulate among people who might otherwise participate in different economies (Catholic, Buddhist, etc.). Reasons are only as good as their ability to compel others who may have different values. But they are vital because only they, in their successful bids to compel others, have, in a postmetaphysical world, any properly coercive power or authority. I give you my reasons for why we should raise taxes to pay for stronger public schools and if you, an enemy of taxation and an advocate for home schooling, come around to my view of your own accord, using your own reason to gauge my reasons, then we are all ruling ourselves freely with the aid of our reason.

But what if you, to the contrary, close yourself off from "the voice of reason"? What if you preemptively decide you will not use your reason to evaluate mine—if you decide to turn to a book instead for answers? Or in John Rawls's language, your comprehensive doctrine will not support a "reasonable balance of political values"?[5] Then, in the liberal view, you are not being rational.

(So there are three kinds of reason: what we offer to others, what we use to gauge others' offerings, and what state we are in.)

Whether addressing domestic politics or international relations, the liberal tradition aims to find means for common accord even among people of different political outlooks. In other words, it accommodates pluralism. But only to a certain extent—everyone should at least agree on a liberal procedure as a proper way of deciding matters. Those who don't agree with solving matters using reason are deemed too irrational to join the conversation. Or, from another perspective, those who disagree with solving matters using secular reason rather than faith exclude themselves from the conversation.

Such are the outlines of the liberal political philosophies put forward by the leading figures of contemporary philosophy of the past thirty years:

Jürgen Habermas, John Rawls, and Richard Rorty.[6] They come out of quite different philosophical frameworks: continental critical theory, Anglo-American analytic philosophy, and pragmatism. Despite their different philosophical orientations, they share the Western liberal view that political matters should be solved with reasons that compel those involved; anyone who disagrees with the authority of reason excludes him- or herself from the political table.

But since 9/11, if not before, this solution is no solution at all when it comes to resolving the world's most pressing political disagreements, which exceed the bounds of liberalism. In domestic politics, these include matters of identity, faith, and community purpose, with "illiberal" parties arguing for the need to subsume the political under these larger questions, for example, by making the political an arena for faith. The liberal solution does nearly nothing at all to address such disagreements, as it deals with the internecine disagreements among those who already subscribe to the notion that faith is a private matter and does not have a place in resolving political questions. I am not saying that God talk should have a place in politics; I am saying that liberals cannot decide by fiat that it does not. It is counterproductive to say that the differences between liberals and nonliberals—about whether God belongs in politics; whether people of various ethnicities or genders have any dignity; whether violence should be used to solve problems; whether "the other" should be tolerated or annihilated—are outside the realm of politics or that politics has no means to deal with them. Rawls's solution, of delimiting where and how an overlapping consensus might arise, does nothing to facilitate rapprochements between parties who disagree over the very role of reason versus faith or capital versus community.[7] Such differences are even more problematic at the international level in disputes between nations that lack any common coin for settling differences. These disputes are usually posed as a schism between East and West, or between the forces of modernization and the advocates of traditionalism, or even as a clash of fundamentalisms. They are characterized as not amenable to reason and hence as properly dealt with through some level of force, whether international pressure or, if this does not succeed, perhaps war. Even the best liberalism has force pick up where reason leaves off.

This analysis of the problem leads to a dead end. We need another course. It is not going to be found in parsing what is reasonable from what is not, by telling some parties that they aren't being good liberals. What do they care? The wise course now might be to try to understand human motivations beyond a narrow conception of reason. I think we need to look carefully at what drives people in their dealings with each other, ranging from the ethical call to heal the world to the nefarious machinations of a will to power born from trauma that uses the cloak of reason to work out its own death-dealing obsessions. On the latter, I think "the West" is as guilty as "the East." Fundamentalists especially, of any religious or mystical tradition, might eschew reason up front and openly. But many avowedly rational parties will use reason disingenuously to cover over a will to power sparked by some unspoken need to have their own way, which is perhaps far removed from any reasons at all. To understand either sort of drive, we need another analysis.

Though I do find liberal theory useful at certain junctures, I think we are in a time that calls for more. In this book I will draw on other traditions and sources that have deeply informed my work and that offer powerful ways of approaching today's maladies. These include psychoanalytic theory, from Freud to Lacan and Kristeva; semiotics, from American pragmatist to poststructuralist; the civic republican tradition, from Aristotle to Arendt; the hermeneutic practices of literary critical theory; and democratic theory and practice, including the theoretical apparatus of discourse ethics and empirical observations of deliberative forums. Together these approaches can focus on the centrality of the semiotic, political public sphere.

One of my central premises is that the human subject cannot be understood in isolation; identity or self-understanding is deeply entwined with the larger community. Here I part company with the prevailing view of modernity that individuation is a process of becoming autonomous. As indicated earlier, the picture I paint here is that development is really a matter of moving from speechlessness to participation, that is, from being an infant to being one who can participate in and contribute to the quintessentially human activity of publicly making meaning. The process of becoming a subject is complex: the ways the discursive public sphere positions us affect our ability to take part in discourse, to make meaning, including the meaning of our own self.

The discursive or semiotic public sphere is both a repository and a transmitter of meaning, including subjective identity. There is a dialectical relationship between the public and the public sphere; each is inextricable from the other. This is true not only in how citizens and the public are constituted but also in how they are harmed. As the first half of this book discusses, a war on citizens is at the same time a war on a public sphere. Recovering from trauma will be a simultaneous re-creation of personal and political subjectivity. Our identity is inextricable from the formation of the *res publica*, this public thing that is neither a place nor an entity but rather an intersubjective space we create among us. The geography of the public sphere is created psychically, and it can be annihilated in the same way, via the kind of psychic damage that survivors of political brutality suffer.

The move from primary to secondary processes, that is, from speech-lessness to signification, depends upon sublimation, the psychoanalytic name for a process of channeling drives rather than simply acting upon them. (The rise of "civilization," society with its norms and taboos, makes the latter unlikely anyway.) From a Freudian point of view, instead of trying to satisfy all libidinal desires through sex, sublimation is used to chan-nel desire via some other expression. Where sex expends libidinal energy through immediate gratification, sublimation can produce cultural arti-facts, events, processes. Instead of lusting after my neighbor, I garden; instead of trying to expend desires, one writes books, sitcoms, Web sites, or any number of other expressions open to interpretation, possible of creating meaning. Just as the story Freud tells in *Civilization and Its Dis-contents* goes: our channeled desires produce buildings, museums, gar-dens, libraries, symphonies. Somatic and psychic drives and energy can be channeled into signifying practices. These may look like orderly symbolic practices after they've been channeled, but they are fueled by desire, the inchoate material of the sociosymbolic order. When desire is channeled well, the sociosymbolic order can function well.

Kelly Oliver's conception of sublimation is broader than Freud's. She sees all drives, or what she refers to as the bodily needs of us biopsychic-social beings, not just sexual ones, as potential material for sublimation. By discharging these drives into language, we fulfill our need for com-munication and communion with others: "all drives make their way into signification—artistic, intellectual, linguistic—through sublimation, Sub-limation is the socialization of drives. Through sublimation, bodily drives and their attenuating affects become discharged in signifying practices; and insofar as signification depends on the discharge of drives, through sublimation drives become signs. . . . The goal of sublimation is connec-tion or communion with others" (Oliver 2004:87–88).

In *Civilization and Its Discontents*, Sigmund Freud notes a homol-ogy between the development of civilization and the development of the individual. Both are "vital" life processes, he writes, in which individuals are melded into groups (Freud 1961:104–110). At the ontogenetic level, the individual must forego the goal of satisfying all his or her desires in exchange for the security that comes with being part of a community. He or she renounces unrestrained gratification of libidinal desire in exchange for the social bonds or aim-inhibited *eros* of the community. As Jacques Lacan and Julia Kristeva have argued, these social bonds are most clearly seen in the symbolic field of signification. For Lacan, the subject's very unconscious becomes structured like a language, a system we share with other speaking beings. For Kristeva, subjects make and remake themselves via their libidinal investments in the symbolic realm. From the psychoanalytic point of view developed by Lacan and Kristeva, one to which Freud probably would have agreed, we become socialized by becoming speaking beings invested in and produced by a sociosymbolic field.

Sigmund Freud and Kelly Oliver are looking at how an individual becomes socialized, though Oliver goes further in seeing sublimation as always already a social process. I take this theory further yet, carrying it over into the global, symbolic, public, political sphere. Oliver describes sublimation as the lynchpin between the psyche and the social. It could be seen as the hinge between them, or rather, I argue, as an overlapping field. The space of sublimation is also *at the same time* the sociosymbolic public sphere. Note that in this book I am not making what some might call "a dangerous homology" between the analysand on the couch and the political public sphere. I am not drawing a *parallel* between the macro and the micro; I am showing the *connection*. I am saying that our particular and collective traumas *show up* in the sociosymbolic public sphere. That is where they *circulate*. It is from there that repression and oppression and potentially liberating media *operate*. Hence, as I argue throughout this book, public talk may serve a psychoanalytic function for the public sphere.

PERIPHERIES OF CONSCIOUSNESS AND THE UNCONSCIOUS PUBLIC SPHERE

Lest I make too neat a division here, consider that both the unconscious and consciousness have peripheries. At the periphery of the unconscious is consciousness; at the edge of consciousness is the unconscious. Nicholas Abraham puts it well, if a bit obliquely:

In Freud's intuition, the Periphery itself includes a Kernel with its own Periphery, which in turn includes a Kernel, and so forth. The secondary, tertiary, etc., Kernels, along with those that precede them in rank, are relate by analogy. Thus the primary Kernel, termed organic, has on its periphery a so-called psychic counterpart or secondary Kernel, which is the Unconscious properly speaking. This, in turn, has in its own Envelope its exterior nucleic counterpart, Consciousness. In summary, the set of Unconscious-Preconscious-Conscious constitutes the doubly nucleic Periphery of the primary Kernel: the Organic. (Abraham and Torok 1994:90–91)

The various realms of the psyche have and share peripheries, making possible interchanges that are not necessarily passages from one side to the other. Looking at memory, Nicholas Abraham turns to Freud's metaphor of the "mystic writing pad," which helps us to see how an inscription occurs

neither in the Unconscious nor in the Preconscious, but in a typically intermediary region: in the region of contact, so to speak, between the Kernel and the Periphery. Without itself being double, the trace of the inscription could lend itself to a twofold use: nucleic, through its side turned toward the Unconscious, and peripheral, through its view toward the Conscious; the former obeying the laws of the Primary Process (in feeding hallucinatory realizations with representations), the latter adapting and bending the trace to the demands of the Secondary Process (discursiveness, temporality, objectality). From this point on, we could proceed to radicalize the concept of the trace and offer the following idea for consideration: the inscription is made possible precisely as a result of different uses to which the trace is put on the two sides, and this doubleness is constitutive of both the Envelope and the Kernel; these would then be simply the poles on the *near* and *far side* of the dividing line where the perpetual nucleo-peripheral differral [*différencement*] pulsates. Envelope and Kernel would have this frontier as substance, instrument, object, and subject simultaneously. (ibid. 91–92)

Hence, the trace is not a static remnant of an event but rather an ongoing activity, "repeating endlessly the alternation of its duplex discourse" (92).

Both the conscious and the unconscious realms of the psyche have borders. Sometimes events occur on the border between them. Sometimes there are passages from one realm to another, and then perhaps retreats. Shots are volleyed, repressed, and come back again. Nicholas Abraham argues that this way of looking at things helps to explain some of the puzzles of repression, how it is both a process of the unconscious (keeping certain thoughts and impulses from coming to consciousness) and something that occurs in the symbolic field. When we understand memory traces as situated on "the nucleoperipheral boundary," we can see how they can be bounced back and forth, sometimes censored, sometimes erupting into consciousness (92).

This helps to make sense of drives that are not successfully sublimated, and especially of the effects of wholesale censorship and marginalization. The return of the repressed is hardly a problem plaguing individuals. Today it is hard to ignore how it plagues the world. "The political unconscious" is the name I am giving this phenomenon of the social and political effects of cultures (conscious political entities) being created by driving unwanted or threatening elements underground. The political unconscious is not an absence but a realm teeming with discontent. It is also the periphery, the border on the edge of consciousness, of political entities. This other, this foreign territory, is never entirely other.

That some entities have not yet found their "voice" could be innocent developments, but often the speechlessness of some bodies in the political unconscious is not at all innocent. Their silence and failure to sublimate could be founded on traumatic repression, oppression, or annihilation of what is deemed foreign, strange, and terrifying. Such exclusions occur most when the sociosymbolic order is founded upon, perpetrates, and continues a conception of identity based upon these very same exclusions. In such situations, the cultural expressions of the sociosymbolic order will lack vital affective, libidinal, and humanitarian force. The semiotic public sphere will carry the signs of a stunted culture. At the same time, the "underground" political unconscious will lack meaningful ways to sublimate wishes and desires, resulting in wholesale silencing of some people and acts of terror by others, all in the vain hope of finding means to transform what has lacked expression into something that is part of the overall culture's popular imaginary, or what is often called the popular imagination.

Many of these entities of the political unconscious recognize the rule of law and widely shared democratic notions. Think of the growth over the years of new social movements that disrupt the complacency of the social order but still abide by basic democratic principles. Others do not, including those that see little space or possibility for making any headway into the prevailing order, such as the movement recently dubbed "ecoterrorism" as well as those movements that dismiss democratic norms altogether, including those that follow revelation or dismiss "rationality" as a mask for power. To the extent that the sociosymbolic order forecloses possibilities for such movements to make their case in the political public sphere, they will seek other means. Recall the Black Panther motto, "By any means necessary." Consider also the post–9/11 renewed insistence on never "negotiating" with terrorists.

Sociosymbolic orders founded on silencing, sacrificing, even annihilating what is other breed the kind of terror they purport to oppose. They create a semiotic public sphere that forecloses the possibility for some to speak and belong and they reenact the trauma of repression and exclusion. They create anything but a democratic society. In the following chapter I consider how two kinds of traumas that founded Western "liberal" societies have created semiotic public spheres that continue to reenact these exclusions, even as reform efforts attempt to chip away at them. Ultimately reform has to address the fundamental maladies, and the means will be what I will turn to in the latter part of this book: political talk, testimony, and deliberation, all ways of *working through* our troubles.

CHAPTER 2

Modernity's Traumas

Tis all in peeces, all cohaerence gone.   —John Donne

State and church, law and customs, were now torn asunder; en-
joyment was separated from labour, means from ends, effort from
reward. Eternally chained to only one single little fragment of the
whole, Man himself grew to be only a fragment; with the monoto-
nous noise of the wheel he drives everlastingly in his ears.

—Friedrich Schiller

At a time when the territorial borders between the great civilisations
are fading away, mental borders are being reinvented to give a second
life to the ghosts of lost civilisations. . . . Ethnicity and religion are being marshaled to draw new borders between groups whose identity
relies on a performative definition: we are what we say we are, or
what others say we are. These new ethnic and religious borders do
not correspond to any geographical territory or area. They work in
minds, attitudes and discourses. They are more vocal than territorial,
but all the more eagerly endorsed and defended because they have to
be invented, and because they remain fragile and transitory.

—Olivier Roy

COUNTING THE DEAD

Modernity's traumas are many, more than can be recounted in a book,
much less a chapter. The war correspondent Chris Hedges gives his quick
and dead-on count:

Look just at the 1990s: 2 million dead in Afghanistan; 1.5 million dead
in the Sudan; some 800,000 butchered in ninety days in Rwanda;
a half-million dead in Angola; a quarter of a million dead in Bosnia;
200,000 dead in Guatemala; 150,000 dead in Liberia; a quarter of a

million dead in Burundi; 75,000 dead in Algeria; and untold tens of thousands lost in the border conflict between Ethiopia and Eritrea, the fighting in Colombia, the Israeli-Palestinian conflict, Chechnya, Sri Lanka, southeastern Turkey, Sierra Leone, Northern Ireland, Kosovo, and the Persian Gulf War (where perhaps as many as 35,000 Iraqi citizens were killed). In the wars of the twentieth century not less than 62 million civilians have perished, nearly 20 million more than the 43 million military personnel killed. (Hedges 2002:13)

And now, less than a decade into the next century, we are certainly faring no better, with genocide in Darfur, civil war breaking out in Iraq, and conflicts continuing in Afghanistan, Burma, Burundi, the Central African Republic, Chad, Chechnya, Colombia, the border of India and Bangladesh, the Cote d'Ivoire, Nepal, and Uganda. These conflicts are devastatingly traumatic here and now for survivors and loved ones. Their effects will be felt well into the future. But they are also the result of trauma, effects felt now from wounds inflicted earlier.

Examining modernity's traumas calls for the genealogical work of uncovering what has given rise to them—and it calls for understanding how trauma that occurs today will have its own long-term effects. We notice that in just trying to make sense of the traumas that go on now, sense is hard to come by. We might catalogue the bloodshed, but it seems impossible to explain; there might be patterns, but nothing rational or explainable. The obvious point is that all these deaths, this bloodshed, these upheavals of the social order represent massive breakdowns in relationships between peoples, sometimes in the form of civil war, other times in clashes between nations. Wars occur for all kinds of reasons, but the most intractable wars result from loss of security or threats to identity and order. Wars purely for economic gain (recall the antiwar mantra of the Persian Gulf War: "no blood for oil") seem amenable to cease fire and intervention: at least we can reason about the bottom line. But there is no reasoning, it seems, about what drives people who live side by side one day to engage the next day in a battle to kill off what suddenly seems to be an ancient and mortal enemy. The end of the twentieth century did not, as Francis Fukuyama once thought (and now, to his credit, no longer believes), bring an end to history and a few ethnic skirmishes; it brought the end of the unifying power of nation-states that could quell such uprisings and the rise of blood enmities, often between brothers. And it brought more genocide and "ethnic cleansing." And all for what?

What really drives the Janjaweed in Sudan? Prior to 2003, attacks by these Arabs on horseback against largely black African farmers might have been motivated by understandable, if not justifiable, competition over scarce water. But as of this writing, something else drives the bloodshed, and even drives the government to back the Janjaweed. This seems to be a nation internally convulsing, struggling with identity and terror. For what? Wars clearly based on self-interest, as in the mantra of *realpolitik*, might be understandable, but more and more wars, especially civil wars, seem to have nothing at all to do with self-interest. To the contrary, they are antithetical to self-interest. They are self-immolating. One day people live side by side, in the nice manner of modern liberalism, and the next they find themselves besieged by wielders of other faiths or identities. Why have we not taken more notice of this obvious fact: conflict is inflamed when religious and clanlike sentiments rise up? Religion and thick conceptions of identity, holdovers from medievalism, disrupt modernity's allegiance to pluralism and tolerance. From Belfast to Beirut, conflict seems to be fueled by religion and identity politics, often oddly in worlds that have been otherwise pluralistic and secular.

TRAUMA AND PSYCHOANALYSIS

I will draw on the tropes of psychoanalysis in an effort to hermeneutically open up what defies explanation. By using psychoanalysis to understand social entities, I do not mean to equate a nation with an individual; the unconscious of the former is of course of a different kind than the latter. Yet there is a connection in how they arise and function, so, as I hope to show, the tools of psychoanalysis can help explain what otherwise seems so inscrutable. The connection is that traumas that beset individuals—and their affective consequences—show up in the public sphere (in thwarted sublimations, repetition compulsions, neuroses, etc.) and circulate there, creating a ripple effect upon others. As Teresa Brennan's work brilliantly demonstrates, these affects move between and among people, becoming shared phenomena. The psychic phenomena become symptomatic in similar ways in people and in a people, especially in the matter of trauma: how it functions in the development and behavior of an individual is uncannily like how it functions in social entities.

Charles Rycroft's *Dictionary of Psychoanalysis* defines "trauma" as follows:

2. In psychiatry and psychoanalysis, any totally unexpected experience which the subject is unable to assimilate. The immediate response to a

psychological trauma is shock; the later effects are either spontaneous recovery (which is analogous to spontaneous healing of physical traumata) or the development of a traumatic neurosis. 3. In psychoanalysis, by extension, any experience which is mastered by use of defences. Trauma, in this sense, produces anxiety, which is followed either by spontaneous recovery or the development of a psychoneurosis. (Rycroft 1995:187–188)

According to Rycroft, Freud's notion of trauma was purely causal. A traumatic event happens to someone without that person willing it, and any effects that result were produced by that event. Freud thought that all neurotic illnesses are the result of traumas that occur in infancy. But Judith Herman, among others, has noted the deleterious effects of traumas that occur in adulthood, from the traumatized soldier to the battered wife. People who weather traumas better—that is, who seem to recover quicker—are those who were more resilient and had stronger social networks in the first place. Those who experience trauma in an already weakened or isolated condition suffer more from post-traumatic stress disorder. Perhaps the latter were already suffering from infantile trauma, which made them less resilient.

What interests me first here are the defenses that arise in order to master traumatization. Defenses work to protect the ego either from unruly aspects of the id (its own desires and drives) or from the outside world. Given that trauma is an unexpected assault from without, defenses help the traumatized subject protect herself from whatever the world might bring again as well as from the memories that still besiege her. Anna Freud listed nine defenses: "regression, repression, reaction-formation, isolation, undoing, projection, introjection, turning against the self, and reversal— plus a tenth, sublimation, 'which pertains rather to the study of the normal than to that of neurosis.' Splitting and denial are also listed as defences" (ibid. 32). Regression is the defense by which the ego reverts to an earlier stage of development to avoid anxiety. Repression is the defense mechanism that renders an unacceptable impulse unconscious. Conversely, reaction-formation seeks to master an unacceptable impulse by exaggerating its opposing tendency. Isolation is the defensive mechanism of psychically separating an occurrence from its effects. Undoing goes even further, denying not only the effects but also the occurrence itself. Projection is the defense of imagining a mental phenomenon as an actual phenomenon, often by locating it in some object or person other than oneself. Introjection can be a healthy process of internalizing something, for example, internalizing external authority into one's own superego; or it may be an unhealthy defense of fantasizing that one has ingested an external object. Turning against oneself is a kind of moral mechanism, such as when a torturer begins to torture himself. Finally, reversal is the process of turning one instinctual vicissitude into its opposite (e.g., sadism into masochism), utilized in reaction-formation.

In the case of trauma, it seems that all of these, save perhaps regression and introjection, would serve as protection. The problem, though, is that relying on these defenses (not including sublimation) for any extended length of time will not help the traumatized subject work through a traumatic experience. It only serves to defer healing and recovery. Moreover, many of these defenses can cause further destruction and damage, either by turning in or against oneself or by projecting one's ills on others. Psychoanalysis offers the traumatized subject tools, namely the tool of the "talking cure," to work through troubles and mourn what has been lost.

Psychoanalysis is both a tool for working through and an analysis of how the psyche forms. Could it be a tool for social entities as well? Much of what I noted above could be applied to societies that have experienced trauma. War's social and political trauma offers strong evidence that the insights of psychoanalysis apply. The defenses at work seem to be variations of reaction-formation, isolation, undoing, projection, and turning against the self. The subject, here the political body (as it is imaginatively constituted in a sociosymbolic sphere), puts up defenses and resists working through, often as if previous trauma shaped it to react as it does. Any war is traumatic, and it is also an acting out of some previous trauma. An act of war or terror is both the result of some trauma and a new instance of it. Both occur simultaneously; they cannot be temporally distinguished.

But they should be distinguished conceptually. In cases of political and social trauma and the accompanying repetition compulsions, there is much to discuss. This chapter considers, with a very broad sweep, originary traumas, the traumas of the modern era that seem to still be doing their destructive work.

ORIGINARY TRAUMAS

Consider the major epochs of human history, at least as we parse time in the West: ancient (roughly until about 333 A.D. with the Roman Empire's adoption of Christianity), medieval or traditional (until about the fifteenth century), modern (from the early sixteenth century until the present), and perhaps now postmodern (Fredric Jameson marks the break, a bit tongue in cheek, at about 1958 with the television and first computer chips). Each shift from one era to the next has been difficult, but the shift from traditional to modern is unparalleled and still not finished. Modernity has not simply been a time in which massive traumas have occurred, it is also something borne of trauma. Modernity *is* the renunciation of tradition's authority, the differentiation of society, the Copernican revolution, meaning both the astronomical and the philosophical shift in our understanding of our own place in the order of things. It *is* the cataclysmic transformations of the world from agrarian to industrial; from feudal to capitalist; from peoples rooted in place to displaced and dispersed around the globe, most horrifically in the Middle Passage of slavery; from a logic of similitude to a logic of identity and difference (black/white; first world/third world; East/West);[1] from the order of traditions to the bewilderment of a life without foundations; from unity to complexity, differentiation, and compartmentalization.[2] For all its comforts, modernity has come about brutally. And for the many who have made these comforts possible, it is far from comfortable.

I do not think that we yet fully fathom, nor have we worked through, this transformation into modernity. Much less have we recovered. Perhaps what we call postmodernism is a kind of blinking of the lights, a look underneath the pretenses of modernity, a belated and still highly intelligent resistance to what modernity wreaks. Habermas has made this point, but in a rather reactionary manner, siding with modernity. I don't mind siding with the postmoderns as well as with traditionalists such as MacIntyre who hesitate and pause before what modernity brings. At the same time, I am a committed modernist, from the aesthetics of architecture and design to the ideals of democracy and self-authorship. Where the traditionalists bemoan the lack of authority that gives meaning to life, I side with the existentialists who say we have to make it up and stand by it ourselves. There is little to appeal to in the way of communicative reason, in what Habermas thinks are the implicit ideals of reason that guide our everyday encounters. These ideals are flimsy and easily abused. Where we are now is life on the edge.

We need to explore several facets of the traumatic birth of the modern and point to the ways we are still acting out rather than working through the changes, from those that are religious and philosophical to those dealing with nation-states, science, and the economy. All of them are deeply interconnected. The economic shift to capitalism requires both modern science and the passing of old traditions and authorities. A new world run according to the logic of profit, expansion, property (including one's own labor that can be bought and sold) and technological know-how cannot have archaic traditions standing in the way. So out they have gone.

We have not fully grieved the loss of tradition or, rather, the loss of traditions that are given in advance rather than made by our own hand. This inquiry will move from the philosophical to the global. I will begin with what Nietzsche looked into, how the world became a fable, and Heidegger's continuation of that inquiry and Weber's sociological analysis of the disenchantment of the world. The philosophical inversion of reality took place against the backdrop of a very real cataclysm that tore apart traditions to make way for colonialism, global capitalism, and an endless war on terror.

HOW THE WORLD BECAME A FABLE . . . AND A PICTURE

At least since Plato, philosophers have divvied up reality between the real and the apparent. In their account, there is what is really real, which can only be grasped through reason, and what is only apparently real, what we gather through our senses. To say that something "seems" to be so is already to doubt it. What seems to us, what comes to be grasped sensuously, is not to be trusted. Plato came on the heels of other ancients, as Heidegger, who had more faith in the senses, reminds us. Or rather, they thought that the world presented itself to human beings and human beings were able to apprehend what opened it:

> That which is, is that which arises and opens itself, which, as what presences, comes upon man as the one who presences, i.e., comes upon the one who himself opens himself to what presences in that he apprehends it. That which is does not come into being at all through the fact that man first looks upon it, in the sense of a representing that has the character of subjective perception. Rather, man is the one who is looked upon by that which is; he is the one who is—in company with itself—gathered toward presencing, by that which opens itself. (Heidegger 1977:131)

This ancient worldview got disrupted and began to be inverted with Plato. As Heidegger writes, "Certainly through Plato's thinking and Aristotle's questioning a decisive change takes place in the interpretation of what is and of men, but it is a change that always remains on the foundation of the Greek fundamental experience of what is" (ibid. 143). Again, this experience is of having to take in what is presencing itself to oneself. Heidegger understands Protagoras's famous dictum—that man is the measure of all things—to mean "whatever at a given time anything shows itself to me as, of such aspect is it (also) for me; but whatever it shows itself to you as, such is it in turn for you. You are a man as much as I" (ibid. 144). Reality might have many aspects, and any one of us may see some particular aspect. This does not mean that truth is relative, but that different aspects of the real might be revealed differently to one person or another. The popular sophist notion that truth is whatever I happen to think it is was wrong; the real "sophist," such as Protagoras, wasn't a relativist. Truth is not based upon the perceiver's take or whim; it is what it is, and we are wise to be as open to it as possible. The preplatonic Greek task was to tarry within the horizon of unconcealment, to try to gather truth and save it, trying to keep a footing while being buffeted by "sundering confusions" (ibid. 131).

Plato enters into a world that experiences the world this sensuous way, and he does preserve that way of knowing in his notion of the apparent world. But he is very worried by the sophism that manipulates appearances at the peril of truth. So he juxtaposes a world of seeming and appearance to a world of unchanging truths. As Nietzsche notes in *Twilight of the Idols*, in the section, "How the 'Real World' Finally Became a Fable: History of an Error," "I. The real world attainable for the wise man, the pious man, the virtuous man—he lives in it, *he is it*. (Most ancient form of the idea, relatively clever, simple, convincing. Paraphrase of the proposition: 'I, Plato, *am* the truth.')" (Nietzsche 1998:20).

In this move, according to Nietzsche, Plato paves the way for the modern notion that the world can only be fathomed as a representation or a picture, as Heidegger puts it, that is created by a knower. "Precisely as a struggle against sophism and therefore in dependency upon it, this changed interpretation is so decisive that it proves to be the end of Greek thought, an end that at the same time indirectly prepares the possibility of the modern age" (Heidegger 1977:143).

With Plato, as Nietzsche notes at the start of his tale, the real world is available to the select few who are wise, pious, and virtuous. It takes a strong ability to measure for reason to ascertain what is real and true. These things cannot be had by people taken in by their senses. Still, what keeps this Platonic view ancient and not properly modern is that, when truth is gotten, the knower is apprehending truth and truth is presencing itself. The real world is not only attainable, "he lives in it, *he is it.*" The philosopher who makes his way out of the cave and into the light of the sun is now living in the real, even if this seems to others (such as Aristophanes) to be living in the clouds.

But the real recedes with the advent of Christianity. In the second step of how the real world became a fable, Nietzsche writes: "The real world unattainable for now, but promised to the wise man, the pious man, the virtuous man ('to the sinner who repents'). (Progress is the idea: it becomes more cunning, more insidious, more incomprehensible—*it becomes a woman,* it becomes Christian. . . .)" (Nietzsche 1998:20). Again, it is a promise made to the select, but they will have to wait. It is promised, but unattainable for now. In medieval times, the real world is deferred until the afterlife. So the schism begins.

The real world is taken to another level of deferment with modernity, with Descartes and then Kant, who in his epistemological writings argues that things in themselves can never be known with certainty, though from a moral perspective the idea of what is right will steer us categorically. "3. The real world unattainable, unprovable, unpromisable, but the mere thought of it a consolation, an obligation, an imperative. (The old sun in the background, but seen through mist and skepticism; the idea become sublime, pale, Nordic, Königsbergian.)" (ibid.).

At each historical step, within ancient thought, in the move to Christianity, and then to the modern era, the real world moves further away. "4. The real world—unattainable? At any rate unattained. And since unattained also *unknown.* Hence no consolation, redemption, obligation either: what could something unknown oblige us to do? . . . (Break of day. First yawn of reason. Cock-crow of positivism.)" (ibid.)

By the nineteenth century with positivism, the real became a quaint metaphysical ideal, and only what could be known empirically had any worth. By the fifth step in his tale, Nietzsche is celebrating the demise of the very idea. "5. The 'real world'—an idea with no further use, no longer even an obligation—an idea become useless, superfluous, *therefore* a refuted idea: let us do away with it! (Broad daylight; breakfast; return of *bons sens* and cheerfulness; Plato's shameful blush; din from all free spirits.)" (ibid.).

Or as David Allison puts it,

What the so-called "true world" entailed or embraced, what it ostensibly signified, was, for Nietzsche, practically a catalogue of Western metaphysics: it included the domain of causality, religion, will, being, science, psychology, morality, and purposiveness. Such a "true world," which effectively defines the Judeao-Christian universe itself, the lives and habits of individuals and their culture, as well as the very discourse of the West, for some two millennia—this entire apparatus of our intelligibility itself, Nietzsche attacks with his celebrated "critique of pure fiction." Such a fictional world, he would remark, in *The Antichrist*, one not even attaining to the status of a dream world, finds its initial motivations in precisely a hatred of the actual, the sensible, world of nature.

But this celebration only really gets under way when the division between the real and the apparent is dashed as well. "6. The real world—we have done away with it: what world was left? the apparent one, perhaps? . . . But no! *with the real world we have also done away with the apparent one!* (Noon; moment of the shortest shadow; end of the longest error; pinnacle of humanity; INCIPIT ZARATHUSTRA.)" (ibid.). The contrast of real and apparent is founded on a metaphysics that distrusts life and experience.

Heidegger's concern goes further. He is worried about how we have stripped ourselves of immediate experience. Where the preplatonic Greeks found themselves in a world of presencing, we find ourselves in a situation where nothing is present to us. Instead we are beings who represent the world to ourselves as a picture. This is twofold: on the one side we become the ground of representations; on the other side the representation is never adequate for real experience. As for the first side, in modernity

man becomes subject. We must understand this word subiectum, however, as the translation of the Greek hypokeimenon. The word names that-which-lies-before, which, as ground, gathers everything onto itself. . . . When man becomes the primary and only real *subiectum*, that means: Man becomes that being upon which all that is, is grounded as regards the manner of its Being and its truth. (Heidegger 1977:128)

As for the other side of this coin, "Man becomes the relational center of that which is as such. But this is possible only when the comprehension of what is as a whole changes" (ibid.). What is is no longer a reality that can be had, certainly not like the reality outside the cave that the true philosopher could enter. In modernity, the best we can do is "get the picture." We might be able to hold the world as picture up to our eyes for scrutiny, but it no longer is present to us. It is at best a representation, and the modern hopes that the representation is a good one. "Hence world picture, when understood essentially, does not mean a picture of the world but the world conceived and grasped as picture." It is, like Baudrillard's simulacrum, a copy without an original.

The real world is now completely deferred, or lost. All we have is a picture we give to ourselves. And we are not in it, except perhaps in some image we have of ourselves that we put in this picture we hold up against ourselves. In modernity, our alienation from the real is complete.

THE DISENCHANTMENT OF THE WORLD

As we tell ourselves in the modern West, the move from the Middle Ages to the Renaissance and then the Enlightenment was a move away from understanding the world as ordered from on high to understanding the world as something that human beings can order and navigate. Though this story gives human beings pride of place in the scheme of things, something that had been vital is lost. In the old order, everything was imbued with meaning and purpose. The new worldview has no room for such enchantments; reason strips away such illusions and lays bare what things are. Describing this loss, Max Weber notes, "The fate of our times is characterized by rationalization and intellectualization and, above all, by the 'disenchantment of the world'" (Weber 1946:155). And a few pages later he describes the subjective loss: "the bearing of man has been disenchanted and denuded of its mystical but inwardly genuine plasticity" (148). Modernity is first and foremost a disenchantment, a casting aside of childish notions such as the traditional ones that everyone has a particular role to fill, a place in the scheme of things. Disenchantment is a kind of trauma, something we, for some reason, visit upon our children with stories of Santa Claus and the tooth fairy. Early in their life, we give them a moment of enchantment, and then on the way to growing up we tear it away. To be grown up in this world is to have been *dis*enchanted.

Were I born into a traditional society, I would be told from the start my place and purpose. I would see myself as a meaningful part of—what Charles Taylor calls embedded within—a larger whole. There is no such narrative structure in the modern era. In fact, the modern chafes at being told what to do. The modern ideal of autonomy is that no one can tell me what I should do with my life. That is for me to decide. But I must also decide what is meaningful and important. Throwing out preordained roles is part of throwing out preordained meaning. In modernity I am free to choose my own purposes and decide what is meaningful. But at the same time I am awash in a world that has no intrinsic meaning or purpose. A world that offers the question "What do you want to be when you grow up?" is a world devoid of intrinsic meaningfulness.

The existentialist response is to choose, to decide by an act of will and performance what is meaningful and right. But there is something unsettling about this state. I could have chosen otherwise. How am I to know whether I am living my life well? What is the standard for deciding what a good life is? If I choose to study and teach philosophy or medicine or art, won't I be haunted by the other things I might have done?

Today we are thrown into a world devoid of intrinsic purpose or meaning. Our place in it is something we choose for ourselves, as best we can. Limitations are seen as failures. Even if I am born into a family or community of deep tradition and faith, this small world is nestled inside a larger one that thinks that faith is a peculiarity. For most people, the disenchanted life, ameliorated with the fabricated rituals and traditions of our made-up communities, works well enough.

Yet even in the sea of modernity, without ready-made life rafts, most people fashion or adopt some traditions and faith, leftovers from an earlier era fashioned to fit comfortably within a modern, secular world. Faith might take up space a day a week, over prayers at dinner, in the rituals of moving from childhood to adolescence and adulthood. There are the children, though, who will rush off in search of something more authentic. The expatriate is this character, leaving home, rejecting the pseudo-truths of his homeland in search of something else, just as the protagonist in Somerset Maugham's *The Razor's Edge*, having returned home after World War I, leaves again, leaving Europe altogether in search of some meaning. The expatriate does this by choice.

Then there are the children of immigrants, or at least those who have left the developing world for developed societies; they are young people growing up in foreign lands, split between tradition, something lost and gone, and modernity. As Olivier Roy writes of second-generation Muslim immigrants, "Contemporary Muslim minorities have to undergo a process of deculturation that has no precedent in history and is not imposed but is the consequence of voluntary displacement and shifts from pristine cultures to a common, uprooted Muslim identity" (Roy 109). He argues that fundamentalism afflicts uprooted Muslims more than established Muslim societies. To be displaced, to be a stranger in a strange land—the sort of displacement so common in modernity—is to be vulnerable to the lure of fundamentalism. Speaking of the situation of foreigners in France, Julia Kristeva, herself a foreigner in France, describes the difficulty facing *les étrangères* of finding a safe home in a land where befriendment tends to come from bleeding hearts, paternalist, perverse people, or paranoiacs. One might suggest, in a strange homage to the International Workers of the World, "foreigners of the world unite," but "things are not so simple," Kristeva writes at the beginning of her book, *Strangers to Ourselves*; "one must take into consideration the domination/exclusion fantasy characteristic of everyone" (24). Even the foreigner finds her own foreigner. In France, she notes, "Italians call the Spaniards foreigners, the Spaniards take it out on the Portuguese, the Portuguese on the Arabs or the Jews, the Arabs on the blacks, and so forth and vice versa" (ibid.). Certainly the same has been so in the United States, where one people after another scapegoats another people after another. Even where links are forged between sets of foreigners, the links "unfailingly snap when fanatical bonds fuse together again communities cemented by pure, hard fantasies" (ibid.).

The fantasies Kristeva refers to, those that some estranged foreigners nurture, are the same ones Roy alludes to now, post 9/11: a "common, uprooted Muslim identity." In my view, this is not a problem peculiar to estranged Islam; it could befall any exile in search of meaning. For the exiled Muslim so seeking, the fantasy can become that of an *Ummah* or universal brotherhood, a fantasy of unity despite or because of estrangement from material and maternal ties. Those who immigrate to a new land are simultaneously, in the very act, emigrants from another, caught in the new land as other and othered from the land of origin, which with distance and time seems more original, sacred, pure. One imagines that the other who others them, that is, the native, is impure; "the foreigner excludes before being excluded, even more than he is being excluded" (24). For those modern nomads, whether Muslims in France or evangelicals in contemporary America, a logic of exclusion is operating as a means of protection, part of a path toward finding purpose and connection in a world that seems to offer none. The result is that "here, on foreign land," Kristeva writes, "the religion of the abandoned forebears is set up in its essential purity and one imagines that one preserves it better than do the parents who have stayed 'back home'" (ibid.). Eerily anticipating the present phenomenon of fundamentalists who have become so as emigrants, she writes, "fundamentalists are more fundamental when they have lost all material ties, inventing for themselves a 'we' that is purely symbolic; lacking a soil it becomes rooted in ritual until it reaches its essence, which is sacrifice" (ibid.). Kristeva may be too cavalier in her characterization of foreigners as all being potential fundamentalists, but her description uncannily accounts for what has happened to those who have gone down this path.

The fundamentalists who boarded and then brought down the planes on September 11, 2001, found their Islam in Europe, among other displaced and alienated youth, not in traditional Islamic countries. Apart from Wahabism in Saudi Arabia, most Muslim countries' brand of Islam is fairly moderate (and even the Saudi extremism can be explained by the huge gap between the wealthy royal family who befriend the West and the poor majority). The point is, fundamentalism is a product of modernity, not traditionalism. Modernity cultivates the alienation that fundamentalism promises to redress.

But as the world goes more global, most traditions are still fabrications, or they are adopted or adhered to in an individualist sense, as a choice that is still somewhat arbitrary. In a truly traditional society these are not matters of choice.

THE RACIAL CONTRACT AND THE RISE OF MODERNITY

One of the most extended, global, and traumatic events of the modern era, namely the fifteenth to the nineteenth centuries, is the trauma of Africans abducted and sold into slavery in the Americas. Upwards of 20 million Africans died in the "Middle Passage," the route of trade between continents in which African slaves were inhumanely and brutally packed and shipped from Africa to the Americas. The slaves were traded for sugar cane and other goods that went to Europe, where they were traded for money and goods that could be shipped off to Africa to purchase more slaves. Vast wealth and empires were made upon this triangular trade. It was the seed for the rise of a modern, global economy. Slavery made modernity as an economic fact possible.

This trauma was repeatedly reenacted over the course of centuries that also saw the rise of European power, including the power of those who emigrated to the Americas as colonists. The American Revolution portrayed itself as an uprising of colonists against the British colonizers, but in many respects it was simply the maturation of those who came to colonize the Americas. The colonized were the indigenous peoples as well as those who were abducted from Africa and brought over to toil for the benefit of European Americans. As Charles Mills argues, the West has conveniently forgotten the way that white supremacy, slavery, expansion, and exploitation helped found modern nation-states. Instead of recognizing racial oppression as a fundamental source, the West invents a hypothetical story of a social contract in which all willingly agree to forego some of their individual liberty for collective security and freedom. Europeans imagine themselves stepping out of the state of nature into a state of political society; the state of nature is hypothetical for them only in the sense that they do not imagine that they could ever sink into barbarity. They construct nonwhites as barbarians, nonhumans; this construction is a heuristic device (not to mention an economic one) used to found the social contract.

Modernity with its ideas of political philosophy and human dignity could not, it seems, be further from the fact of trading in and brutalizing human beings. Yet in these very same years, political philosophers from Hobbes to Locke developed an idea of a social contract that began with the radical freedom and dignity of human beings. Charles Mills explains the seeming contradiction with his concept of the racial contract, which underlies the social contract by delineating what is "civilized" through a construction of the uncivil as nonwhite. Civil and rational and free and equal all add up to white and European, providing a layer of rationalization to justify expansion and conquest of other lands. In the story of the West, Europeans can lay claim to other lands not just because of their military and economic power but also because of their superiority and uprightness as protectors and agents of civilization.

According to Mills, the racial contract is not just an idea but a historical reality. It is "historically locatable in the series of events marking the creation of the modern world by European colonialism and the voyages of 'discovery' now increasingly and more appropriately called expeditions of conquest" (Mills 1997:20).

We live in a world which has been foundationally shaped for the past five hundred years by the realities of European domination and the gradual consolidation of global white supremacy. Thus not only is the

Racial Contract "real," but . . . the Racial Contract is global, involving a tectonic shift of the ethicojuridical basis of the planet as a whole, the division of the world, as Jean-Paul Sartre put it long ago, between "men" and "natives." (Mills 1997:20)

To rationalize these moves, European social contract theory and practice divide up the world between white and nonwhite; people are placed in hierarchical order, with some taking license in the name of rationality and civilization to dominate others.

COLONIZING THE SEMIOTIC PUBLIC SPHERE

Charles Mills's analysis makes sense and seems obvious. What is scandalous is that it is so easy, especially for white people, not to think about it.

How can this be? How is it that those of us who are Euro-Americans can so easily forget the magnitude and the enormity of a process that helped found the modern social order, the West's economic power, the division of the world between the haves who are overwhelmingly light-skinned and the have-nots who are almost always of color? How can the founding trauma of white privilege go unnoticed? Shannon Sullivan gives a brilliant analysis by developing the concept of a "collective raced unconscious" formed via individuals' psychosomatic habits, which have been handed down from one generation to another (Sullivan 2006:94–96). This collective unconscious is not the Jungian sort, which, Sullivan argues, confuses habit with instinct (97), but one that arises culturally and historically and is passed down from one group to another, a collective unconscious that haunts subsequent generations. Drawing on the work of Nicolas Abraham and Maria Torok, Sullivan calls this collective unconscious a phantom: "an unspeakable secret from previous generations that will not die, that has a murky but very real presence amongst the living" (110).

Via their connections to this phantom collective unconscious, both masters and slaves bequeathed to subsequent generations modes of bodily comportment, ways of interacting with others, that flowed from their position as master or slave. Unconscious, these habits can go undetected. As Sullivan writes,

What I find interesting about collective unconscious habits of white privilege is that, from the perspective of the individual, they both do

and do not seem to exist. Often the impact of the collective unconscious on an individual is uneventful. No one has ever sat down and
explicitly explained to me, for example, the (alleged) superiority of
white people. There is no specific event to point to. Nothing seems to
have happened, and no collective knowledge about white superiority
seems to exist. Yet it does. A white privileged collective unconscious
has slipped, undetected, into my individual habits. Because of this
slippage, I unconsciously "know" that white people are superior to all
others, and I manifest that knowledge in my psychosomatic engagement with the world. (Sullivan 2006:95)

Drawing on the work of Frantz Fanon and contemporary psychoanalysis, Sullivan describes the collective unconscious as a traumatic inheritance that can "haunt" contemporary individuals (101). These inheritances
need not be bequeathed straightforwardly. A black man who had grown up
in French Martinique, a predominantly black French colony, Fanon realized later, after traveling to France, that his culture had inherited the white
values of France that held that whiteness was good and blackness bad.
Fanon, along with the rest of his culture, grew up identifying himself as
white and making all the usual French (Western) associations of whiteness
with purity. This ethical slippage (*glissement éthique*) passed into Antillean
culture via literary, visual, and aural media. Through "history textbooks,
songs, and especially magazines and movies . . . black schoolchildren in
the Antilles were explicitly taught to identify with 'our ancestors, the Gauls'"
(98). Hence, "the collective unconscious of '*homo occidentalis*' became that
of the Martiniquean, and the Martiniquean also learned to distrust blackness as symbolizing everything sinful and evil" (97–98).

Earlier I described the public sphere as a discursive or semiotic space
through which signifying human beings try to fashion and refashion the
meaning of life, the shape of their communities, and political direction,
through language, signs, and symbols. I suggested that the matrices and
grids of these intersecting and dynamic signifying processes are so prevalent that people often do not notice them for what they are: ways everyday
reality is constructed. Now, to make things even more interesting, Fanon's
work and Sullivan's discussion of it reveal one more level of complexity.
The public sphere carries not only today's attempts at making meaning
but also unconscious meanings carried over from the past. In the case of
Fanon, Sullivan describes how the entertainment media carried the trau-

matic past and its distortions into his present world. The public media of Martinique carried the signs and symbols of a racist culture in such a way that racist values became part of the frame of everyday life, the "natural" order of things. Likewise, the media in any public sphere have this power to structure reality in a way that the structures become invisible as such. Sullivan notes that

> because the ethical slippage from France to Martinique operated by means of media images, it was difficult to detect and, as a result, especially effective. As Fanon comments, "the black man among his own in the twentieth century does not know at what moment his inferiority comes into being through the other." Magazines, comic books, movies: these generally are seen as frivolous and pleasurable, as mere entertainment, but their frivolity is what makes them so insidious. The values they convey slip into one's thinking subtly, smoothly—this is what is conveyed by the particular term *un glissement éthique.* (98)

The media in Martinique not only carried the message of white superiority, they also carried the trauma of slavery and the inheritance of racism. Growing up, Fanon had never experienced directly the insults of white-on-black racism—he grew up without encountering any whites at all—yet once he was a university student at the Sorbonne, surrounded by white people, he immediately developed the neuroses symptomatic of racist trauma. Though he was not physically or personally traumatized in childhood, the media images of white superiority traumatized him nonetheless.

Kelly Oliver puts it another way: "it is the fact that the colonized are oppressed by the preformed stereotypical image of themselves propagated by the colonizer that makes their alienation unique" (Oliver 2004:26). She notes that the colonized are "thrown into a world of meaning not of their making," a meaning that includes the meaning of the colonized, beings incapable of making meaning themselves (ibid.). From this perspective, the trauma of colonization is finding oneself foreclosed by semiotic systems over which one has no control, being caught in a realm of being that is semiotically structured but unable to have any part in refashioning it. Colonialism works its evil by foreclosing the possibility for those who are colonized to sublimate their desires and affects, to channel inchoate energy into meaningful semiotic structures. Rendered speechless, deprived of subjectivity, they cannot "find themselves" in the semiotic public sphere.

Despite Marshall McLuhan's pithy phrase to the contrary, the media in fact do carry a message, but not in the form of transmitting information from sender to receiver. The media are the medium in which political trauma moves from one generation to another. Or to put matters in a different frame, the semiotic, discursive public sphere carries within it the traumas that gave rise to itself in its current form. As with the example above, the trauma of slavery was part of a racial contract, forgotten as such but reformulated in the West's (false) consciousness with the concept of a social contract. In that modern Western myth, all people freely consent to give up some of their own prerogatives in exchange for the security or freedom that will come with the formation of political society. But in fact political society as we know it is founded on the traumatic subjugation and exploitation of people of color throughout the world. As other writers have noted, the contemporary conservative call for a "color-blind" society masks the fact that the social order is still ridden with color divisions and hierarchies. To be color-blind today is to turn a blind eye to the problems that affect people of color. The political Right calls for consciously forgetting color, but media images and messages still transport, in whatever thinly veiled form, a racist collective unconscious.

MYTH AND THE BACKLASH OF FUNDAMENTALISM

Myths are efficient ways of speaking by means of which some situation or other comes about and is maintained. We know how: by carrying out, with the help of their manifest content, the repression of their latent content. Myths, therefore, indicate a gap in introjection, in the communication with the Unconscious. If they provide food for understanding, they do so much less by what they say than by what they do not say, by their blanks, their intonations, their disguises. Instruments of repression, myths also serve as a vehicle for the symbolic return of the repressed. (Abraham and Torok 1994:94)

Premodern truth, as Lyotard has noted, is based on narratives such as religion and myth. If the earliest myths are responses to the fact of being thrown into a world of much danger and uncertainty, stories that manifestly offer explanations of human purpose and place in the world, their latent meaning is that perhaps there is no such purpose or place, that such hopes for certainty are human fabrications and all such values are only contingently true, even if necessary for equilibrium. Myths offer reasons in a world that lacks them; they offer a sense of identity and place to peoples who lack anything certain on which to hang identity or on which to ground themselves. Myths evolve into religions that offer the same comforts. But over time these stories and traditions of purpose, meaning, identity, and place are stories responding to events that shatter illusions of purpose and place, that upturn established boundaries and identities.

The Copernican revolution. The Crusades. The fall of Constantinople. Nine-eleven. From originary myths that gave a people security until today, myths have changed from tales of purpose to tales of trauma. The stories of the Jews are stories of exile; the stories of the Christians are ones of persecution; the stories of Muslims are stories of splintering within and attack from without. And through the interlocking histories, since all three "peoples of the book" have occupied the same lands, their stories and the identities they provide have become ways to account for themselves in relation, often in opposition, to others.

CONCLUSION

Trauma presents a choice: either work through it or cover it over with denial and fabrications. The traumas of our modern times—from the Middle Passage of slavery that founded contemporary empires to the brutal disenchantment that has exchanged the sacred for the profane and arbitrary—are manifestly still wrenching the public worlds we inhabit. They have produced their own stories, the metanarratives of modernity, which say history is marching forward for the sake of freedom, justice, progress. A modern story "legitimates itself with reference to a metadiscourse," writes Lyotard, yet these metanarratives have become unraveled in the postmodern unraveling and unveiling of them as myths in their own right. Still wedded to stories such as "we have gone to war for the sake of democracy" or "our aims are beneficent and righteous," we find ourselves creating debauched situations like Abu Ghraib. The myth of democratic intentions gets frayed and we begin to see that the real aim may simply be power. These untended traumas, covered over, still largely denied, prompt a repetition compulsion. Today's peoples of the book, Christians, Jews, and Muslims—those who try to maintain sacred spaces and identities in a world that resists them—and agnostics and other apostates all face the task of creating meaning anew, but not on the bloody shards of old traumatic events. Otherwise we are doomed to revisit these traumas without end.

CHAPTER 3

Targeting the Public Sphere

In appearance, speech may well be of little account, but the prohibitions surrounding it soon reveal its links with desire and power. This should not be very surprising, for psychoanalysis has already shown us that speech is not merely the medium which manifests— or dissembles—desire; it is also the object of desire. Similarly, historians have constantly impressed upon us that speech is no mere verbalization of conflicts and systems of domination, but that it is the very object of man's conflicts.

—Michel Foucault, from "The Discourse on Language"

TRAUMA'S DEFENSES AND THE MODERN STATE

The last chapter charted the traumatic birth of the modern and ended with the choice trauma presents: either to work through it or to cover it over with denial. For the most part, modernity has chosen the latter. Maintaining denial, given the enormity of some of these traumas, requires major defenses. We saw some of these in the last chapter, enumerated in Anna Freud's list: "regression, repression, reaction-formation, isolation, undoing, projection, introjection, turning against the self, and reversal" (Rycroft 1995:32). To what extent are these defenses tied up with the meaning of modernity itself? Charles Taylor describes modernity as a "historically unprecedented amalgam of new practices and institutional forms (science, technology, industrial production, urbanization); of new ways of living (individualism, secularization, instrumental rationality); and of new forms of malaise (alienation, meaninglessness, a sense of impending social dissolution)" (Taylor 2004:1). In this very nice list there is a notable omission: the rise of the nation-state, a political entity to which many cities and peoples can belong and that eventually becomes the representative of the sovereign people, a political but also a cultural entity to which we can pay fealty, loyalty, and patriotism and with which we feel solidarity. Certainly this development was caused by numerous factors, but might it also be the product of many defenses against the cataclysmic loss of an enchanted world in which leaders were ordained by the established order of things?

Could the nation-state be, at least in part, a product of repression, reaction-formation, isolation, projection, and introjection? So much power needs to be enlisted to bring together people spread across hundreds of miles into one national identity, for them to even think of themselves as a nation. Could defenses against modernity's traumas have had such power and made possible the necessary coalitions and coalescences?

The instability and unease of modernity certainly called for new social identities, new ways of fortifying oneself. With the defense of isolation, a nation can attempt to ward off external threats and avoid conflict. In the case of the United States, for example, a policy of isolationism could serve as a denial of the New World's guilt in the slave trade, the global trafficking in human beings on which American wealth was created and that gave the lie to the central precepts of the United States' founding documents. The explicit policy of isolationism that remained in place until World War II (even with the brief interlude of World War I) served to sever U.S. indebtedness to other peoples; it also served to shield the United States from becoming enmeshed in European politics. Ensconced between oceans to the east and west and between acquiescent neighbors to the north and south, the United States, especially in its heartland, seemed safe. It still sought to be a world power, but without becoming entangled in the affairs of the world. After World War II, the United States left isolationism behind, but then mustered another defense to fortify itself: repression, most acutely in the paranoia of McCarthyism, where any "dangerous" elements that seemed to threaten national security were silenced with anticommunist oaths or exiled from the mainstream of culture, society, and economic prosperity. Unease easily translates into threat, threat into enemies (reaction-formation, projection, introjection). Joseph McCarthy was a textbook case of these classic defenses, imagining enemies in every crevice of government, the media, and society. Later Richard Nixon, mired in Vietnam and then Watergate, came up with his own enemies list.

A goal of isolationism is sovereignty, being an inviolable subject with no master but oneself. Yet when sovereignty is sought through defensive means that turn offensive, a reaction is formed; sovereignty is sought aggressively by denying the sovereignty of others. In a post–9/11 world, the United States leads the way in this neurosis. Writing shortly after 9/11, Judith Butler notes that while nations

> are not the same as individual psyches . . . both can be described as "subjects," albeit of different orders. When the United States acts, it establishes a conception of what it means to act as an American, establishes a norm by which that subject might be known. In recent months, a subject has been instated at the national level, a sovereign and extra-legal subject, a violent and self-centered subject; its actions constitute the building of a subject that seeks to restore and maintain its mastery through the systematic destruction of its multilateral relations, its ties to the international community. It shores itself up, seeks to reconstitute its imagined wholeness, but only at the price of denying its own vulnerability, its dependency, its exposure, where it exploits those very features in others, thereby making those features "other to" itself. (Butler 2004:41)

Like Pearl Harbor, 9/11 shattered the illusion of U.S. sovereignty. Its borders were permeable, fragile, vulnerable, even though these were, in the case of Pearl Harbor, borders of a territory and not the United States proper. In both cases, to reestablish imagined sovereignty and power, to deny its vulnerability, the United States waged war on others. Pearl Harbor brought the United States into a world war that was already raging. Nine-eleven led it to wage a new war on stateless but transnational enemies who might take refuge in the caves of Afghanistan or on the borders of Iraq. Battling these elusive others is difficult; establishing sovereignty by making them vulnerable is nigh impossible, unless we begin to conflate the enemy with the innocent people who harbor them. And so we waged war with our mighty weapons and high-tech drones, setting our sights on Al Qaeda or Saddam Hussein's national guard, but in fact murdering countless innocents.

REGRESSION, ABJECTION, AND THE PSYCHOTIC STATE

In addition to isolationism and the other defenses that Anna Freud had noticed, there is one noticed by Julia Kristeva: abjection (Kristeva 1982). In Kristeva's account, abjection precedes other defenses. Something that is abject is "an 'object' of primary repression (in scare quotes because at this stage of development, showing up in the very first year or two of development, there is no self/other distinction at work, though the abject continues to haunt or police the self into maturity)."[1] The abject is a quasi-other that we imagine on the way to becoming a member of a symbolic world with others. Abjection is a step toward becoming a subject, a "one" distinct from others. In this first step of primary repression, we abject what threatens to keep us in the animal realm.[2] "The abject confronts us . . . with those fragile states where man strays on the territories of animal" (ibid. 12). How does abjection work in social bodies? "Primitive societies," Kristeva writes, "have marked out a precise area of their culture in order to remove it from the threatening world of animals, or animalism, which were imagined as representatives of sex and murder" (ibid. 12–13).

The birth of modern nation-state identity seems to have called for a more advanced abjection. The Hobbesian imaginary of the state of nature, a world in which life was nasty, brutish, and short, seems to be part of this abject consciousness. Recall Charles Mills's observation discussed in the last chapter, that the state of nature served as a hypothetical, let us now say imaginary,[3] construct to separate whites from nonwhites, for Europeans could never imagine themselves sinking into that kind of brutality. But they could and did imagine nonwhites there, so the nonwhite became the limit of the social and hence the negative designation of what the social is. The nonwhite, non-European "barbarian" served as the basis for the social contract; it was the abject other of the modern nation-state. But this other is not outside; it is abject because it is within, but part of oneself that, it seems, must be expelled in order to construct a clean and proper identity. Yet even in the state of abjection, the abject cannot be expelled. Note Mills's observation that the slave trade was also the economic basis for the rise of the modern economy. Economically, the modern nation-state could not arise without bringing nonwhites into its fold; they became constitutive but always threatening elements of nation-state identity.

The abject is not quite other, not entirely foreign; it is on the periphery of identity, something we imagine must be expelled in order to constitute orderly boundaries. A psychoanalytic lens helps us see how political societies can be formed by abjection of uneasy elements of the self. The nation-state forms, but some of its members seem to threaten its purported identity. They may be productive and objectively useful members of the whole, but the whole cannot conceive of them as proper to itself. So it tries to banish them. Isn't something like this the fate, still to this day, of undocumented immigrant labor, the untouchables in India, the Roma in Europe, migrant workers in the farmlands, blacks in America? We have had millennia of such misadventures, attempts to found identity by denying identity and agency to others, to fashion a "we" by an exclusion of others. Instead of being founded through social eros, community is founded on negation of "abject" others. The libidinal energy that might tie people together twists back in a narcissistic and defensive self-aggrandizement. Are we at some level still in the throes of abjection, still in—or back in—a state of primary repression that doesn't even have the resources of a neurotic (who at least has symbolic capacities)?

To return to Freud's account in *Civilization and Its Discontents,* phylogenetically, civilization is the product of many individuals developing mores that bind them together. Very cautiously, Freud suggests that the processes that help create individual identity might also be at work in the development of social identity, and that the disorders that befall the individual might also befall the society. In its journey from being a dispersion of presocial individuals to its aim of being a social body, civilization might suffer developmental setbacks similar to the kinds of neuroses suffered by individuals. "If the development of civilization has such a far-reaching similarity to the development of the individual and if it employs the same methods, may we not be justified in reaching the diagnosis that, under the influence of cultural urges, some civilizations, or some epochs of civilization—possibly the whole of mankind—have become 'neurotic'? An analytic dissection of such neuroses might lead to therapeutic recommendations which could lay claim to great practical interest" (Freud 1961:110). Freud refers to these setbacks as neuroses, which in psychoanalytic terms are disorders that plague individuals who are otherwise comfortably situated in the sociosymbolic order. Under the heading of neuroses, psychoanalysts would include anxieties and compulsions.

A repetition compulsion is usually a sign of neurosis. Colloquially speaking, a neurotic person may have problems, but he or she is definitely sane, that is, in touch with reality. Conversely, psychotics suffer from disorders through which they lose their foothold in the sociosymbolic order. Psychoses include schizophrenia, bipolar disorders, extremely severe depression, and paranoia. These maladies evidence a regression from the sociosymbolic order to an archaic stage of development—what looks like the stage of primary repression (including abjection) and the autoimmunity of narcissism. This can be signaled by an inability to speak and by a general disassociation from what we normally call reality. The psychotic has lost the bounds of ego and the bonds of sociality that demarcate and situate him or her in a world with other subjects. The psychosis severs the subject from the sociosymbolic field.

Certainly there are ways societies become neurotic, perhaps when their authoritarian agencies (analogous to an individual's superego) begin to excessively monitor and control elements within the social body, especially those that seem to threaten or undermine the stability of the social field and the identity of the body politic. But there are also ways societies become psychotic, losing hold on the signs and symbols that tether the social world together. Brutal regimes of the past century, from Hitler's Nazi regime to Cambodia's Khmer Rouge and those leading massacres in Rwanda, Darfur, and the Balkans, seem to be societies stricken, rendered psychotic by some party's design—by unraveling the bonds that held them together. For the sake of winning something—but what?—they destroy their sociosymbolic public sphere. Neurotic societies take aim at other nations, but psychotic ones take aim primarily at themselves, attacking internal "enemies" in a manner that is thoroughly self-defeating. Such regimes terrorize parts of their own body politic or try to excise some parts of it, largely by attacking their members' position in a human or public space. The extreme, genocide, begins with dehumanization (making it easier for soldiers to cut down these "others" and making victims less than human or the walking dead). More run-of-the-mill terror isolates subjects from each other. Their civil wars are not waged by attacking the sociosymbolic order directly—for there is no entity as such; it is an intersubjective field, an array of signs, laws, structures, and customs that have meaning by virtue of its members' observance of them. Civil or oppressive internal war is waged by striking the members' membership in this field, leaving them bereft of an ability to partake in and maintain the realm of signs and symbols that make a mass of people into a community.

WITHOUT SUBLIMATION

Speculating on what life must have been like for early human beings as they underwent a transformation from instinctive to thinking beings, Nietzsche writes, "these semi-animals, happily adapted to the wilderness, to war, free roaming, and adventure, were forced to change their nature. Of a sudden they found all their instincts devalued, unhinged" (Nietzsche 1956:217). Without the "guidance of their unconscious drives," they were "forced to think, deduce, calculate, weigh cause and effect—unhappy people, reduced to their weakest, most fallible organ, their consciousness!" (ibid.). Their old instincts had not gone away, but now they could rarely be satisfied, or satisfaction could only be found covertly. It was Nietzsche, not Freud, who first articulated drive theory: "All instincts that are not allowed

free play turn inward," he writes. "This is what I call man's interioriza-
tion; it alone provides the soil for the growth of what is later called man's
soul. Man's interior world, originally meager and tenuous, was expanded
in every dimension, in proportion as the outward discharge of his feelings
was curtailed" (Nietzsche 1956:218). In a social world, drives and instincts
that threaten society become taboo and are turned inward, creating what
Nietzsche calls "bad conscience."

In the Freudian picture, much like the Nietzschean one, energy needs
to be discharged, lest it reverberate and haunt the self. Desire needs to be
cathected, that is, connected to some one being or to many, so that it does not
turn back on itself. In the Lacanian picture, desire reaching outward fuels our
entry into a sociosymbolic world. And as Kristeva has noted, failures to sublimate render us back into a presymbolic, mute—but not peaceful—existence.

In what must have been most painful research into the memoirs of victims and survivors of death camps in the twentieth century, Terence Des
Pres began to see the interconnection between the body and the psyche,
and the ways an attack upon one is an attack upon both, or, that is, upon
the whole human/bodily person.

> The basic structure of Western civilization or perhaps of any civiliza-
> tion, insofar as the processes of culture and sublimation are one, is the
> division between body and the spirit, between concrete existence and
> symbolic modes of being. In extremity, however, divisions like these
> collapse. The principle of compartmentalization no longer holds, and
> organic being becomes the immediate locus of selfhood. When this
> happens, body and spirit become the ground of each other, each bear-
> ing the other's need, the other's sorrow, and each responds directly
> to the other's total condition. If spiritual resilience declines, so does
> physical endurance. If the body sickens, the spirit too begins to lose its
> grip. There is a strange circularity about existence in extremity; survi-
> vors preserve their dignity in order "not to begin to"; they care for the
> body as a matter of "moral survival." (Des Pres 1976:65)

When such failures afflict social entities, not just individuals (leaving
aside for the moment that no person ever exists in isolation), an internal
war can go on inside the body politic. Instead of successful sublimation,
we can have malformations of public spheres. The energy that is neither
sublimated nor discharged is often driven back underground into what

we call the unconscious, here the political unconscious. There are misfired attempts at sublimation, but rarely healthy ones. There is thwarted
sublimation, signs of the scarring of a public sphere founded on abjection
and annihilation of others, or on a closing of the ranks of a "we" imagined
to be threatened by others. Like any energy, the energy that fuels these
misadventures moves into "cultural" expression: whether the "culture" of
Jim Crow and all its stereotypical representations of black people, or the
screeches of Rush Limbaugh and all his invective against "feminazis," or
the slightly more subtle but no less effective cultural depictions of Muslims and other others. To be sure, even "misfired" and "thwarted" sublimations can produce great art; they can circulate in the sociosymbolic sphere.
And sometimes they can be part of a process of working through trauma
whose result may well be healthy for the public sphere and lead to a more
democratic and inclusive society. My point here is that, as often as not,
what becomes sublimated and circulates in the sociosymbolic sphere may
serve to perpetuate and reinforce injustices.

The residue of desires that are not successfully sublimated, that is,
transformed into meaningful sociosymbolic culture, are driven back into
a political unconscious that continues to try to discharge its energy. The
political unconscious is not something separate from a political entity; to
the contrary, it is part of the very soil and foundation of the political, an
absent presence, a periphery that continuously seeks entry, a source of
energy and undoing, a doing that threatens to undo what is overtly present.
Along these lines, Judith Butler writes, "The public sphere is constituted in
part by what cannot be said and what cannot be shown. The limits of the
sayable, the limits of what can appear, circumscribe the domain in which
political speech operates and certain kinds of subjects appear as viable
actors" (Butler 2004:xvii). This is not pure circumscription, for what is outside the system continuously seeps in, triggering vigilance and abjection.

What is unconscious may be forgotten, but it is not released. Whether it is
a product of repression due to the taboos that make "civilization" possible, a
trauma experienced from some cataclysmic event, or a loss yet to be mourned,
the content of the unconscious continues to shape and impinge upon the conscious psyche. When unconsciously some parts of the self are felt as abject,
as threats to the integrity of the body politic, then who can "appear as viable
actors" is a decision shot through the political realm, affecting both those who
are abjected and those who abject: that Jews could not be part of a public world
in Nazi Germany, that they were less than human, was a thought that issued

from a political unconscious teeming with abjection. This was a trauma stemming from Germany's failure to develop a modern, political, Christian identity, or from an older inability to develop a Christian identity that could neither
forego nor welcome the Jew that Christ was first and always. Perhaps it was a
trauma of secularization, of nation-state building.

There are profound effects of such failures to sublimate, namely two
kinds of phenomena: civil wars that seek to banish some from membership in the political community and international wars that seek to preserve the security of one nation at the expense of another's. Such a distinction—between civil and international wars—works to a point, but even it
fails when war waged by one country on another leads to civil war within
the besieged nation, or in the case of genocide, when this loathed other is
perhaps a projection of internal demons, abjected selves (just as Hitler's
attempt to annihilate the Jews must have been somehow connected with
his own Jewish blood). In the remainder of this chapter I consider how
these traumas are acted out in internal conflicts, civil wars, and other brutal repressions. Chapter 4 looks more broadly at how untended traumas—
whether suffered yesterday or hundreds of years ago—can give rise to a
repetition compulsion and an endless war on terror.

THE AIMS OF BRUTALITY

We live in a time of terror: not just the terror of suicide bombers and fun-
damentalist cells but also the terror that a people can inflict on itself. One
need only consult the tragic roster of brutal and repressive regimes that
have systematically sought to decimate vital portions of the body politic:
South Africa's recently felled apartheid government, the Khmer Rouge in
the killing fields of Cambodia, the marauding rape squads in Rwanda,
the death squads in the mountains of Guatemala, and now those bent on
genocide in Darfur. Beyond reason and rationale, barely speakable, theirs
are political crimes inflicted on their own people. One can barely fathom
the motives, but the effects are clear: in addition to being callously inhumane, brutal regimes silence and eventually annihilate the invisible fabric
that connects people as a society, culture, civilization, or state. That fabric
is woven via a public space where meaning and norms are made. As the
war correspondent Chris Hedges notes,

> War breaks down long-established prohibitions against violence,
> destruction, and murder. And with this often comes the crumbling of

sexual, social, and political norms as the domination and brutality of the battlefield is carried into personal life. Rape, mutilation, abuse, and theft are the natural outcome of a world in which force rules, in which human beings are objects. The infection is pervasive. Society in wartime becomes atomized. (Hedges 2002:103–104)

War crimes are not just those that affect individuals' welfare (again, not to suggest that welfare can ever be purely individual); they are those that strike at shared understandings of what is right and wrong, that undermine a people's ability to make such distinctions.

Brutal regimes range from those engaged in civil war and torture to the milder repressive and authoritarian ones. Yet all share key features. Political crime may begin mildly, banning public associations and preventing people from joining organizations not controlled by the state, as in China, where the only public associations allowed are those sanctioned by the Communist Party. Even in the midst of liberalization, reformers have focused upon liberalizing the market rather than on liberalizing the public sphere.

When there are no places in which people can gather to discuss matters of public concern, there is little opportunity for a public to denounce the regime as illegitimate. This phenomenon was exemplified just before the fall of the Berlin Wall. In East Germany and in Czechoslovakia, civil associations began to form at the same time that the Soviet Union was pulling back its coercive power over the Eastern Bloc. Without this enforcement, communist party governments began to tolerate some associations. These began to denounce the "people's" governments as illegitimate, as anything but representatives of the people. Within a matter of days, the governments stepped down and the undisputed communist party reign ended, testifying to the power of public associations.

More fundamentally, without public spaces, no entity can form that we might recognize as a public. Instead there will be the mass of people, each concerned with the continuance of his or her own private life. To keep a people from becoming a public, authoritarian regimes often take as a first step the banning of public associations or gatherings.

More brutal and repressive regimes go further. They attempt to destroy some or all of citizens' self-understanding as citizens. They do this systematically, through any number of practices—racism, torture, rape, making citizens "disappear," and other forms of brutality. In "Violence as Self-Sacrifice: Creative Pacifism in a Violent World," Aaron Fortune makes a similar claim about violence in general:

The relevant aspect of violence . . . is its forceful reduction of possibility to actuality. This structure works on many levels, some more concrete than others. If I kill you, I concretely end your possibilities for becoming in this world. If I maim you, physically or mentally, I impair your future by reducing your physical and/or mental capabilities for future action, perhaps handicapping you or traumatizing you such that you think of nothing except ways to get even. More abstractly, forcefully reducing your possibilities for becoming characterizes your possibilities as unworthy of realization or less valuable than mine. I limit your freedom of personal becoming by telling you your possibilities are no better than your actuality and your actuality is not valuable enough to exist. Any act that has this effect or intent is at least abstractly violent, regardless of its level of physicality.[4]

While torture is at the extreme of violence, even verbal and legal assaults that undermine one's sense of possibility work on the same plane, denying someone an equal footing in his or her own culture.

These practices might be carried out by a regime seeking to annihilate opposition movements or a party in a civil war. At first glance, incidents of brutality may seem to be an assault upon one private individual after another. I contend that they are better understood as assaults upon the public sphere, conducted by undoing individuals' participation in that sphere. Without collective participation, the public sphere dissolves into nothing, for it is in the first place the fact of participation by many in a common world with others.

Both the civic republican tradition and psychoanalytic theory help show how such practices strip subjects of their identity as agents in a political community. Republicanism, understanding the institutions of a polity as *res publica*, things created by the public, calls for participation from all members. To be prevented from being able to shape the direction of the republic, is to undermine the public sphere itself (Viroli 1999:101–103). Psychoanalytic theory, as I have been drawing on it in this book, shows how participation is in large part a matter of being able to use semiotic energy, to sublimate, in order to help shape and define what is meaningful and important in the public sphere. As Viroli notes, "Men and women learn citizenship when they go to union meetings, join sports groups, attend city council hearings, participate in church activities, or become members of a political party: all these practices occur in places and contexts that are culturally dense, specific, meaningful" (Viroli 1999:102). But it is not enough simply to be in the room or to absorb the norms of citizenship; one should be able to help shape what happens in that room, to have a say in what should be. To be deprived of the ability to sublimate individual drives into public meaning is to be cut off from a central aspect of citizenship. From both traditions, one can see that membership in a political community, that is, citizenship, is granted not only with a piece of paper but through affective, somatic, and psychic participation in a polity's sociosymbolic field. When brutal regimes humiliate and silence any citizens, they effectively strip them of their ability to participate in a common world. They dispossess people of their title as citizen, "title" literally meaning belief in one's legitimate place as someone to be heeded by others, someone who can contribute to thinking with others about matters of common concern.

Barbaric regimes and sometimes parties in civil wars use terror to unravel the sociosymbolic field of their society. Some may be psychotically bent on self-destruction; others may hope to replace this field with one they find more attractive; others still may simply not want a space available for any public deliberation. Whatever their ultimate aim, the immediate effect is that a certain way of being in the world is lost. As I indicated in chapter 1, this is a *public* way of being. Following Aristotle as well as the republican tradition in Western thought, I think that human beings flourish best when they partake in a public world with others, when they have the opportunity to deliberate with others about the shape and future of their life in common.[5]

Such deliberation requires what Hannah Arendt called a "space of appearance" (Arendt 1958). This is more than a visual field in which we appear to others; it is also, as I am suggesting above, a sociosymbolic order, which from a political perspective is called the public sphere or, sometimes, civil society. It is not a place as much as an occurrence, optimally an occurrence that is ongoing, continuously engaged in and re-created through the sociosymbolic activity of its members. The best way, then, to destroy this field is to halt its members' participation therein.

This way of thinking about the public sphere helps, I think, to explain how repressive and brutal regimes set out to undermine it. First they set out to undermine public expectations that rights or the rule of law will be respected. As Rajeev Bhargava writes, "In a barbaric society, where basic procedural justice is dismembered, the entire mechanism of negotiation and arbitration has vanished. Usually, the violation of norms of procedural justice begins with the politically motivated deployment of excessive force. In the early stages of regression into barbarism, gross violations of basic rights—that is, physical intimidation, torture, murder, and even massacres—occur on a fairly large scale" (Bhargava 2000:47). These acts are not aimed, primarily, at brutalizing individuals. They are aimed at destroying the political sphere. As a result, "active deliberation and opposition is brutally terminated. As indifference and submissiveness are routinely generated in a depoliticized environment, the initial use of excessive force makes physical coercion more or less redundant" (Bhargava 2000:47). Bhargava persuasively argues that these evils are political ones. They can be distinguished from nonpolitical crimes in their means and intents:

> A person who is robbed on a highway or systematically exploited on agricultural land or in a factory is a victim, but not a political victim. Political victims are those who are threatened, coerced, or killed because of their attempt to define and shape the character of their own society, and to determine the course of what it might become in the future. When political victims suffer violence, they are not merely harmed physically, however. The act of violence transmits an unambiguous, unequivocal message, that their views on the common good—on matters of public significance—do not count, that their side of the argument has no worth and will not be heard, that they will not be recognized as participants in any debate, and, finally, that to negotiate, or even reach a compromise with them, is worthless. In effect, it signals their disappearance from the public domain. (Bhargava 2000:47)

Bhargava's depiction of political violence rests on a republican vision of what the public domain is: a thing that belongs to all, a space in which all members help to shape and determine their life in common.

Political theorists argue about whether the republican view is apt, but the evidence left by brutal regimes bolsters the idea that the ability to partake in a public realm is a central aspect of citizens' self-understanding as political beings. Seeking to annihilate the public space central to the republican view, they testify to this idea's reality and import. Sometimes a phenomenon is best known through its absence or, in the present case, destruction. If brutal regimes are in fact attempting to undermine the public being of citizens and their polities, the regimes are implicitly attesting to something true about politics as it normally occurs.

Where I use the terms "the public sphere" or "the sociosymbolic order" to describe our world in common, Elaine Scarry uses the terms "the human world" and "civilization," referencing both the artifacts created by advanced cultures and the practices that bind them together. Though the terms can be semantically distinguished, in practice they map onto each other, especially in the practice of their destruction. In her powerful book, *The Body in Pain: The Making and Unmaking of the World*, Scarry describes how torture aims to do much more than inflict pain and produce a "confession," though that is certainly a large part of its purpose. It also aims to sever the victim from a human world, in fact to disintegrate the victim's experience of that world. First the civilized expanse of creations that protect and further human flourishing is reduced to one barren room. The objects in the room that normally serve the welfare of the person—the bed, the bathtub, the chair—are turned into weapons of destruction: the victim chained to a bed, beaten with a chair, submerged and electrocuted in a bathtub.

> Beside the overwhelming fact that a human being is being severely hurt, the exact nature of the weapon or the miming of the deconstruction of civilization is at most secondary. But it is also crucial to see that the two are here forced into being expressions and amplifications of one another: the de-objectifying of the objects, the unmaking of the made, is a process externalizing the way in which the person's pain causes his world to disintegrate, and, at the same time, the disintegration of the world is here, in the most literal way possible, made painful, made the direct cause of the pain. That is, in the conversion of a refrigerator into a bludgeon, the refrigerator disappears; its disappearance objectifies the disappearance of the world (sky, country, bench) experienced by a person in great pain; and it is the very fact of its disappearance, its transition from a refrigerator into a bludgeon, that inflicts the pain. (Scarry 1985:41)

Torture is a matter not just of inflicting physical pain but of annihilating the hope and reality of a world that otherwise had provided comfort, of a culture that brought fraternity. In the forms of artifacts, in the space of the room, "civilization is brought to the prisoner and in his presence annihilated in the very process by which it is being made to annihilate him" (Scarry 1985:44).

To be a victim of political brutality, whether through surveillance, coercion, or torture, is to be marked as unfit and unable to shape the course of one's own society; more, it is to be exiled from that society while physically remaining within it. Even after the brutality stops, the legacy of silencing remains. Because of the toll that terror and trauma take, the survivor continues to suffer their effects, and renewed public participation remains a long way off.

FROM PSYCHOLOGICAL TRAUMA TO POLITICAL TRAUMA

With their double maneuvers, depriving some members of the political community of their effective membership in that community and foreclosing any space for a public and a public will to form, repressive regimes destroy the possibility for democratic action to occur. When a brutal regime tortures and terrorizes individuals, it robs them of their sense of being subjects able to inhabit this public space.

In this sense, psychological trauma can be inflicted for political purposes. Then it is, as Bhargava argues, a political crime. In her groundbreaking book, *Trauma and Recovery*, Judith Herman documents the effects of many of the traumas of the twentieth century, from the "shell shock" of World War I to battered wife syndrome, Stockholm syndrome, and post-traumatic stress syndrome. Though their causes vary widely, they can be understood as one sort of malady, all of a piece. Such trauma occurs without warning and shakes one's sense of security and order. It affects the powerless—enlisted soldiers, women, children, the vulnerable—more than the powerful.

As mentioned in the previous chapter, trauma's effects are most pronounced on those who have fewer social bonds. But trauma also has a way of loosening any bonds that do exist: "Traumatic events call into question basic human relationships. They breach the attachments of family, friendship, love, and community. They shatter the construction of the self that is formed and sustained in relation to others" (Herman 1997:51). Traumatic events—from life in the extremity of death camps to the life of a battered wife—are extraordinary and overwhelming. "Traumatized people feel utterly abandoned, utterly alone," Herman writes, "cast out of the human and divine systems of care and protection that sustain life" (Herman 1997:52). When one can neither flee nor resist, traumatic events have long-term effects. Even years later, a survivor's ability to go through everyday life is disrupted. In Herman's analysis, survivors experience a disorganization of arousal, emotion, cognition, and memory. Past events and memories intrude unexpectedly and repeatedly. Under severe and prolonged trauma, the psyche becomes fragmented and one becomes disassociated from oneself.

Specifically, Herman helps identify five clusters of symptoms of sustained and long-term trauma. In *hyperarousal,* the survivor startles easily, sleeps poorly, reacts irritably, and suffers from a chronically stimulated nervous system and extensive psychophysiological changes. In *intrusion,* long after the fact, trauma keeps intruding on normal life; normal development is arrested; linguistic encoding of memory may be inactivated; traumatic memories may become frozen and wordless, be shorn of verbal narrative and context, and contain vivid sensations and images. With *reenactments and the repetition compulsion,* the survivor may suffer from a compulsion to repeat a trauma or defense, experience an innate tendency to return to earlier conditions and a drive to return to the inanimate (the death instinct). This repetition compulsion must be remedied by a process Freud called "working through." In *constriction,* the survivor may find herself numb and in a state of surrender, as one of "the walking dead." *Disconnection* is the rending of the victim's sense of connection to others and understanding of his or her safety in the larger world.

> The damage to relational life is not a secondary effect of trauma, as originally thought. Traumatic events have primary effects not only on the psychological structures of the self but also on the systems of attachment and meaning that link individual and community. Mardi Horowitz defines traumatic life events as those that cannot be assimilated with the victim's "inner schemata" of self in relation to the world. Traumatic events destroy the victim's fundamental assumptions about the safety of the world, the positive value of the self, and the meaningful order of creation. The rape survivor Alice Sebold testifies to this loss of security: "When I was raped I lost my virginity and almost lost my life. I also discarded certain assumptions I had held about how the world worked and about how safe I was." (Herman 1992:51)

Of all the consequences of trauma, this last one, disconnection, shows most profoundly the relationship between the psyche and the social. It is one thing when one person is brutalized; but when a group of people are selected for brutality, even if just some representatives are pulled out and tortured, all who identify with this group become afraid to connect, to speak, to share in the public world. The more pervasive fear and distrust become, the more difficult it will be to re-create a public sphere, a sociosymbolic order to which all might feel connected. Such brutal mass disenfranchisement leaves profound and long-lasting scars. Even if dispelled in the short term, its phantom hovers for generations.

SILENCING THE PUBLIC SPHERE

States at war silence their own authentic and humane culture. When this destruction is well advanced they find the lack of critical and moral restraint useful in the campaign to exterminate the culture of their opponents. By destroying authentic culture—that which allows us to question and examine ourselves and our society—the state erodes the moral fabric. It is replaced with a warped version of reality. (Hedges 2002:63)

In order to escape accountability for his crimes, the perpetrator does everything in his power to promote forgetting. Secrecy and silence are the perpetrator's first line of defense. (Herman 1997:8)

As Kelly Oliver notes in *Witnessing*, trauma undermines people's very subjectivity and voice. These regimes make people afraid, or even unable, to speak in public, even in the quasi-public space of a car or a restaurant. When people cease speaking together about matters of common concern, there ceases to be a truly public sphere. In his reading of Hannah Arendt's work on this point, Jürgen Habermas wrote,

Every political order that isolates its citizens from one another through mistrust, and cuts off the public exchange of opinions, degenerates to a rule based on violence. It destroys the communicative structures which alone power can generate. Fear heightened to terror forces each to shut himself off from every other; at the same time it destroys the distances between individuals. It takes from them the power of initiative and robs their interaction of its power to spontaneously unify what is separated: "pressed together with everyone, each is totally isolated from all." (Habermas 1977:10)

Regimes of terror decimate public space by destroying what we might call psychic space, a person's mental and affective world with its geography that orients him or her to others in the community. As chapter 1 discussed, maturation occurs through sublimation. To be a recognizably *human* being is to be one whose sublimations circulate in a sociosymbolic field. Through whatever capacity a person has, becoming human is a matter of making meaningful their own concerns, desires, and aspirations, whether through language, art, performance, or some other kind of creation. If one's own world is purely inner, if it finds no social or public manifestation, one hasn't becoming part of the human world. I use the word "human" here with qualification. Those who are unable to express inner worlds outwardly are still physically human beings, but the deprivation (note the root, de-prive, to strip of publicity, to render one private) of social expression is a serious insult and injury to beings who, I think, long to participate in a world with others.

Those who are the most bereft of relationships are the most vulnerable to trauma, and perhaps few have ever been as bereft as prisoners of Nazi and Soviet camps, caught in a life of extremity.

> To pass from civilization to extremity means to be shorn of the elaborate system of relationships—to job, class, tradition and family, to groups and institutions of every kind—which for us provides perhaps ninety percent of what we think we are. In the camps prisoners lost their possessions, their social identity, the whole of the cultural matrix which had previously sustained them. They lost, in other words, the delicate web of symbolic identifications available to men and women in normal times. In Nazi camps they lost even their names and their hair. They were reduced to immediate physical existence through a process of desublimation so abrupt and thorough that—in the plainest, starkest sense— nothing remained of what the self had been. (Des Pres 1976:182)

To illustrate desublimation's effects, Des Pres quotes a survivor of Birkenau, Seweryna Szmaglewska:

> You lost the capability of proving to yourself, in a moment of doubt, that you are still the same human being you were when you came here. That being is gone, and only a miserably wretched creature remains in her place. A naked creature deprived of everything and avidly covering her body with someone else's sweat saturated garments in spite of keen disgust. (ibid.)

Nazi death camps created the strongest evidence for the dehumanizing power of deprivation: the walking dead, *der Muselmann*, who, silenced and rendered animal in their being and comportment, gave up on life altogether before departing physically from the world. "They died inwardly," Des Pres writes, "and as their spirit withered their outward aspect was terrible to see" (De Pres 1976:88). Bruno Bettelheim describes *der Muselmann* thus: "They behaved as if they were not thinking, not feeling, unable to act or respond. . . . Typically, this stopping of action began when they no longer lifted their legs as they walked, but only shuffled them. When finally even the looking about on their own stopped, they soon died" (152–153).

Des Pres's phenomenal compilation and account of life in extremity, as told by survivors, is governed by an ideal that survival is possible so long as desublimation is not complete. Those completely stripped of their humanity quickly fell into the state of *der Muselman*.[6] Only those who retained some will to tell, to warn others, to communicate the story of what had happened, survived. They repeatedly stated that their desire to tell this story, to not let it all be forgotten or erased, was what kept them alive. Survivors are those who can manage to hang on to an imagined social network, into the future, that will hear and heed the worlds of their testimony.

But in situations of extremity the urge to tell is constantly countered by the phenomenon of silencing.

> Silence, in its primal aspect, is a consequence of terror, of a dissolution of self and world that, once known, can never be fully dispelled. But in retrospect it becomes something else. Silence constitutes the realm of the dead. It is the palpable substance of those millions murdered, the world no longer present, that intimate absence—of God, of man, of love—by which the survivor is haunted. (Des Pres 1976:36)

This is the terrible dialectic of terror: its aim is to unravel the psychic bonds that allow some select members of the world to have a hand in shaping that world. It targets their ability to participate, debilitating, disconnecting, and silencing them. But the only documented way to counter this terror is through refusing to be silent. Speech itself becomes the battleground.

CHAPTER 4

The Repetition Compulsion or the Endless War on Terror

A surprising fact gradually emerges: the work of the phantom coincides in every respect with Freud's description of the death instinct. First of all, it has no energy of its own; it cannot be "abreacted," merely designated. Second, it pursues its work of disarray in silence. Let us note that the phantom is sustained by secreted words, invisible gnomes whose aim is to wreak havoc, from within the unconscious, in the coherence of logical progression. Finally, it gives rise to endless repetition and, more often than not, eludes rationalization.

—Nicholas Abraham (Abraham and Torok 1994:175)

In general, "phantamogenic" words become travesties and can be acted out or expressed in phobias of all kinds (such as impulse phobia), obsessions, restricted phantasmagorias or ones that take over the entire field of the subject's mental activities . . . [while the phantom effect may fade over generations] this is not at all the case when shared or complementary phantoms find a way of being established as social practices along the lines of *staged words*. . . . We must not lose sight of the fact that to stage a word—whether metaphorically, as an alloseme, or as a cryptonym—constitutes an attempt at exorcism, an attempt, that is, to relieve the unconscious by placing the effects of the phantom in the social realm.

—Nicholas Abraham (Abraham and Torok 1994:176)

THE INTERNATIONAL PUBLIC SPHERE

I have been arguing for understanding the public sphere as a space that people create as they use semiotic modes to participate in a world with others, to coordinate action and produce outcomes; a space in which public employments of semiotic structures, discursive and otherwise, construct meaning, identity, purpose, and political direction. By "public" I mean what John Dewey meant in *The Public and Its Problems*: an array of people who are related by common interests or concerns. As Dewey put it, "The public consists of all those who are affected by the indirect consequences of transactions to such an extent that it is deemed necessary to have those consequences systematically cared for." As I discussed in chapter 1, members of a public need not share the same views on these things, but they find themselves to be a public when they see that they are affected by the same things. The public sphere is a *res publica* created through the semiotic investments of members of political communities. It can be unmade through the work of oppressive regimes that try to excommunicate some swaths of society from membership in the political community.

There can also be a *res publica* internationally, something that can be a resource more powerful than liberal reason. This international public sphere is created through the semiotic investments that peoples make in fathoming shared concerns and possible courses of coordinated action. As of this writing, this process is currently at work in the area of climate change. For example, *The New York Times*'s op-ed page of March 4, 2007, carried pieces from around the world offering perspectives on the consequences of global warming. These were the perspectives of individuals. An international public sphere really begins to form when peoples, not just people, begin to see how they are jointly affected by common problems.

But the promise of an international public sphere is undermined when some nations fail to take part, or are barred from taking part, in this space-. Countries that have sunk into civil war psychosis are states that John Rawls would call, in a most understated way, non-well-ordered (Rawls 1999:89). In their external relations, they are likely to become threats to international peace and stability. But even if externally they behave appropriately, internally non-well-ordered states can violate the minimum standards of decency and exact injustices and social evils upon their own people to the point that well-ordered societies, especially liberal ones, are loathe to tolerate them, for they violate a fundamental principle of a law of peoples: to honor human rights (Rawls 1999:37).

Rawls holds out hope that forums for international reasoning and talk can persuade non-well-ordered peoples to change their ways. "For well-ordered peoples to achieve this long-run aim," he writes, "they should establish new institutions and practices to serve as a kind of confederative center and public forum for their common opinion and policy toward non-well-ordered regimes." Through the United Nations or other international alliances, confederations of well-ordered states can formulate and express their views about "the unjust and cruel institutions of oppressive and expansionist regimes and their violations of human rights" (Rawls 1999:93), and in exposing them help to bring these wrongs to an end. Now, shame is indeed a powerful weapon against barbarism, but barbarous regimes can still be impervious, especially, I'd add, when they have been traumatized and lost their foothold in the sociosymbolic realm. When shaming doesn't work, sanctions may, especially sanctions that deprive such states of the benefits of membership in an "international society of cooperation" (ibid.).

   That there is or can be an international society of cooperation is a central feature of Rawls's practically utopian ideal. The members are not states but peoples, he argues, because peoples, not states, have these two moral powers: "a capacity for a sense of justice and a capacity for a conception of the good" (Rawls 1999:92). Political doctrines that think of states as the prime international actors, namely international realism, hold that what motivates international action is crass self-interest that is impervious to moral reasoning. But states are instruments of peoples, Rawls argues, not the other way around. Their authority emanates from their peoples and can be stripped just the same.

   Though Rawls's language and mine differ, we share a common picture of an ideal international realm. As I would put it, this ideal is not just a not-yet-realized utopia; it is also a regulative ideal that can prompt and guide action. Internationally, peoples have an imago of a space of relationship, of connections, indebtedness, obligation, friendship with others. This international space of cooperation is constructed imaginatively, but being an imago makes it no less powerful than anything concrete. It is even more powerful, for it is both a self- and a collective understanding of connections and obligations. Moreover, it is not confined to the actions of states and official governments; as the world becomes more globally connected through new media, technologies, transnational nongovernmental organizations (NGOs), and economic relations, we are developing an international public sphere, a sociosymbolic realm of peoples' sublimations in which peoples strive to participate, to "see themselves."

   Rawls's language and framework, steeped in abstract reason, pay short shrift to the power of the imaginary, the limits of reason, the causes of barbarity, and, to an extent, the ways supposedly reasonable and well-ordered peoples (or at least their leaders) can dissemble and rationalize their actions. Insofar as an international society of peoples is constituted psychically

and imaginatively, international political relations can be driven by fundamental psychological factors. That a people can be well ordered all the way
down is highly unlikely, especially given the fact that most peoples have
not worked through their traumas or properly grieved their losses. Most
peoples (and I mean here *qua peoples*, not individuals) are still acting out,
not working through, their troubles, so even if seemingly well ordered, they
can be driven by a will to power (or security or vengeance) that they cloak
in innocent garb. Their relations with others may be less than benevolent.
Their actions toward those they deem threats may have as much to do with
annihilating the other's identity internationally as with self-defense.

International policy formed under some given rationale may be driven
by underground motivations to harm or make politically invisible other
peoples, along the same lines as the kind of political harm done to individuals by oppressive or barbaric regimes. Recall Rajeev Bhargava's powerful discussion:

> The act of violence transmits an unambiguous, unequivocal message,
> that their views on the common good—on matters of public signifi-
> cance–do not count, that their side of the argument has no worth and
> will not be heard, that they will not be recognized as participants in any
> debate, and, finally, that to negotiate, or even reach a compromise with
> them, is worthless. In effect, it signals their disappearance from the
> public domain. (Bhargava 2000:47)

Bhargava is referring to political crimes within barbaric regimes, but the
same phenomenon is at work internationally when parties are at war. Those
on whom war is waged are effectively stripped of their title and standing in
an ideal international realm of cooperation. In an era of globalization, the
public domain is not just a national phenomenon but a global one. The violence of war and even the harshness of sanctions are signs, to say the least,
that other options have either been exhausted or will not be considered. War
is a way of making the other politically disappear from the civilized global
public domain. Ironically, though, it also signals that the one waging it has
given up on politics and is resorting to coercion or violence.

THE REPETITION COMPULSION

At the heart of this book are two questions: Is it possible for people with
few, if any areas of agreement on fundamental questions to find a way to

live together peacefully? Can political solutions be found in matters where what counts as properly political is itself in question? I have been arguing that the rational framework is now inadequate and a new one is needed. A new framework involves seeing the vital role of an imago of an international realm of cooperation to which peoples want to belong. Differences that are not resolved often lead to war, but we cannot understand this if we focus on reasons and ignore traumas and how they are, in the Freudian sense, acted out rather than worked through. This is not a novel idea. As Shoshana Felman argues in her book, *The Juridical Unconscious*, the whole of the twentieth century used trials and the judicial system, often imperfectly, as means for peoples to work through their traumas. As I discuss in later chapters, other forms of engagement are needed, such as long-term unofficial dialogue and truth commissions. But for the moment, I want to show the consequences of failing to work through trauma, of getting mired in a repetition compulsion.

To see an example, we don't have to go any farther than the morning paper. The remainder of this chapter takes up the example of the U.S. war on terror to make a case that seems all too obvious: war is not the answer. To the contrary, it is a way of acting out, a repetition compulsion, stemming from unresolved trauma and the common occurrence of non-well-ordered peoples. The end of the Cold War was an opportunity for the United States to participate in creating a more peaceful and stable global order. But instead, the first Bush administration set about, in the words of Colin Powell, being "the bully on the block." During the end of that Republican administration, Dick Cheney, with the help of Paul Wolfowitz and other then mid-level national security strategists, devised a defense planning guide designed to keep the military at Cold War levels, with a strategy that advocated preemption and unbridled U.S. global power. As David Armstrong writes,

> In January 1993, in his very last days in office, Cheney released [the] Defense Strategy for the 1990s. . . . The goal [was] to preclude "hostile competitors from challenging our critical interests" and preventing the rise of a new super-power. Although it expressed a "preference" for collective responses in meeting such challenges, it made clear that the United States would play the lead role in any alliance. Moreover, it noted that collective action would "not always be timely." Therefore, the United States needed to retain the ability to "act independently, if necessary." To do so would require that the United States maintain its massive military superiority. Others were not encouraged to follow suit. (Armstrong 2002)

The plan was put in place just before the Clinton administration took over, but was tacitly scuttled as soon as Clinton came into power (Armstrong 2002). However, Clinton did little to create a multilateral global order; he barely paid any mind to foreign affairs at all. When the next Bush administration came in, so too did the crew that had devised the earlier defense planning strategy. Here was an administration with a defense plan that would ensure U.S. sole superpower status, but no plausible rationale for why the American people should pay for it or the world should tolerate it.

But matters changed on September 11, 2001, in a way that psychoanalysis is able to explain better than political theory. Eli Zaretsky describes that moment:

> We call an event like that of September 11 a trauma. A trauma is an event whose impact does not occur at the level of consciousness and which therefore tears open the fabric of everyday existence in a way that consciously experienced acts do not. The confusion, the self-questioning, the civility and even vulnerability of New York City street life, however temporary, the constant replaying of images of the towers in flames, the towers collapsing, the compulsive visits to "ground zero"—these can all be understood as response to trauma. The mind was unprepared for the event. The upset and rupture took place at a different level of the psyche from the one on which the mind normally functions. Afterward, the mind goes back to the event, reliving it as if preparing to encounter it again. The driving force is the effort to master the event that mastered it, to master it by incorporating it back into an ordinary, everyday consciousness. (Zaretsky 2002:99)

The trauma of 9/11 called for a response. Under the cover of this collective trauma, the Bush administration unveiled a supposedly "new" policy of preemption. The post–9/11 Defense Planning Guide (DPG) was a thinly revised version of the old one: "Signed by Wolfowitz's new boss, Donald Rumsfeld, in May and leaked to the *Los Angeles Times* in July," Armstrong writes, "it contains all the key elements of the original Plan and adds several complementary features. The preemptive strikes envisioned in the original draft DPG are now 'unwarned attacks.' The old Powell-Cheney notion of military 'forward presence' is now 'forwarded deterrence.' The use of overwhelming force to defeat an enemy called for in the Powell Doctrine is now labeled an 'effects based' approach."

In short, it was a policy of unilateral U.S. action that violated most of the norms of just war theory. Granted, some of the more sober just war theorists supported the U.S. use of force following 9/11, but not because they favored preemption; they thought that Afghanistan and then Iraq presented imminent threats, against which just war theory can condone military action. But the "new" U.S. doctrine itself stretched the definition of "imminent" beyond recognition.

One cannot say for sure whether the second Bush administration was acting out from trauma or just being calculating about this opportunity to enact its plan. Regardless, the United States as a people was stopped short in the process of working through the trauma. This allowed the country to take the course of a repetition compulsion or, in other words, an endless war on terror. In the following section I point to some signs that this was what in fact occurred.

TERROR AND SUICIDAL AUTOIMMUNITY

In the case of 9/11 and the war on terror waged in its name, there is a complex array of motivations, of *ressentiments*, at work that drive U.S. policies. Even the naming of the event, with the seeming certitude of "9/11," is a complex result of what was both unexpected despite being expectable (in the sense, as Derrida noted just weeks afterward, the United States had already experienced, in Oklahoma, the bombing of a federal building and that only a few years earlier, the Twin Towers had been bombed) and experienced yet still incomprehensible: "The telegram of this metonymy [9/11]—a name, a number—points out the unqualifiable by recognizing that we do not recognize or even cognize, that we do not yet know how to qualify, that we do not know what we are talking about" (Derrida, in Borradori 2003:86). What made 9/11 so momentous and devastating was its incomprehensibility. In Derrida's view, to be an event in the strongest sense of the word, something must happen in a way that is not quite experiencable: "The event is what comes and, in coming, comes to surprise me, to surprise and to suspend comprehension: the event is first of all *that which* I do not first of all comprehend. Better, the event is first of all *that* I do not comprehend. . . . [It is] my incomprehension" (ibid. 90).

It is hard to see how the Rawlsian "practical" fiction of a well-ordered society and international arena is of any help when policies issue from, that is, are (dis)ordered by, traumatic events. Even the naming of the thing that happened is a form of distancing or numbing:

> We repeat this ["9/11"], *we must* repeat it, and it is all the more neces-
> sary to repeat it insofar as we do not really know what is being named
> in this way, as if to exorcise two times at one go: on the one hand, to
> conjure away, as if by magic, the "thing" itself, the fear or the terror
> it inspires (for repetition always protects by neutralizing, deadening,
> distancing a traumatism, and this is true for the repetition of the tele-
> vised images . . .), and, on the other hand, to deny, as close as pos-
> sible to this act of language and this enunciation, our powerlessness
> to name in an appropriate fashion, to characterize, to think the thing
> in question, to get beyond the mere deictic of the date: something
> terrible took place on September 11, and in the end we don't know
> what. (ibid. 87)

In Derrida's view, even just the naming of the whole of that event with the date, "September 11," or the abbreviation, "9/11," is defense against its traumas, and in the course of the interview from which I'm quoting, he argues that the meaning of the event surpasses the number of the dead, the violation of borders, the method of attack. "I believe always in the necessity of being attentive first of all to this phenomenon of language, naming, and dating," Derrida says, "to this repetition compulsion (at once rhetorical, magical, and poetic). To what this compulsion signifies, trans-lates, or betrays . . . to try to understand what is going on precisely *beyond* language and what is pushing us to repeat endlessly and without knowing what we are talking about, precisely there where language and the concept come up against their limits: 'September 11, September 11, *le 11 septembre*, 9/11'" (ibid. 87–88).

Beyond the overwhelming calamity of that particular day, what wound does this repetition compulsion signify? What trauma does it betray? And what does the significance of this trauma say about the repetition compulsion that has gone on in the intervening years since the interview occurred—the compulsion to react against the trauma itself?

What makes the events of September 11 so overwhelming is not just the sheer number of deaths, though Derrida does not deny the singu-larity of each of the thousands of lives lost. Beyond these quantitative measures, qualitatively, there is a belief about the United States and its place in a post–Cold War order. "The obvious fact is that since the 'end of the Cold War' what can be called the world order, in its relative and precarious stability, depends largely on the solidity and reliability, on the *credit*, of American power" (ibid. 92–93). This is the case on many levels at once: "economic, technical, military, in the media, even on the level of discursive logic, of the axiomatic that supports juridical and diplomatic rhetoric worldwide, and this international law" (ibid. 93). The attacks of September 11 violated more than borders, buildings, and lives; they violated the discursive and rhetorical power (which is more than economic and military, though these aspects are formidable) that holds the global system in place:

> What is legitimated by the prevailing system (a combination of public opinion, the media, the rhetoric of politicians and the presumed authority of all those who, through various mechanisms, speak or are allowed to speak in the public space) are thus the norms inscribed in every apparently meaningful phrase that can be constructed with the lexicon of violence, aggression, crime, war, and terrorism, with the supposed differences between war and terrorism, national and international terrorism, state and nonstate terrorism, with the respect for sovereignty, national territory, and so on. (ibid.)

U.S. hegemony underlies U.S. authority to make all such distinctions. (And note that the relationship between hegemony and authority is circular; there is a kind of positivism driven underground beginning with the Enlightenment: by having global power, the United States is "authorized" to deem who is powerful and what is legitimate.) U.S. hegemony underlies notions of what kinds of actors and operations are credible and what are not. Hence, with 9/11's traumatic wound to U.S. power, what was "touched, wounded, or traumatized by this double *crash*" was not just the immediate casualties but even more the "hermeneutic apparatus that might have allowed one to see coming, to comprehend, interpret, describe, speak of, and name 'September 11'—and in so doing to neutralize the traumatism and come to terms with it through a 'work of mourning'" (ibid.).

There is a destructive autoimmunity at work in these phenomena. Derrida compares it to a response that can befall a biological organism: the defenses it musters to fight off a foreign agent turn back upon the organism itself. He identifies three overlapping autoimmune reactions. First is the manner in which the attacks came: not from without but from within. The hijackers were trained in the United States to use technologies developed in the United States; they hijacked U.S. planes that departed from U.S. cities; and they aimed them at vulnerable but powerful U.S. symbols. Moreover, the hijackers came from networks that the United States had helped create. In the last throes of the Cold War, in its attempt to get the Soviet Union out of Afghanistan (or even earlier, to dupe the Soviet Union into going into Afghanistan in the first place), the United States teamed up with its royal allies in the Middle East, the Saudis, to develop networks to fund the *mujahadeen* who would fight against the Soviets (Armstrong and Trento 2007). These networks remained in place long after the Soviets pulled out of Afghanistan, and they funded the next generation of militant Islamic fundamentalists, including Al Qaeda.

Second, the suicidal autoimmunity at work issues from the nature of a powerfully traumatic event. Departing from the classical notion of trauma, rooted in its historicity as an event in the past that one cannot assimilate in the present, Derrida identifies the salient feature of trauma as the haunting sense that there might be something worse still to come. To be sure, the classical account notes that trauma becomes a problem when it causes anxiety, and anxiety is surely a forward-looking, forward-fearing symptom. But Derrida argues more that what is traumatic is the thought of what might yet happen *"worse than anything that has ever taken place"* (Derrida, in Borradori 2003:97). Were it possible to be assured that nothing as terrible as or more terrible than 9/11 would ever happen again, Derrida argues, the wound would not be so debilitating. We could do the "work of mourning" and move on. But this is not at all the case. There is traumatism with no possible work of mourning when traumatism is produced by the *future*, by the threat of the worst *to come*, rather than by an aggression that is "over and done with" (ibid. 97).

What might come and is so terrible and fearful are again things that the United States helped wreak: the biotechnology that can unleash deadly nerve agents and organisms; the nuclear technology developed during the Cold War, because of the Cold War; and, with its triumph in winning the Cold War, enemies that are shadowy and elusive. When the United States became the global superpower, it became the sole "protector" of the world order. When no other state could counter it, a rival power began to form in nonstate actors, many of which, as just noted, the United States helped create and fortify in the first place. David Armstrong and Joe Trento describe how the U.S. government under Carter lured the Soviets into Afghanistan, knowing this would be the Soviet Union's own Vietnam, and did all it could to get assistance in this project from Pakistan, despite knowing that Pakistan had developed and was circulating nuclear technology. Fixated on winning the Cold War, the United States began to seed a new threat. Defending U.S. secret operations in Afghanistan that gave rise to Taliban control, former National Security Adviser Zbigniew Brzezinski asked in a 1998 interview, "What is most important to the history of the world? The Taliban or the collapse of the Soviet empire? Some stirred-up Moslems or the liberation of Central Europe and the end of the cold war?" (Armstrong and Trento 2007). Looking back, it is painfully clear that these defensive measures against a known threat were doomed to fuel a worse one.

That this is a terror of what might come, what might issue from some unknown place and unidentifiable enemy, leads to the third aspect of suicidal autoimmunity: repression. As a terror that can hardly be formally recognized, named, or fought, it is both hard to grasp and easy to deny. Paradoxically, "even if this terror is the very worst, even if it touches the geopolitical unconscious of every living being and leaves there indelible traces," because it is so unidentifiable and fleeting, it can easily be "denied, repressed, indeed forgotten" (Derrida, in Borradori 2003:99). But attempts to "attenuate or neutralize the effect of the traumatism . . . are but so many desperate attempts . . . which produce, invent, and feed the very monstrosity they claim to overcome" (ibid.). Describing this vicious circle of repression, Derrida says:

> It cannot be said that humanity is defenseless against the threat of this evil. But we must recognize that defenses and all the forms of what is called, with two equally problematic words, the "war on terrorism" work to regenerate, in the short or long term, the causes of the evil they claim to eradicate. Whether we are talking about Iraq, Afghanistan, or even Palestine, the "bombs" will never be "smart" enough to prevent the victims . . . from responding, either in person or by proxy, with what it will then be easy for them to present as legitimate reprisals or as counterterrorism. And so on ad infinitum. (ibid. 100)

One needn't be a philosopher to anticipate the consequences of such defenses against trauma. The investigative reporter David Armstrong assessed the situation on October 2002, on the eve of the war with Iraq:

This [United States] once rejected "unwarned" attacks such as Pearl Harbor as barbarous and unworthy of a civilized nation. Today many cheer the prospect of conducting sneak attacks—potentially with nuclear weapons—on piddling powers run by tin-pot despots.

We also once denounced those who tried to rule the world. Our primary objection (at least officially) to the Soviet Union was its quest for global domination. Through the successful employment of the tools of containment, deterrence, collective security, and diplomacy—the very methods we now reject—we rid ourselves and the world of the Evil Empire. Having done so, we now pursue the very thing for which we opposed it. And now that the Soviet Union is gone, there appears to be no one left to stop us.

Perhaps, however, there is. The Bush Administration and its loyal opposition seem not to grasp that the quests for dominance generate backlash. Those threatened with pre-emption may themselves launch pre-emptory strikes. And even those who are successfully "pre-empted" or dominated may object and find means to strike back. Pursuing such strategies may, paradoxically, result in greater factionalism and rivalry, precisely the things we seek to end. (Armstrong 2002)

Since the above-quoted pieces were published, the fallout of the U.S. response to 9/11 has become even more suicidal and toxic. The war in Iraq has been disastrous, creating a situation on the verge of civil war that breeds more animosity to the United States and more opportunities for the likes of Al Qaeda to multiply and pose even worse threats. Derrida noted the repetition compulsion at work in the coining of the name 9/11. Certainly it is also at work in how the United States has waged war on a country that clearly had nothing to do with 9/11.

Surely the United States is not alone in the folly of suicidal autoimmunity, in trying to deal with unresolved traumas by acting out, rather than working through, what it has experienced. But at this point in time it stands alone as the world's only superpower, authorizing itself as the world's policeman. As of this writing, I am beginning to hear rumblings from the White House about "grave" threats to democracy posed by new socialist governments in South America. How long until the world's policeman heads south?

TRANSITIONS AND REPETITIONS

The past century has seen many wars waged in the name of freedom and democracy. Sometimes force may be necessary to end repression, but war *prima facie* cannot bring about democracy. Even if the force is used to install ballot boxes and other apparatus of democratization, transitioning to democracy will succeed only to the extent that old wounds are healed. Desire for justice needs to be tempered with a desire for creating a new and inclusive political community. Wherever there is a need to stop perpetrators and hold them accountable, there is also a need for recovery and reconciliation. Absent means of recovering from trauma, a political community will doubtless continue its repetition compulsions, whether by repressing seemingly dangerous and abject members or by going after seeming enemies abroad.

The acting out and concomitant repetition compulsions also figure into criminal tribunals. Even when they follow the rule of law, tribunals and criminal proceedings may be masks for vengeance and retribution, not just ways of achieving accountability and deterrence. Certainly sometimes such trials are warranted; despots do need to be called to account. But as means of helping a people work through, as catharses, they are severely limited. To answer the question, as David Crocker puts it, "How should a fledgling democracy reckon with severe human rights abuses that earlier authoritarian regimes, their opponents, or combatants in an internal armed conflict have committed?" many are developing the idea of transitional justice. "Sometimes the term 'transitional justice' is used to refer exclusively to penal justice and even to retributive interpretations of trials and punishment," Crocker notes. But he and most others involved in the field are usually more interested in the kind of justice that can compensate those who have been wronged and restore the community to a more sound footing. "The challenge for new democracy is to respond appropriately to past evils without undermining the new democracy or jeopardizing prospects for future development" (Crocker 2000:99).

In embarking on a path of transitional justice, a people can ask what they are seeking and then consider what measures are most conducive to their project. Those engaged in transitional justice tend to lean in one of two directions: upholding human rights through international criminal tribunals and the rule of international law or working for reconciliation, healing, and even forgiveness that might pave the way for a new society. (In fact, the title of a book on which I am drawing takes a cue from this division: *Truth v. Justice*, edited by Robert Rothberg and Dennis Thompson.) These options are not mutually exclusive. The South African truth and reconciliation process, for example, retained the right to deny amnesty to perpetrators who were then still subject to criminal prosecution. And perpetrators can be held accountable even as a people goes through the process of working through and recovering from trauma. My point is that any single-minded focus on prosecuting human rights violations may stall or deflect attention from the need to work through. It may even be a subconscious repetition compulsion. (Who beside Bosnian Serbs did not feel some pleasure at the trial of Slobodan Milošević?)

And even though criminal proceedings involve public testimony, the format does not allow such testimony to have much, if any mending power. As Martha Minow writes,

> The trial as a form of response to injustice has its own internal limitations. Litigation is not an ideal form of social action. . . . Victims and other witnesses undergo the ordeals of testifying and facing cross-examination. Usually they are given no simple opportunity to convey directly the narrative of their experience. Evidentiary rules and ruling limit the factual material that can be included. Trial procedure makes for laborious and even boring sessions that risk anesthetizing even the most avid listener and dulling sensibilities even in the face of recounted horrors. The simplistic questions of guilt or innocence framed by the criminal trial can never capture the multiple sources of mass violence. If the social goals include gaining public acknowledgment and producing a complete account of what happened, the trial process is at best an imperfect means. (Minow 2000:238)

Countries recovering from brutality do indeed need to restore basic political justice. But this alone is not enough to heal a nation or restore a sociosymbolic field. Wounds to the *polis* can outlast a regime. I saw this phenomenon first hand as a teenager visiting family in Greece. Three years after the fall of the authoritarian regime known as "the colonels," Greek citizens still would not even whisper in public about political matters. Although they were putting political structures back in place, the restoration of a discursive public sphere was long in coming. With much struggle, opposition movements sometimes can remove old regimes and install new ones. But democratic change has little chance unless old traumas are brought to light and some measure of restoration occurs—restoration simultaneously to citizens of their title as citizens and to the nation of its public sphere.

∎

These last few chapters have visited the complicated and many-layered process by which communities attempt to found themselves. The process misfires when they attempt to build commonality on the backs of some or when a trauma provides cohesion while maintaining a constant "threat level." Such communities are easily destroyed. Even when they are maintained, the happiness and welfare of those whose backs are made to suffer, of those who are silenced, are destroyed. The trauma is doubled because, it seems, human beings and peoples thrive in community and suffer when banished or outcast. The suffering can be so extreme it renders the survivor less than human.

Recovering from this condition, as I will begin to argue now, calls for recovering or reconstituting community. This takes place performatively and discursively, in the process of claiming membership in something public. It cannot be done alone. If no one is present to hear and to respond to the claim, only further suffering ensues.

CHAPTER 5

Recovering Community

Analyzing the problem to this point is easy compared to what comes next: trying to fathom how a people and peoples can work through these traumas so that they are not doomed to continuously act them out. There are many people focusing on these issues, from international conflict resolution and sustained dialogue efforts in various regions of the world to the work of new citizen media in the developing world that allows those who have not been able to voice their concerns to do so.

I want to point to what I think is a significant resource: the international society of cooperation that I discussed earlier in this book, drawing largely (though rather liberally) on John Rawls's *The Law of Peoples*. It is an imago of international relations, a global public sphere, a regulative idea that could promote mutual respect among peoples, and a motivation to talk across difference. It seems to me, and I think to Rawls as well, that peoples—even hermits like North Korea—dearly want to be seen and respected as members of this international society. It is vital to their self-image to be members in good standing, to be acknowledged as able to help shape the fate of the earth.

What does it mean for an international public sphere to be a regulative idea? It means that we act "as if" it were true. Or, as with William James, it serves as a concept that regulates our transactions with the world. Much like the idea of humanity, which we rarely if ever see actually instantiated, the idea of an international society of cooperation can regulate the behavior of peoples in such a way that they seek out respect from other peoples and extend it to them as well. When it operates in international institutions and international law, this regulative idea provides spaces for peoples to work through their disagreements, to find just redress for harms, to deliberate and negotiate about the matters that concern them in common. In short, it provides a space for working through issues that might, untended, lead to counterproductive repetitions.

The unilateral actions of the United States after 9/11, like other unilateral actions of other nations in the past, violate this regulative ideal. Such actions are often aimed at asserting power over the global public sphere, power garnered through asserting the ability to decide who can be a member, who can be excommunicated, who can be "disappeared." Peoples do not want to be "disappeared" from an international society. After a great trauma that seems aimed at a people's standing therein, it is understandable that their reaction might be to strike out at those who created the threat, but U.S. unilateral action abroad, aimed at making terror disappear, has ironically diminished the United States' own standing in this international order. Not just the supposedly non-well-ordered peoples of, say, Syria or Palestine condemn the way the United States has behaved these past years. The well-ordered peoples of Europe and other continents also do. Through its war on terror, the United States has become something of a global pariah, even though its power protects it from physical harm.

While the U.S. administration may plunge ahead, the people of this country have begun to have serious second thoughts. The political realignment happening internally in U.S. politics is, I think, an attempt by the American people to again become members in good standing of an international society of cooperation. Perhaps peoples are becoming more sensitive than their governments to the regulative idea of an international society of cooperation; if so, it is all the more important for democracy to flourish within nations.

When Cheney and company, under the cover of 9/11 trauma, began gearing up for the war on terror, and before that when the administration began its rhetoric of "either you're with us or you're with the terrorists," the budding introspective American dialogue asking, "Why do they hate us?" was cut short. When the U.S. media initially rallied around the government, it also quashed the kind of working through that could have gone on. Thankfully, such measures have their limits. The blogosphere opened up space for dissent and introspection; the media became more skeptical; the people grew more appalled at a war that only seemed to breed more terror and diminish the United States' standing in the world. This is not to say that in the end bad things will run their course and all will be well, but to point out the vital resource of an imago of an international society of cooperation and the need for democratic space to be sensitive to it. Moreover, there is a need to turn this idea into more of a reality, to strengthen and respect the function of the United Nations and an international rule of law. Through such international spaces, conceived more broadly and inclusively than Rawls does, through the law that is formed there, peoples can help create narrative understandings of past traumas. They can talk from their seemingly irreconcilably different perspectives on what counts as properly political, as they try to fashion a new global political order.

■■■

There is a certain posture needed for a country, indeed for a world, to transform itself and to set or continue a democratic course. The posture ought to be one where members of a political community ought to lean toward each other, rather than digging in their heels and leaning back. This is the posture one finds in public deliberations, from the New England town meeting to the televised national deliberative public opinion polls or the scene of a truth and reconciliation commission where a victim and perpetrator come to terms. For meaningful transformation to occur, there needs to be an inclination to be open to others and to change. What are the conditions for such a posture and inclination? It would be naïve to be too sanguine. But one vital condition seems to be an ability to imagine coherently such a possibility.

If an endless war on terror is the result of acting out, of a repetition compulsion, then ending the seemingly eternal return of suffering and retribution will call for working through our trauma. Just as the analysand works through her troubles using the "talking cure" of psychoanalysis—even if we agree with Lacan that any "cure" is dubious—then perhaps the political analogue will also be a kind of talk. There are many varieties, from the old New England town meeting to testifying on a witness stand to participating in a deliberative forum to staking out a corner of the blogosphere.

RESTORING PUBLIC BEING AND PUBLIC SPACE

As Kelly Oliver's work on witnessing suggests, the way to restore public voice and subjectivity to survivors of political trauma is to afford them opportunities to bear witness to what they have suffered. This process helps subjects work through rather than act out or suffer the repetition of trauma. It helps restore their subjectivity as well as the sociosymbolic world in which their words can be heeded. In the very process of bearing witness to the traumas that tore away their dignity and membership in the sociosymbolic field, survivors begin to re-create this field and their membership therein. Another important function of testifying about trauma is that the testimony and the way it is taken up by the community allow for the possibility of integrating experience. Traumatic events fracture experience; suffering is often private and becomes even more surreal when its reality is publicly denied. Testifying makes it possible to integrate what has been fractured and privatized into a more coherent narrative ordering of events, so that survivors can see the larger political malfunctions and crises that sundered their experience. While the senseless and brute dumb facts of trauma can imprison the subject and the social in repetition compulsion and obsessions, testimony can give these facts new meaning. In short, witnessing to trauma not only helps those who have suffered privately, it helps build new connections between the psyche and the social in that space I described earlier as the overlapping space of the psyche and the social: the space of sublimation that is simultaneously the person's space for joining humanity and the space of a political humanity.

A need for such restoration seems to underlie many recent efforts to transition to democracy. For example, to heal their nation, many countries have held truth and reconciliation commissions. From South Africa to El Salvador, these commissions have given thousands of survivors of past regimes the opportunity to stand before their nation and tell the story of the brutality they underwent. In the process, these individuals reclaim their dignity and title of citizen. At the same time, they create the conditions for the possibility of politics: a discursive field and an affective identity with others. Brutality undermined victims' sense of dignity, humanity, and public worth (all necessary to effective agency as a citizen); the process of testifying in public helps to restore their sense of being citizens able to help steer their communities.

When those who have been muted begin to speak in the presence of others, they begin to re-create their mental and affective world with its geography that orients them to others in the community. On the remains of a decimated public sphere, testifying in public to trauma reconstitutes the subject as a member of a political community while simultaneously re-creating that community or sociosymbolic field. The process puts a subject back in an intersubjective field and creates a space in which newly healed citizens begin to talk together again.

MORAL DISAGREEMENT AND THE NECESSITY
OF DEMOCRATIC POLITICS

In this book, I have focused largely on situations of extremity. As I move into discussing the process of reintegration, restorative justice, and democracy, I should note that the key method at work is *public talk*, the most basic form of sublimation that can allow the traumatized sociosymbolic field (which, again, is also the space of people's thwarted or successful sublimations) to work through trauma, to free itself from imprisoning fixations. These processes are necessary for recovering from extremity, but they are also needed in seemingly well-functioning democracies.

On the cover of their book *Democracy and Disagreement*, first published in 1996, Amy Gutmann and Dennis Thompson include an interesting tagline: "Why moral conflict cannot be avoided in politics, and what should be done about it." This may have been apt in 1996, but it is not so fitting today. The truth now is that politicians and citizens alike seem to be doing a good job of avoiding moral conflict, mostly by avoiding each other. Many residents of the new exurbs say they moved there because they sensed that their neighbors would share their conservative values. Young urbanites stick to the cities for opposite, but similar reasoning. We have become so adept at avoiding disagreement and each other that we have imagined myriad ways in which those "other" people are evil, corrupt, irresponsible beings. There are two related worries here. One is that we are so different we cannot begin to fathom each other. The other is that, in our emotivist culture, there is no reason to think that people with different predilections would seriously consider our point of view or any reasons we might offer in support of it. The outcome of these worries, as Alasdair MacIntyre notes in his book *After Virtue*, is that instead of trying to converse with each other—having little faith that our words might move someone different from us—we take to shouting. In an emotivist culture where value is seen as little more than personal, arbitrary preference, we tend to think that the only way to prevail is to emote louder than the next person. It is the force of the louder argument, not the force of the better argument, that wins. For there is nothing objective that could make any argument *better* than any other. We measure the effect of our protests by how much press coverage we get, how many people show up, what great rhetorical lines are left ringing in the air.

Against the emotivists are the rational, deliberative democratic proceduralists, who have great faith that the force of the better argument, not rhetorical or strategic force, will and can and should prevail; that no matter how great our differences, we share an ability to reason with others reasonably. Both the emotivists and the rational proceduralists reject the possibility that we might be *affectively* capable of and interested in finding ways to understand each other. The rational proceduralist might take issue with this characterization. I think that affects and solidarity can be greater resources than this school of thought generally acknowledges.

The reality may be that, affectively, we are really not so different as we imagine. And even when we hold rather different values, someone else's values, if one hears them out, can be remarkably appealing. There is a way of talking across differences, but it is not quite the way that the rational proceduralists imagine. It is more hermeneutic and Gadamerian than rational and Kantian. The emotivists and kindred spirits like Lyotard and Rorty are wrong in thinking that we are closed up in our own language games, destined to babble on, intelligible only to ourselves. And the rational proceduralists are wrong to think that feeling, emotion, and desires have no place in rational deliberation. The third way that I am charting in this book is the path of developing and conversing and living well together through our existential desire to be a part of a larger human project, what we readily call "humanity."

Born of the rational procedural camp, Gutmann and Thompson wrote *Democracy and Disagreement* only a decade after "the culture wars," when the cultural and political elite were busy trying to tell each other why they were wrong. The United States was still a nation that reveled in conversation and disagreement. But five years after their book came out, 9/11 happened, and "the other" became not an interlocutor but a mortal enemy. Even domestically, if you were not "with us," our attorney general said, "you were against us." The new "sign" of one's values, of where one stood in the war on terror and other wars, was the presence or absence of certain stickers and flags on one's car or home. More signs, less need to talk. If your signs are like my signs, then we needn't deliberate because we already emotively agree; if they're diametrically opposed to mine, then deliberation would probably be fruitless—and terribly unpleasant—anyway. Likes stick with likes to minimize political quarrelling, but the outcome is a bipolar nation. By 2004, polarization had fiercely set in and with it a new national self-understanding: one nation, divided between red and blue.

Against that backdrop, consider this op-ed published in *The New York Times* in December 2006, titled NO "RED" OR "BLUE" IN THE GREEN ROOM. The author, Anne Kornblut, begins:

DONNA BRAZILE calls them green room conversions.

One of her more recent went something like this: Ms. Brazile, the garrulous Democratic strategist, found herself in the waiting room—known in the world of television talk shows as the green room—with Senator Rick Santorum, the conservative Republican from Pennsylvania who campaigned to defeat her candidate, Al Gore, in the 2000 presidential campaign.

The two, awkwardly thrown together with little to do except contemplate the pastry spread, started to chat politely.

"Santorum and I, we're both Catholic, we're both from large families and we just struck up a conversation that ended up continuing, and I went over to his office one morning and had breakfast," Ms. Brazile said, ticking off the issues, from AIDS to faith-based institutions, on which the two have consulted since. "I have met a lot of people I would normally not even talk to," said Ms. Brazile, a regular on the talk show circuit. "Somehow in the green room you put all that aside. It's time for small chatter."

Kornblut recounts a number of green room conversations. "In an earlier, less polarized era—in the days when senators in opposing parties played poker, when partisan fund-raising had not yet become a blood sport—the camaraderie inside green rooms might not have been so noteworthy," she writes. "But as the tenor in Washington has grown more rancorous over the last decade, bipartisan socializing has dwindled. With Republicans in control of both houses of Congress and the White House, there are ever fewer reasons for the two sides to exchange views, or even pleasantries."

In a fascinating way, these conversations result in "conversions." They don't really lead to people changing their views on issues; they lead to them changing their views of other people. In the green room,

the White House communications director, Dan Bartlett, who is often too busy to return reporters' phone calls, found himself swapping parenthood stories at the height of the 2004 campaign with Tad Devine, a Democratic rival on the Gore and John Kerry campaigns.

"You come to find out they have the same experiences and challenges you do: a family, balancing a campaign and kids," Mr. Bartlett said. "I wouldn't want to say it was a surprise, but it was good to see."

This comment sadly indicates that before the green room conversation, the other could be imagined as devoid of any concern for family, work, and responsibility. The more we think that those with whom we disagree are less than human, the more impossible civil politics becomes. And the more we configure ourselves on a polarized landscape, and the more we avoid each other. We need more "green rooms" for democracy, spaces in which we can stop avoiding moral conflict and work through our disagreements. I suspect that one of the first things we'd find is that we don't disagree as much or as deeply as we imagine—and the "signs" we rely on are not very reliable.

Gutmann and Thompson orient their book as a way to deal with the problem of moral disagreement—which they say is "formidable," and with which they say that democratic politics has so far not been able to cope. *Democracy and Disagreement* adopts a rational-proceduralist version of deliberative democracy as a way to deal with these disagreements because it "secures a central place for moral discussion in political life." Where other forms of politics allow members to avoid difficult conversation, deliberative democracy puts such conversation squarely at the center.

The authors note the salient features of moral disagreement that give rise to central qualities of deliberative democracy. Our moral disagreements are on the whole disagreements about how policies can be designed so that they apply to everyone equally and are fair to all. And they involve people in public office—including the "public office" of citizenship—deliberating publicly with a view to mutual accountability. Deliberative democracy nicely responds to these features because it is

> a process that seeks deliberative agreement—on policies that can be provisionally justified to the citizens who are bound by them. Accountable agents reach out publicly to find reasons that others who are motivated to find deliberative agreement can also accept. When citizens and accountable officials disagree, and also recognize that they are seeking deliberative agreement, they remain willing to argue with one another with the aim of achieving provisionally justifiable policies that they all can mutually recognize as such. (16)

Gutmann and Thompson's ideal of deliberative democracy is very much based on a philosophical tradition aimed at reaching agreement through the give-and-take of reasons. They see the process as a sort of philosophical point-counterpoint, with the back-and-forth of reasoned argument that continues until all agree on what principles and policies are justifiable, that is, until, as Jürgen Habermas puts it, the force of the better argument prevails.

"In politics, disagreements often run deep," the authors write. "If they did not, there would be no need for argument. But if they ran too deep, there would be no point in argument. Deliberative disagreements lie in the depths between simple misunderstanding and immutable irreconcilability" (16). Deliberative democracy can only get off the ground if there is something uncertain and contested that we as a community need to decide, but also only if there are limits to the uncertainty and contestedness. It also only gets off the ground if we are inclined to take part. This is where many deliberative theorists falter. Their account for why people join deliberative public forums rests on the notion that citizens are amateur rational philosophers who "are motivated to find deliberative agreement."

My sense—based on much observation—is that people are not motivated to participate in public deliberation by a desire to reach rational agreement; rather, they attend deliberative forums because they are worried about what is happening to their communities and because they want to have a say in setting things on the right course. They want to make sure that their own concerns and perspectives are taken into consideration, even if that mucks up the chance of everyone agreeing on a course of action.

Moreover, only a small portion of deliberation follows the course of rational argument and the give-and-take of reasons. For the most part it proceeds with people explaining how they came to have the views they have and what their experiences are that shaped their sense of the world. In the course of these conversations, much like in green room "conversions," participants change their views of others' views. They enlarge their understanding of problems and begin to appreciate the complexity of how issues affect other members of the community. Sometimes, instead of reaching agreement, participants leave saying that they are more uncertain than ever. Deliberations can be very sobering as people learn more about the unintended consequences of their favorite policies. At the start they may have had simple views of the problem and the solution, but at the end that simplicity is devastated.

The salient feature of these deliberations is not a search for agreement but a sensitivity to others. To quote Harold Saunders, "politics is about relationships." In a deliberative conversation we change the way we relate to others and revise our views of policies because of what they will do to these others.

A decade after *Democracy and Disagreement*, we might change the line on the cover from "why moral conflict cannot be avoided" to "why we need to stop avoiding moral conflict." The polarization we've sought to keep us safe has only exacerbated the central political danger of damaged relationships that let us demonize other people and their views. Fortunately, we have an inclination stronger than the one to seek safety by retreating into enclaves: the inclination to have a hand in shaping and healing public life, to participate in the whole. I charted this in the first chapter of this book when I described human development as moving from speechlessness to participation in a world with others, rather than the usual story that we move from helplessness to independence.

THE POLITICAL WORK OF MOURNING

The usual story covers over the vulnerability that we experience as bodily beings. Considering the question of what it is to be human, Judith Butler writes, "each of us is constituted politically in part by the social vulnerability of our bodies—as a site of desire and physical vulnerability, as a site of a publicity at once assertive and exposed. Loss and vulnerability seem to follow from our being socially constituted bodies, attached to others, at risk of losing these attachments, exposed to others, at risk of violence by virtue of that exposure" (Butler 2004:20). Because of this vulnerability, we suffer when we lose people we love. And this suffering calls for mourning. Contrary to Freud's notion that the work of mourning involves substituting a new object for the old one, Butler argues that "one mourns when one accepts that by the loss one undergoes one will be changed, possibly forever," without knowing in advance how one will change (21). Grieving involves submitting to the loss of something enigmatic; it is a process that leaves us more heightened to the sense of our connections with others. "Something about who we are is revealed, something that delineates the ties we have to others, that shows that *these ties constitute what we are, ties or bonds that compose us*" (22, emphasis added). "[Grief] returns us to a solitary situation and is, in that sense, depoliticizing. But I think it furnishes a sense of political community of a complex order, and it does this first of all by bringing to the fore the relational ties that have implications for theorizing fundamental dependency and ethical responsibility."

If we call these collective ties to others, which we make affectively and discursively, the realm of humanity, we can begin to see how the work of mourning helps us to reinhabit humanity itself. In a sense, the public sphere is the human realm. To be cut off from it—like exiles from the city-states of ancient Greece—is to be cut off from the possibility of human flourishing. The atrocities that occur in situations of extremity effectively cut people off from humanity. Perpetrators traumatize victims into an abject, inhumane state, themselves acting inhumanely in the process. Turning a barbaric society back into a human space, as those involved in South Africa's truth and reconciliation process found, calls for mourning and public testimony. "This thing called reconciliation . . . if I am understanding it correctly," said Cynthia Ngewu before the South African Truth and Reconciliation Commission, "if it means the perpetrator, this man who killed Christopher Piet, if it means he becomes human again, this man, so that I, so that all of us, get our humanity back . . . then I agree, then I support it all" (quoted in Minow 2000:250).

Butler explains the power of testimony to transform us. "In the asking [for recognition], in the petition, we have already become something new, since we are constituted by virtue of the address, a need and a desire for the Other that takes place in language. . . . It is to solicit a becoming, to instigate a transformation, to petition the future always in relation to the Other" (44). This way of thinking about humanity unsettles the old Cartesian picture of the self as the center of being. As Butler puts it, "My very formation implicates the other in me . . . my foreignness to myself is, paradoxically, the source of my ethical connection to others" (46).

Butler takes the "death of the subject" to a positive place: loss of sovereignty, vulnerability, leads to responsibility: "I cannot think the question of responsibility alone, in isolation from the Other" (46). "For if I am confounded by you, then you are already of me, and I am nowhere without you. I cannot muster the 'we' except by finding the way I am tied to 'you.' . . . You are what I gain through this disorientation and loss. This is how the human comes into being, again and again, as that which we have yet to know" (49). Those who have lost their world in situations of trauma and extremity find it again through connecting with others.

Judith Herman describes the process that she has noticed in those recovering from post-traumatic stress disorder. Before any public work can go on, the person has to find a safe zone. He or she is too fragile at the start to try to make connections with others. But once this safety is found, the work of recovery begins. It starts with remembrance and mourning and continues with reconnection. "Having come to terms with the traumatic past, the survivor faces the task of creating a future," Herman writes. "She has mourned the old self that the trauma destroyed; now she must develop a new self. Her relationships have been tested and forever changed by the trauma; now she must develop new relationships. The old beliefs that gave meaning to her life have been challenged; now she must find anew a sustaining faith. . . . In accomplishing this work, the survivor reclaims her world" (Herman 196). During this third stage of recovery, "survivors are ready to reveal their secrets, to challenge the indifference or censure of bystanders, and to accuse those who have abused them" (Herman 200). Their task becomes to reconnect with themselves and with others, not by trying to forget the past but through public truth-telling, by finding what Herman calls a "survivor mission." The survivor speaks truth (what I later describe as narrative truth) in public not only for her own sake but also for the sake of the body politic. On this point, Herman quotes Hannah Arendt: "The wrongdoer is brought to justice because his act has disturbed and gravely endangered the community as a whole. . . . It is the body poli-tic itself that stands in need of being repaired, and it is the general public order that has been thrown out of gear and must be restored. . . . It is, in other words, the law, not the plaintiff, that must prevail" (Arendt, quoted in Herman 210). However therapeutic the testimony might be for the survi-vor, witnessing is a way of re-creating the commons. It is a political act.

BEARING WITNESS IN THE POLIS

Conventional understanding of political discourse sharply distinguishes between the public and the private, culture and nature, thought and bod-ies. But this conventional understanding cannot make sense of the kinds of political witnessing that go on today, that indeed have gone on for a century. In times of trouble, people testify in public to the wrongs that have afflicted their entire beings, public and private, psyche and soma. Note the advent of the Truth and Reconciliation Commission (TRC), con-vened in places from South Africa to Haiti.[1] In such political discourse, the distinctions between what is properly private and what is public begin to disintegrate.[2] By speaking in public of the devastating crimes committed, often clandestinely, that robbed victims of their humanity, these speakers begin to restore their own and their nation's soul, especially its public space and public being. By attending to this kind of "public talk," we can recall, through a new framework, the old feminist mantra: the personal becomes political.

Julia Kristeva is one of the few philosophers of our day to provide a language for thinking about how the personal becomes political, namely, how affective and somatic forces enter into language and culture. While it is true that, since Nietzsche, most every Marxist, pragmatic, and Wittgensteinian account of language has considered how subterranean forces make their way into public discourse, these accounts generally attend to the dynamics among people (historical, productive, and cultural) rather than the dynamics within them.[3] Kristeva (ever indebted to Freud, Klein, and Lacan) focuses on how inner tumults make themselves felt in our shared language and world. Kristeva's engagement with Hannah Arendt suggests how affective forces might enter into and transform political space.[4] While Kristeva is curiously silent on how her own theory of language can supplement Arendt's philosophy of the public sphere, her engagement resurrects the Aristotelian idea that what makes human beings political animals is language. As Aristotle writes in the *Politics*, "Nature makes nothing pointlessly, as we say, and no animal has speech except a human being. . . . Speech is for making clear what is beneficial or harmful, and hence also what is just or unjust. For it is peculiar to human beings, in comparison to other animals, that they alone have perception of what is good or bad, just or unjust, and the rest. And it is community in these that makes a household and a city-state" (1253a7–18). In other words, human beings possess the ability not only to discern but also to talk, to share their inner world in public and so to create a public space, what Arendt call a "space of appearance." In Arendt's thoroughly Aristotelian view, if people do not take part in this space, then they haven't actualized their potential to be political beings. Following Aristotle, Arendt calls on people to enter this plural world.

But what happens when people are denied entrance—when their title as citizens is revoked, not simply by overt disenfranchisement but through trauma and terror, political crimes of torture, rape, and other humiliations, or everyday but debilitating instances of racism?[5] As humanity has too often witnessed, brutal regimes systematically destroy their victims' sense of dignity, humanity, and public worth, which are all necessary to effective agency as a citizen. They thus strip victims of their identity as agents in a common world with others. They often push victims back to the recesses of a presymbolic, mute existence and deprive them of dignity and humanity, of the right to participate in a common world. When those who have been muted begin to speak in the presence of others, they begin to re-create their mental and affective world, with its geography that orients them to others in the community. In the remainder of this chapter, I use Kristeva's work on Arendt as an opportunity to explore how testimonies in the public sphere can transform political communities trying to recover from regimes of terror. First I examine how Kristeva's ideas can be used to understand the political dynamics of bearing witness in the public sphere.

WITNESSING

When I say "witness," I draw on the meanings Kelly Oliver has given the term in her book *Witnessing: Beyond Recognition*. She distinguishes eyewitnessing, with its notions of evidence gathered through vision, from bearing witness, which usually offers a testimony of something that cannot be seen, and draws on this second meaning to develop a theory of subjectivity radically different from the Hegelian model of recognition—and different as well from most Western theories of how subjectivity arises. The usual, Hegelian model of subjectivity arising from recognition takes for granted that recognition is conferred by one person upon another. This model supposes that the social realm is hierarchical and antagonistic. Oliver notes that many social theorists advocating for those who have been marginalized or demeaned accept the recognition model and try to wrest recognition from those in power. She wants to do something else entirely: to offer instead a model of subjectivity that develops through witnessing. In her view, subjectivity can be achieved through bearing witness to one's own humanity, sometimes by voicing the pain that is inflicted whenever subjectivity is denied. For example, a victim of torture has suffered more than pain; she has suffered being treated as less than human. Her torturer may have humiliated her until she is too wounded to speak of what has occurred. If she escapes, she will have to do more than heal her physical wounds. In order to recover her humanity, she will need to bear witness to the ways her humanity and subjectivity have been violated. Thus, at the very moment that she is voicing how it had been lost, she will performatively re-create her own subjectivity.

Oliver develops this conception of witnessing for two reasons: to address the needs of those who have been denied subjectivity and to offer another way of thinking about the social realm. Here I use it for a third purpose: to reconsider the functions and purposes of testimonies or narratives proffered in the public sphere, in what Arendt calls the "space of appearance."

Oliver draws on Kristeva to develop her theory of witnessing. Key here is Kristeva's notion of psychic space. In *Tales of Love* she describes it as an innerness, a "space of psychic solitude" (377). In *New Maladies of the Soul* she argues that without psychic space, we fall prey to all the anomie and emptiness that plague people in modern consumer societies. When people lack any meaningful psychic life (what Arendt would simply call the ability to think), they seek meaning in the lures of consumer society, such as drugs, alcohol, consumer goods, images—in short, "the society of the spectacle" (she says, borrowing from Guy Debord). Alternatively, by developing and nurturing our imaginative capacities—our abilities to create psychic space and meaning where otherwise there might be none—we can find meaning and transform our lives. Oliver points to the importance Kristeva places on imagination, which gives us access "to our bodies and ourselves and other people" and allows us to represent experience. Taking Kristeva a step further, Oliver argues that this imagination "is inaugurated and nourished through relations with others" (Oliver 2001:71). "This is to say that we are psychically alive by virtue of our relations. And without acknowledging our fundamental ethical dependence on otherness through which we become ourselves, we lose our innovative capacities. Without imagination, that divine space created between people, we lose our ability to represent our experience. We lose our ability to find meaning in life" (2001:71–72). Oliver extends psychic space from a purely inner zone to an imaginative region that extends from within one person to the being of those around her. Through this communal space, a subject creates meaning, including the meaning of life.

In Oliver's view, bearing witness to trauma helps to re-create this intersubjective psychic space. Oliver focuses on the way that bearing witness, telling stories, and making meaning can, in the regions between people, transform individual lives. She is not thinking about this transformation occurring at the level of the *polis*, but imagine that it does: imagine that narrative testimonies could transform communities. Such imagination means, I think, conceiving psychic space even more broadly as a mental and affective world with a geography that orients oneself to others in a community. In this view, psychic space is my imaginative placement of myself in a world of others. This view, I think, overcomes some of the individualistic tendencies in Kristeva's thinking. Even though Kristeva argues that subjectivity is constituted dynamically by heterogeneous processes, the subject seems always to be by herself. She is a speaking being creating herself. Oliver's work moves the Kristevan subject from an almost solipsistic inner zone to a space in which she is coming to be (or reclaiming herself) in the company of others. When we see witnessing as a political enterprise, we can go even further, seeing the way that bearing witness in a political community can transform the community itself.

It might seem wrong to call for bearing witness as an imaginative transformation in settings such as truth and reconciliation commissions, where one might hope that mimesis and accuracy would reign. However, an imaginative transformation is not a transformation of "the truth" but the telling of a truth that can transform communities. Some call such truths "narrative" truths as opposed to "microscopic" or "forensic" truths (Boraine 152). In the TRC process, notes André du Toit, "the relevant sense of justice, which is intimately connected with that of truth as acknowledgment, is that of *justice as recognition*" (136). The process requires settings in which victims speak for themselves: "What is at stake when victims are enabled to 'tell their own stories' is not just the specific factual statements, but the right of framing them from their own perspectives and being recognized as legitimate sources of truth with claims to rights and justice" (du Toit 136). TRC theorists repeatedly note that such storytelling is an integral part of progress toward reconciliation. As Martha Minow writes, "Bearing witness to their deaths, disabilities, and lost hopes; considering what could help those who survived to return to living; and redressing the dehumanization that both presages and endures after mass violence: each of these aspirations calls for a process that focuses on the voices and lives of real individuals" (254).

While many theorists link bearing witness to social transformation, little attention has been paid to how these personal testimonies draw on affective and somatic forces to transform the political. Minow comes close: "the trauma story is transformed as testimony from a telling about shame and humiliation to a portrayal of dignity and virtue; by speaking of trauma, survivors regain lost worlds and lost selves" (Minow 243). Kristeva's work can take us even closer.

POLITICS AND THE HUMAN CONDITION

In a broad sense, both Julia Kristeva and Hannah Arendt are concerned with the human condition. In her book by that title, Arendt argues that human beings are primarily, as Aristotle thought, political beings who

are best realized or actualized in the public sphere, the "space of appearance" where their words and deeds can be memorialized via other people's
recordings. In the private sphere of the *oikos* or household, human beings
are mired in the realm of necessity, in the repetitive tasks needed to ensure
the survival of the species. In the household, there is no history, no actions
worth commemorating, no freedom, no politics. It is not until people enter
into the public realm that they can begin to leave their mark or legacy. But
their mark isn't made in just any nonprivate way, certainly not by *poeisis*,
making things, production. Claiming her difference from Marx, Arendt
insists that human beings should aspire to more. We should not be satisfied with being *homo faber*, a being realized through what he makes and
perhaps sells. And so the *agora*, the marketplace, is not our destiny. "The
impulse that drives the fabricator to the public marketplace is the desire
for products, not for people, and the power that holds this market together
and in existence is not the potentiality which springs up between people
when they come together in action and speech, but a combined 'power of
exchange' (Adam Smith) which each of the participants acquired in isolation" (Arendt 209–210). Arendt will settle for nothing less than the *polis*,
the city, the "space of appearance," where true action can occur and be
memorialized and where "the 'who,' the unique and distinct identity of the
agent," can be revealed (Arendt 180).

  With these distinctions, Arendt offers her tripartite scheme of modes
of living: labor, work, and action, which correlate respectively with the
oikos, the *agora*, and the *polis*. Through labor we (merely) reproduce ourselves (primarily through the life-maintaining labor of the household) and
through work we try to produce things that will have an objective reality.
But only through action—word and deed—are we able to "insert ourselves
into the human world" (Arendt 176). Action means bringing about something new. Human beings demonstrate themselves as free, as initiators,
when they do something new, unprecedented, and improbable, that is,
when they act (177–178).

  Unlike cultural feminists of the past twenty years, Arendt finds little
of value in the household or its ethos of care. She has little sympathy for
materialist interest in production, in the condition of *homo faber* and the
site of the *agora*. She focuses on what takes place in the *polis*, "the organization of the people as it arises out of acting and speaking together" (Arendt
198). In this public space people develop a common sense of an objective
world's reality: "The only character of the world by which to gauge its real-

ity is its being common to us all, and common sense occupies such a high rank in the hierarchy of political qualities because it is the one sense that fits into reality as a whole our five strictly individual senses and the strictly particular data they perceive" (Arendt 208). But unlike the liberal individualism that has for so long prized the public over the private realm, Arendt is no individualist. She shares the Aristotelian conviction that people are political, social beings, which is manifest in her rendering of the *polis* as an arena where one is always acting in relation with others. She holds that true action is pointless unless it is done in the company of others who will recount it. The story of its occurring needs to be told; action has no meaning unless it is accompanied or followed by a narrative. The narrative will offer others in the *polis* a way to think about the political, namely the way that Aristotle described: *phronesis*, i.e., prudence or practical reason.

WORKING THROUGH, THROUGH NARRATIVE

These are the points that Kristeva emphasizes in the story she tells of Hannah Arendt's *The Human Condition*. On one level, Kristeva's account is quite faithful to Arendt. But in a gentle, deconstructive spirit, Kristeva reads Arendt carefully enough to draw out of her texts meanings and purposes that are not manifestly evident. For example, she reads into Arendt's text—rightly, I think—a conversation that Arendt is implicitly carrying on with Martin Heidegger. In Kristeva's view, Arendt shares Heidegger's love of the Greeks but differs with Heidegger over the kind of reason the Greeks are employing in public life. Heidegger believes the dominant mode of thinking is, and ought to be, *sophia*, theoretical wisdom, which if employed properly can be attuned to being. Arendt argues that in public life, especially in the speeches that accompany action, *phronesis* is at work. Instead of the wisdom of theory, public actors need the wisdom of how to act, that is, practical reason or prudence. Kristeva writes, "Arendt's main point here is that if thinking is *sophia*, political action accompanies it and transforms it into a *phronesis* that knows how to partake of the plurality of the living. It is narrative, and not language itself (although language is the pathway to narrative), that provides the mechanism for innately political thinking" (Kristeva 2001a:86).

Kristeva highlights the way Arendt distinguishes *poiesis* (production) from *praxis* (action) (ibid. 70). Where *poiesis* leaves behind an artifact that may crumble and pass away, *praxis* "applies to all activities that do not pursue an end and that leave no work behind but that 'exhaust their full meaning in the performance itself'" (ibid. 71). While the meaning of a *praxis* is spent in the event, it need not be lost. If the conditions are right, it could become part of history. The prime condition is that an action should occur in the *inter-esse*, the in-between, of people in a *polis*, that is, in their "web of relationships" (Arendt 183). Then "the spectators are the ones who 'accomplish' history, thanks to a thought that follows the act," Kristeva writes, recounting Arendt's view. The spectators "make the polis a productive place to organize memory and/or history and stories" (ibid. 72).

As Arendt puts it, the *polis* provides occasions in which people could win immortal fame (Arendt 197) and offers "a remedy for the futility of action and speech," which in themselves leave nothing behind. The presence of others guarantees, she says, drawing from Pericles's Funeral Oration, "that those who forced every sea and land to become the scene of their daring will not remain without witness and will need neither Homer nor anyone else who knows how to turn words to praise them" (197). The *polis* "is a kind of organized remembrance" (198).

Though Arendt points out the difference between the enacted story (the events) and the related story (the narrative), she pays little attention to the art of narrative, that is, to the way it is a fabrication or *poiesis*. The narrative that follows an event need not—in fact could not—be a pure mimesis of the event. Via its structural elements, its choice of beginning, middle, end, and plot, the narrative gives the event a *meaning*. Though she resists the idea that narrative is a fabrication, she does observe that it somehow "crystallizes" what occurred. Moreover, the event is never really completed until it is thought through and narrated. A narrative must not just convey the meaning of an action but complete it. Even in this sense, it is a kind of production or *poiesis*. This fact is implicit in Arendt's formulation, but not acknowledged—for she denigrates *poiesis* as mere fabrication (done for the sake of something else), the stuff of work and production, not true *praxis* or action (carried out for its own sake).

Kristeva rightly points out this tension. Arendt acknowledges that narrative is not mere mimesis: the narrated story is not an exact replica of lived experience, but neither does it operate independently of experience. In fact, the narrative helps disclose what occurred and who acted, thus completing the action. "In truth," writes Kristeva, "history owes its very existence to humans [as spectators], but it is not 'made' by them, according to Arendt and Plato. If we get too wrapped up in the coherence of a plot, we forget that the main goal of plot is to disclose" (2001a:74). For Arendt, the main task of the narrator is not to invent a story but to recognize "the moment of accomplishment" and to "identify the agent" of the story.

This disclosive function, Arendt suggests, is best served when the narrative is as devoid of style as possible. For example, she praises Franz Kafka's language for its "extreme parsimony." Kristeva notes that when Arendt engages narrative, she prefers to "bypass technique in favor of disclosing social mechanisms" (ibid. 91–92). For Arendt, "the art of the narrative resides in the power to condense the action into an exemplary space, in removing it from the general flow of events, and in drawing attention to a 'who'" (ibid. 73). Arendt would like to consider narrative as action, not production, but here the line between the two activities blurs, especially given the fact that the kind of narrative that interests her is "memorializing" and to remain so must be recorded, a story turned artifact. So it is hard to see how she can escape the fact that narrative is a fabrication.

Kristeva seems to agree with Arendt that we can set aside the more complicated questions of narrative, questions of style, subjectivity, and rebellion. But I think we should ask whether such an ideal is possible or even desirable. Could there ever be, as Arendt thinks there is, a Kafka-esque purging of style from public stories?[6] In my own reading experience of Kafka, his minimalism is itself chilling. Could this be because his pared-down prose pares away the semiotic force that makes events meaningful? Many of his texts are about the senselessness of modern life, so the absence of style may in fact "signify" an absence of meaning in life. When narratives attempt to signify more than a lack, should they be purged of style? Would Martin Luther King Jr. have been a better narrator of the public woes and deeds of African Americans if his language had been "pared down"? Would Vaclav Havel have been a better leader had he not also been a dissident and a playwright? These and other public testimonies call for close readings, because an important area for inquiry is the extent to which public testimonies are imbued with semiotic content, the way this content *gives meaning* to events. Kristeva's term for this phenomenon is *signifiance*, what Kristeva's translator, Leon Roudiez, identifies as "the work performed in language (through heterogeneous articulation of semiotic and symbolic dispositions) that enables a text to signify what representative and communicative speech does not say" (Kristeva 1980:18). Were it not for the telltale signs of the semiotic chora in public testimonies—the very signs Arendt would have us strip away—there would be no meaning given to events.

The reason I am pressing this point is that to the extent that a narrative is *poiesis*, it is not really an "eyewitness" account of what in fact occurred (as a mimetic reproduction might be). It is a testimony that draws on the experiences and psyche of the narrator to give meaning to events. Whether it is a fabrication or an action, the narrative that Arendt describes calls for psychic investment from the narrator. We rely on the narrator's hermeneutic capacities, political insights, and rhetorical skill, her ability to bear witness to something vital but invisible (not just what happened but how it is important). The narrator is the medium through which the events crystallize. Arendt seems to think that the narrator is transparent to herself, not embodied and desiring. Concerned primarily with communicability, Kristeva notes, Arendt denies the salience of any affect (pleasure or displeasure, anguish or desire) in favor of a repressive communicability (Kristeva 2001a:225–228). Following Kant's lead, Arendt tries to found political community by repressing what is other to the symbolic—the semiotic aspects of language.

When we bring Kristeva's analysis of the speaking being to bear on Arendt's views of narration, this conception will need to change. Kristeva's theory of the speaking subject points to the difficulty of reading or rendering any political narrative as a straightforward, mimetic "report" of the meaning of events. In the context of testifying to political crimes, the narrative meaning produced can draw on the pain, tension, and trauma that have, in silence or without a public audience, had nowhere to go. In a political crime, the victim who survives is not only brutalized and stripped of her title as a citizen with dignity but also robbed of a community of aid. She cannot go to a public for help because she has been banished from fellowship in that public. She can only search in private for aid, from those few friends and family in whom she dare confide. The TRC setting begins to reverse this double trauma: it simultaneously helps to reinstantiate her subjectivity and her membership in the community. Narratives of trauma do double duty, both completing a story and helping those involved work through the trauma itself. Moreover, the meaning that comes through in such testimonies will be the meaning that results from the speaking being's "working through" instead of her "acting out" (in the Freudian sense) the turmoil that she has experienced.

Where Kristeva focuses on the analytic session as the scene for such working through, I would like to consider the analogous setting of a truth and reconciliation commission. The witness is akin to the analysand, and the commissioners and community are akin to the analyst. To the extent that this kinship is apt, there might be a transference relation at work in public testimonies. Like an analysand, the witness narrates her story that she offers to the community for interpretation. Despite Oliver's claim that witnessing bypasses the recognition model, certainly a witness does seek some kind of acknowledgment, validation, and bestowal of dignity from the community. Hers is the hopeful attitude at work in a caring relationship. Kristeva notes that the analysand looks at the analyst as one who knows and who can cure, thus she looks at the analyst with love. The analyst too experiences love, just as the community looks with something like love, or perhaps simply good will, at the witness. "Countertransference love is my ability to put myself in their place; looking, dreaming, suffering as if I were she, as if I were he. Fleeting moments of identification. Temporary and yet effective mergings. Fruitful sparks of understanding" (Kristeva, *Tales*, 11).

I don't think we need to follow Kristeva all the way down to conceiving these relations as loving. In political situations, the aspiration is not love but solidarity. Still, I think Kristeva's work helps explain the countertransference at work in the TRC process, especially in light of the experience of those present. One South African commissioner, Archbishop Desmond Tutu, writes that even after mental health care workers prepared the commissioners for how wrenching it would be to hear the stories, "we were shattered at what we heard and we did frequently break down or were on the verge of it."

> One commissioner's marriage broke down. . . . Many reported disturbed sleep patterns; some were deeply concerned that they were more short-tempered, quarreled far too easily with their spouses, or were drinking far more than they should. The journalists who reported on the commission regularly were also affected. Some had nervous breakdowns, or cried far more easily than they had known themselves to do previously. (Tutu 286)

Tutu recounts how difficult the process was for the translators, for they had to speak in the first person, sometimes as victim, other times as perpetrator: "'They undressed me; they opened a drawer and then they stuffed my breast in the drawer which they slammed repeatedly on my nipple until a white stuff oozed.' 'We abducted him and gave him drugged coffee and then I shot him in the head. We then burned his body and while this was happening, we were enjoying a barbecue on the side'" (Tutu 286). No doubt, translators must have found speaking the words of either party to be very traumatic. Even those far removed from the testimonies, Tutu noted, would end up in tears.

In these poignant and powerful interchanges, those taking part in a TRC, including those witnessing on the stand and those witnessing as they listen to the radio, exemplify the relationship of systems open to one another, open in a way that destabilizes identity ("in the direction of its 'desire-noise' as well as its 'memory-consciousness'" [Kristeva, *Tales*, 15]) but also makes way for renewal. Time after time, observers have noted the cathartic power of testifying to trauma and the transformative effect this process has had upon political communities.

I believe we can account for these outcomes both by drawing on Kristeva's description of the analytic process and by attending to the ways political bodies (both citizens and communities) benefit. In her examination of *The Human Condition,* Kristeva reads Arendt generously and avoids applying her own linguistic and psychoanalytic views to Arendt's conception of narration. She does, almost in passing, raise a few concerns, which she seems to brush aside:

> We might fault Arendt for failing to grasp that the poetic language of a narrator—such as Proust—is a way to join the "thinking ego" and the "self as it appears and moves in the world." . . . We might be worried by Arendt's Lukács-style sociology that allows her to declare [in praise] of Kafka, a bit too hastily, that "style in any form, through its own magic, is a way of avoiding the truth . . .]." We might further regret that Arendt did not recognize the need for rebellion—an intrapsychic need but a historical one as well—that led the century's avant-garde to an unprecedented reevaluation of narrative structures, of the word and the self. . . . Art, and in particular the art of narrative, has a history that does not repeat past problems [*enjeux passés*] and old solutions. Today's narrative is more akin to clinical protocol than to moral judgment. It is up to us to discover the causes and the fate of this history, not to stigmatize it. (Kristeva 2001a:92–93)

"It is up to us," Kristeva writes, but apparently not just yet, for in the very next moment she excuses herself from the task: "But that is not what really interests Arendt, who seeks the optimal solution to the 'frailty of human affairs.' Through this political lens, narrative art is subordinated to the just act that it may or may not illuminate" (93). But what if we decided *not* to subordinate narrative art—and instead saw narration as a way to heal and restore fractured communities? In political narrative, art cannot be subordinated, for the very *meaning* of the political act, which results from our decision about what that act means *for us*, can never be ascertained apart from the art of interpretation and narration. Arendt insists that political narratives may be about matters that are supposedly objectively true, but at the same time, they reveal something that is variable and uncertain, the "who," the identity of the speakers and their relations with their fellows, i.e., "the in-between" (Arendt 182). "Most action and speech is concerned with this in-between, which varies with each group of people, so that most words and deeds are *about* some worldly objective reality in addition to being a disclosure of the acting and speaking agent" (182). Now, even if we disagree about the "objective reality" of the world, we might agree with Arendt that narratives performatively create and reveal "the who" and the "in between." Or we might go further, in the direction that Gadamer and Kristeva have, and say that speech is precisely not a performance of human agents. Rather, speech itself performs something for human beings.[7] Likewise, testimonies in the public sphere attend to the wounds in the *polis*, giving back to citizens their title as citizens and to the polity its public space of appearance in which people can come to be together.

To move beyond Kristeva's reading of Arendt, I think we can press Arendt's theory of political reason beyond the simple choice between *phronesis* and *sophia*, toward a phenomenological understanding of what we might call "public knowledge." This does not require using Kristeva's particular theory as much as the phenomenological tradition to which she is heir. To explain, let us return to the debate Arendt implicitly carries on with Heidegger. Narratives construct our understanding of occurrences. In this sense they call for *sophia* because they are knowledge of what has happened and thus what is. They testify to a past truth. But, as Arendt realized, narratives also call for *phronesis*, because they shape past events into a meaning that suggests what ought to be done hereafter. In the dispute Kristeva discerns between Arendt and Heidegger, Arendt argues that *phronesis*, not *sophia*, is the dominant mode of reasoning in political discourse. Following

Aristotle (in his *Nicomachean Ethics*), she argues that this is because political speech revolves around the question of what to do and thus how to act. Both Arendt and Heidegger are observing Aristotle's taxonomy of knowledge that distinguishes *sophia, phronesis,* and *techne* (technical knowledge or know-how). These are useful distinctions, but following them devoutly while trying to understand the public sphere leads to a certain blindness, as I will explain in a moment.

As I have noted throughout this book, by "public sphere" I mean the nongovernmental space in which people come *to be* together. I put this ambiguously on purpose: from an Aristotelian point of view, we have not become fully human until we make use of an opportunity (present in a proper city) to be with others but not in silence, "for speech is what makes man a political being," Arendt writes. "Men in the plural, that is, men in so far as they live and move and act in this world, can experience meaningfulness only because they can talk and make sense to each other and themselves" (Arendt, *Human Condition*, 3–4). When they carry on these conversations, they create a public (themselves) and a public sphere. As Jürgen Habermas puts it, wherever two or more people come together to talk about matters of public concern, there is the public sphere (Habermas, *Theory*, 231). It is the occurrence of our conversations about our past (what is given to us, our facticity) and our future (what we should do). As Kimberley Curtis writes in her book on Arendt, "the significance of the public realm arises not only because it houses the mutual promising and common deliberation of the future-oriented actor but also because it is the site for these conversations with the past—conversations that, transformed by the spectator into stories, illuminate what otherwise is a welter of bewildering occurrences" (Curtis 112). We need to tell stories of what the past means both to work through trauma and to decide how to act in the future. The public sphere is the communicative site where we respond to what Curtis calls "the phenomenal richness of our shared world" (Curtis 113).

Knowledge of this "phenomenal richness" is more than either *sophia* or *phronesis* alone. For want of a better term, I call it "public knowledge." When people create or recover meaning as a public, they are knowing phenomenologically, from the standpoint of a lifeworld. By this I mean something closer to what Habermas calls the "everyday concept of the lifeworld" rather than the "communicative-theoretic" understanding. The former refers to the perspective from which "communicative actors locate and date their utterances in social spaces and historical times. . . . [This] lay concept of the lifeworld refers to the totality of soiocultural facts" (*Society and Politics* 172). Here there is no sharp demarcation among different ways of knowing, for example, science, morality, and art. People telling stories from a lifeworld perspective not only describe what happened but also evaluateit, normatively and aesthetically.

Habermas (following the sociologists Weber, Luhmann et al.) argues that as societies become more modern, these ways of knowing become specialized ventures; society becomes more differentiated (Habermas, *Society and Politics*, 165–187). In contrast, Arendt, Kristeva, and other heirs of an alternative tradition, phenomenology, are more likely to vaunt the synthetic way of knowing in the lifeworld. They generally hold, for example, that there is no independent reality "behind" what presents itself to experience (contra Plato's theory of forms) and thus participants need not have a specialized theoretical knowledge stripped of affective dimensions and normative values. Members of a lifeworld do not hesitate to construct together in their testimonies a multilayered meaning (of values, hopes, observations, etc.) for what is present before them. Obviously, poststructuralist critiques of immediate, "given" experience unsettle a simple phenomenological view, but they do not call for turning away from the goal of making sense, as best we can, of the world we inhabit. From this standpoint, sharp distinctions between *sophia* and *phronesis* keep us from seeing that our story of what is will shape our decision about how to act. Paying little heed to distinctions between scientific and practical knowledge, public testimonies create a knowledge of the world that respects participants' need for a meaning that can guide action.

In sum, testifying to political trauma in public is a step in the process of working through trauma, and it helps reconstruct public ways of being and subjectivities shattered by horror, terror, torture, and degradation. We can rethink Arendt's notion that the "who" is disclosed through testimony by way of Kristeva's theory of language, in which subjectivity emerges through the speaking beings' struggles while negotiating the semiotic chora's disruptions into its symbolic communications. Witnessing helps survivors translate what is felt immediately and inchoately into a public language by which community can begin to mend and emerge. When those who have been muted begin to speak in the presence of others, they begin to heal not only their own psyches but also their societies.

CHAPTER 6

Deliberative Democracy

In chapter 1, in discussing the public sphere, I began to describe what I mean by democratic politics. As noted there, democracy takes place in this public realm where public meaning and purpose are created, ultimately the meaning and purposes that steer a political community. A true democracy begins early and deep, in the abilities of all members of the polity to feel themselves members of a common public space with a hand in shaping its contours. Democracy takes place in the assembly and the town meeting, not merely in the private space of a voting booth. A democracy is not an agglomeration of free individuals; it needs a public, in the Deweyan sense, that can develop judgment and set direction about things common. My approach is very Aristotelian, but it does not require importing all of Aristotle's metaphysical biology or politics. It simply means thinking that human flourishing involves being part of the project of forming a public life together. (Those who want to mind only their own business may want nothing to do with this, though they should be aware that abdicating public business also involves severely curtailing what counts as one's own affairs.) Yet even as it is Aristotelian, my view is highly informed by both poststructuralist and pragmatist thought. The result is a nonfoundational theory of politics that goes much further than the work of many to whom I am indebted, including Iris Young and Jane Mansbridge. In the last half of this book I develop a model of deliberative democracy that I call integrative, for it sees participants in deliberative discourse as weaving their various and partial perspectives into a view of the whole that might guide their actions.

This view of democracy and politics merges uncannily well with the psychoanalytic theory of sublimation and human development. What matters in both democratic politics and sublimation is what happens in public. Dealing with trauma that besets the public sphere calls for public work, not private decision making. This is not just a theoretical edifice. Let me describe how it works in practice, internationally in some of the most challenging parts of the world.

SUSTAINED DIALOGUE

Describing the downfalls of forced democratization efforts, Randa Slim, the vice president of the International Institute for Sustained Dialogue, who has worked extensively as a practitioner in dialogue and peace-building processes in the Middle East and Central Asia, writes,

> Elections, it seems, may exacerbate societal divisions rather than heal them. Elections lead to a winner and a loser and, as in the case of many countries in the Middle East, the loser may be a group that has long enjoyed privileges and power that it is not willing to give up without a fight. Elections tend to equate the act of being a citizen to that of becoming a voter. By so doing, it limits the whole responsibility of citizenry to that of choosing among a slate of candidates. Most often it is a solitary act, performed by the individual in the confines of a small voting booth. In divided societies, the challenge for any political intervention aimed at promoting sustainable democratic change is to move the individual from the confines of his or her self (often defined by the tribe or ethnic identity) to the wider realm of a citizen actor, often defined by the national identity. This transition from one narrowly defined identity component (tribe/clan/confession) to a more inclusive one (the nation-state) is the major challenge to any democratic transformation in a divided society. Representative democracy, per se, is least capable to help with this transition. (Slim 2007)

For societies in the process of transitioning from oppressive regimes to democracy, much more than voting booths are needed:

> What is needed is the creation of dialogue spaces, deliberative meetings, and opportunities for collaborative work that provide testing grounds where one citizen may listen to the other and understand where he or she is coming from, may try joint safe activities like brainstorming together, and eventually, may understand the self and what and how the individual has to change in order for societal change to happen. The story of Nelson Mandela is great testimony to the reality that

self-induced change in one's own attitude about the other side, one's image of "the other," is a necessary precursor to a changed *relationship* with that other. What is missing from the work of most international organizations involved in this area is just this embracing of a broader concept of democracy that moves beyond technical assistance (with its mere machinery) to the promoting of sustainable and safe spaces where people can, over a sustained period of time, learn and test the basic underpinnings of citizenship on which democracy rests. (Slim 2007)

Slim works closely with Harold Saunders, an architect of the Camp David Peace Accords and a prominent career diplomat until 1981, now the chairman and president of the International Institute for Sustained Dialogue. They have both been writing about a "citizens' peace process," which focuses on working with the unofficial sectors of societies and regions in conflict. Their work continues a project begun under the Eisenhower administration, when Eisenhower asked Norman Cousins to try to get some kind of unofficial but high-level dialogue going between the United States and the Soviet Union. The two nations, mired in the Cold War, couldn't talk with each other officially, but Eisenhower understood that it was vital for some kind of discussion to occur. Cousins was on the board of the Charles F. Kettering Foundation, which he enlisted to help. The first meeting of former officials from both countries was at Dartmouth College, and all the many subsequent meetings were dubbed the Dartmouth Conferences. The participants met regularly throughout the remainder of the Cold War and developed modes of relating that largely involved each side talking about its own affairs, not opining or railing about the other's affairs. I think these conferences were a vital part of preventing the Cold War from ever becoming catastrophic.

As the Cold War ended, the Dartmouth Conferences became regional conflicts task forces. Participants began to focus on and draw in people from regions in conflict throughout the world. During the 1990s Saunders and Slim worked in Tajikistan, starting a citizens' peace process to get through the country's civil war. As of this writing they are working with unofficial leaders from various parties and sectors in Iraq, bringing them to safe places outside the country to start to find some way to forge a nation together. The key task in all such work, Saunders writes, is for the parties to develop relationships, by which he means "the continuous interaction within and among clusters or associations of citizens that make up a whole body politic" (Saunders 2005:55). In a peace process that has involved deeply conflictual and traumatic pasts, Saunders sees five dimensions of relationships that need to be developed. First there is identity, which is largely founded on a people's experience.

> No person, group, or country can be fully described in terms of a snapshot or measurement of physical characteristics at a particular time. It is essential to know where a person or group "is coming from." What developmental process or interactions with others have brought them to the present place and moment—shaped their worldviews and their approach to others? How individuals are taught to "remember" past interactions—traumatic experiences that produced a sense of grievance or victimhood or of great achievement—may be more important in shaping their present sense of identity than knowing objectively what happened. Each party to an experience depicts, mourns, or lauds it differently. People do not easily forgive. Some may let go of past pain; others will hug the pain close. (Saunders 2005:66)

Identity thus includes the "chosen traumas" and "chosen glories" that Saunders's friend and colleague, eminent psychoanalytic theorist Vamik Volkan, described. Volkan, whom I quoted at the very start of this book, writes that he uses the term "chosen trauma" to describe the collective memory of a calamity that once befell a group's ancestors (Volkan 1997:48). A chosen trauma is "more than a simple recollection; it is a shared mental representation of the event, which includes realistic information, fantasized expectations, intense feelings, and defenses against unacceptable thoughts" (ibid.). Volkan uses the word "chosen" in this context not to indicate that the group volunteered for the trauma or its psychic consequences but because "the word *chosen* fittingly reflects a large group's unconsciously defining its identity by the transgenerational transmission of injured selves infused with the memory of the ancestors' trauma" (ibid.) He lists a handful of examples, including Czech identity founded on the defeat in the 1620 Battle of Bilá Hora that deprived the Czechs of freedom during 300 years under the Hapsburg monarchy; the Lakota people's memory of defeat in the battle of Wounded Knee in 1890; the ways the Jews will "never forget" the Holocaust; and the Crimean Tartars' definition of themselves by their 1944 banishment from Crimea. I could add the traumatic identity of the Roma in central Europe, the Kurds in Turkey and Iraq, the Basques in

Spain, the Armenians in Turkey, and much of the eastern Mediterranean countries vis-à-vis the Turks/Ottoman empire. How such groups deal with or work through their chosen traumas shapes the kind of relationships they might be able to forge with others.

The other four factors, according to Saunders, include:

(2) *interests*, both concrete and psychological—what people care about—that bring them into the same space and into a sense of their dependence on one another, *interdependence*, to achieve their goals, (3) *power*, defined not only as control over superior resources and the actions of others but as the capacity of citizens acting together to influence the course of events with or especially without great material resources, (4) *perceptions, misperceptions, and stereotypes*: and (5) the *patterns of interaction*—distant and close—among those involved, including respect for certain *limits on behavior* in dealing with others. (Saunders 2005:56)

Emerging political relationships need to be dynamic, evolving, and continuous. Their work proceeds in steps; it involves creating space for talking together and new mindsets optimistic about the capacity of unofficial sectors of society to effect change. Eventually, these dialogues need to be merged into the larger communities.

Through all these aspects of developing political relationships following conflict and trauma, the ability of participants to work through trauma is crucial. Every step of the peace process involves creative talk and what Christopher Bollas calls unconscious freedom. Peoples will not be free to imagine and forge new relationships if they are imprisoned by past traumas. So the talk that goes on in any peace or transitional process must always also involve a working through from trauma to freedom of and for the political unconscious.

A DELIBERATIVE PUBLIC

Much political philosophy of the late twentieth century takes its cue from Immanuel Kant, certainly and rightly a hero for those championing democracy and justice. In the deontological tradition, perhaps less in Kant's own theory than in contemporary "projects of Enlightenment," such political theory postulates that the aim of public deliberations is agreement on questions of justice, mutual understanding of and agreement on what courses of action can pass the test of universalizability. Such theory calls on participants to strip themselves of particular attachments and proclivities in order to adopt a universal point of view.

Where such theory seeks universal answers to moral and political questions, democratic theories that draw from the pragmatic tradition and kindred continental philosophical traditions offer a vision of deliberation as a practice that helps a public to find or make itself, helps this public develop an understanding of the political topography of its problems, and aims for integrating multiple, particular points of view into a provisional public judgment that can be used to create just and sustainable public policy. Note that the third feature can work hand-in-glove with a psychoanalytic understanding of "working through" loss and trauma. Even in a deliberation on a matter as mundane as energy policy, there are, when plumbed, deep choices about sacrifice, potential and real loss, that have to be grieved or worked through.

I draw on Dewey, Derrida, and other allies to develop a pragmatic understanding of the public and of what deliberative public judgment might be.[1] Where deontological approaches try to strip themselves of particularity (at least in their logical tests for universalizability, though less so in the form of the humanity principle), integrative and pragmatic approaches aim to unearth the richness of particularity. In deliberatively trying to understand problems, this richness has two sides: the manifold aspects of a problem itself as well as its consequences for all involved; and the meaning it has for all of us in connection with our own ever-evolving values, concerns, and purposes. When we look for the meaning of an event or a problem, it is not just what *it* means but what it means *for us*. Public deliberation helps elucidate the topography of a problem and the range of political permission on what can be done. In fact, in deliberations, a seemingly inordinate amount of time is spent trying to understand the problem itself (whether it's crime, immigration, the U.S. role in the world, or anything else). This may be the case because understanding the problem and its meaning for us is a matter not just of excavation and discovery but also of creation, interpretation, and working through. In articulating what a problem means for us, we also begin to articulate (both retrospectively and prospectively) the meaning of "us": who we are, what we want to stand for, and with whom we are in relation, including those who might have seemed to be our enemy.

The meaning of "us" in a deliberative context provides a way of thinking about who we are as a "public." Investigating the meaning of "public" in "public deliberation" is, I think, worthwhile. Let me start by saying, much as I think Dewey knew, that the public is not a thing, and this nothing we call a public is quite intriguing and baffling. We often refer to it with the definite article, *the* public. To use the term "publics," as some with multicultural sensibilities sometimes do, is to twist the word beyond recognition, for "public" seems designed to connote a collectivity, really an uber-collectivity of members of a political community (on whatever scale); if there is more than one collectivity, then any one of them isn't a collectivity or a public at all. Instead of a public, we might call it a faction.

I say the public, whatever it is, is not a thing. By that I mean that it is not waiting in the wings. It is ephemeral. It seems to come together one day and disperse the next. A public is always in relation to something else, whether a problem that can, upon recognition, band people together, or a cultural production or a speech. Yet with the latter, "a public" seems to mean anyone paying attention, and calls for little more than paying attention. That's what we call an audience, not a public.

Since public deliberation calls for participants, not observers, we need to try to understand what this public is in a civic dimension rather than a spectator sense. But civically speaking, there is a widespread concern that perhaps, as Walter Lippman claimed, the public is a phantom. We invoke the phantom public to make ourselves feel that we have a real democracy. But look around, he noted; people seem to be unable to fathom the complexities of the problems that beset them, and much less are they able to engineer solutions. They barely know what is going on. They are like the theatergoer who shows up in the middle of the second act and leaves before the curtain closes, having stayed just long enough to figure out who the villains and the heroes are.

Well, maybe you are right, John Dewey replied. The public is inchoate, but this is largely because people have not found a way to fathom the problems that beset them—and each other. "At present, many consequences are felt rather than perceived," Dewey wrote; "they are suffered, but they cannot be said to be known, for they are not, by those who experience them, referred to their origins. . . . Hence the publics are amorphous and unarticulated" (Dewey 1954:131). To become a public, people need something that brings them together *as a public*. "An inchoate public is capable of organization only when indirect consequences are perceived, and when it is possible to project agencies which order their occurrence" (ibid.). When people seem unable to cohere as a public, to grasp problems or identify solutions, the remedy is not to take away their authority but rather, Dewey argued, to find ways to help the public find itself.

Identifying problems and beginning to see how these problems affect them and their fellows helps a public start to find itself. Dewey noted two other essential processes: the public needs to be able to produce a knowledge of what could be done to address the problems, in the form of public opinion, public judgment, or public will, knowledge that ideally could help shape public policy; and members of the public need to be able to communicate together to help create this public knowledge. "Systematic and continuous inquiry into all the conditions which affect association and their dissemination in print is a precondition of the creation of a true public. But it and its results are but tools after all. Their final actuality is accomplished in face-to-face relationships by means of direct give and take. Logic in its fulfillment recurs to the primitive sense of the word: dialogue" (ibid. 218).

The public can find itself, or to put it more aptly, *make* itself by coming together to talk about the pressing problems of the day, to identify their sources, see how the problems differentially affect others, and try to decide together what should be done. Out of these processes, which all amount to what we call public deliberation, might emanate informed public opinion about what should be done. This information has a special status. Dewey put it this way: "The man who wears the shoe knows best that it pinches and where it pinches, even if the expert shoemaker is the best judge of how the trouble is to be remedied" (ibid. 207). The public may enlist experts or governments to fix its problems, but it alone is the best judge of what needs to be addressed and whether the remedy is successful.

Dewey's clarification still leaves us with many problems. For one, how in fact the public can make itself, especially when its members have been polarized or wounded; what help it needs; who can help; and how. For another, how the public creates its intelligence, opinion, or judgment. And finally, how the public's understanding of what should be done can have any impact on those in the business of governing. Dewey might have had a nice rejoinder to Lippman, but history took its cue from Lippman, not Dewey, and the political system generally proceeds as if citizens are merely clients, taxpayers, and occasional voters, not a potential public with any valuable knowledge or authority to shape public policy.

A public makes itself performatively. It is in the process of doing public work that people become a public. Recently I heard a talk where the author made such a claim about the body itself (Morris 2006). If we notice what happens when a part of the body is immobilized, say, when a broken arm is put into a cast, we notice that over time, as the bone heals, the muscles atrophy. After the bone mends, its strength is only recovered when it is repeatedly tested. Physical therapy involves putting the body to work precisely when and where it is not yet up for that work. The bone is not healed until it is able to withstand stress, and it only can come to withstand stress by doing the work when it's not ready. It becomes a body by bodying. The body is an effect of a body working.

Likewise for the public. Writing in the 2004 issue of the *Higher Education Exchange,* David Mathews proposes that "a sovereign or democratic public comes into being only when people begin to do the work of citizens, which Harry Boyte of the University of Minnesota calls 'public work.' This way of conceptualizing the public sees it as a dynamic force rather than a static body of people. . . . In other words, the public doesn't just do the work—doing the work creates the public" (88). This process-oriented view suggests that there need not be unity or unanimity in advance of the public work of deliberation; whatever might emerge will do so in the process.

The problem with a performative answer to the question of how a public makes itself is, ultimately, a chicken-and-egg problem: where to begin. If public making occurs through a public working, how did this public find itself in the midst of this work? If public making, as Mathews writes, "isn't separate from collective knowing, deciding (deliberating), and acting," if "it *is* those activities," how does it find itself there?

I think that individuals become a public when they come together, with their individual opinions, preferences, and complaints, and begin to talk together, or whenever they are thrown together and start to figure out how and why they were thrown together. A few years ago I heard an Argentinean woman describing a moment outside the bank doors, when once again the political system was in crisis and the financial markets in turmoil. She was standing in line with hundreds of other people similarly worried about their savings, and then she and others looked around and at each other and begin to identify themselves as a public *created* in this moment of recognition, of this connecting of the political crisis, the financial crisis, and their collective welfare.

If individuals are treated only as individual complainants, or even as individual citizens to be surveyed, addressed, assured, a public cannot come into being. If politics proceeds by recording individual preferences or adding up individual votes, nothing like public work can take place. The major problem of our day is that Lippman and later Joseph Schumpeter convinced political thinkers and leaders that democracy can happen so long as individual views are aggregated. So long as public policy is consistent with individual preferences, they argued, a society is democratic. But this view of democracy is more about satisfying individuals, like a well-functioning market (in fact, it entirely takes its cue from market logic), than about rule by the people, that is, if we are to think of "the people" as some kind of collective public.

There are two problems here. One is that the aggregated sum of individual views is inferior to the public understanding that comes about when people compare notes. An aggregated sum adds up partial perceptions and blind spots, but public understanding results when people begin to fill in and interconnect partial views. When people deliberate together about issues, in a conversation that might ramble among stories, reasons, interpretations, and perspectives, an integrative process takes place. Together they unfold a problem through the back-and-forth of conversation, offering perspectives, anecdotes, and concerns. As this process goes on, participants create an understanding of the topography of a political issue and begin to see how various options would or would not be able to navigate that terrain. No aggregation of preferences on an issue could ever approximate what deliberation produces.

The other problem is that aggregating individual views does not do any of the work of deciding what should be done. The task of politics is ultimately to decide what to do, work that still has to occur after an aggregation; but in this model the work is done by officials, not the public. Unlike democracy, here officials take the aggregation of individual views *under advisement* as *they* do the work of deciding what to do. In a democracy, it is the considered opinion or judgment of the people, the *demos*, the *demes*, that charts the course.

Despite the hold that Walter Lippman's and Joseph Schumpeter's desiccated notions of democracy have on us, there is something else about public opinion that has an even stronger hold. Politicians continually refer and defer to it, even well between election cycles. There seems to be some kind of democratic ideal that gives public opinion gravitas even as the usual ways of gathering public opinion leave much to be desired. Asking a mass of individuals for their views, never tempered through public deliberation, and then tabulating the results delivers a table of preferences, not a *public* opinion.

Putting this more poetically, Jacques Derrida writes, "public opinion is *de jure* neither the *general will* nor the *nation*, neither *ideology* nor the sum total of *private* opinions analyzed through sociological techniques or modern poll-taking institutions" (Derrida 1992:87). No public comes into being through aggregation. If public opinion is to be more than "the silhouette of a phantom," to borrow Derrida's wonderful phrase, it must be something other than the aggregation of private opinions. Instead of asking individuals what they think, people need to come together to decide what to do, to render a judgment on matters affecting the polity: "Opinion, as its name indicates, is called upon to pronounce itself by means of a *judgment*," Derrida writes. "This judgment is not some knowledge, but an engaged evaluation, a voluntary act. It always takes the form of a 'judgment' (yes or no) that must exercise power of control and orientation *over* this parliamentary democracy" (Derrida 1992:90–91).

The ideal of public opinion is that it guide public policy, that the people be ultimate arbiters of what the polity should do, where its policies should go. The democratic hope is that public opinion be both authoritative and more able to grasp what is at stake than elected officials might. "As the place of a potential electorate," Derrida writes, "public opinion is an assembly of citizens called upon *to decide, by means of a judgment,* issues that are within the competence of legal representation, *but also* issues that escape them, at least provisionally, in a zone that is being extended and differentiated today in an accelerated way, thereby posing serious questions about the present functioning, if not the very principles, of liberal democracy" (ibid. 91–92).

The problem today is that the representative system of liberal democracy produces a gap between the public and its representatives, and any opinion that a public manages to form must be heard, and represented, by these representatives, who no longer have much interest in heeding or taking seriously what the public might deem important. But I am getting ahead of myself.

The mystery, if there is a mystery, of how a public performatively creates itself is not in its finding itself doing the work. It is not that people might occasionally come together to talk—though we could certainly use more opportunities and occasions. The mystery may be in the work itself. What is this work? What is this public doing? Derrida says it is judgment, not a knowledge; a deciding what should be, not an ascertaining of what is true or false.

Compare Derrida's view to that of one of the leading theorists of deliberative democracy in the Kantian mold, Jürgen Habermas, as he criticizes the communitarian movement. Notice how Habermas disparages deliberations aimed at public self-understanding and public making in favor of deliberations aimed at reaching understanding about what is universally right for all (the moral equivalent of "true or false," not the ethical judgment Derrida calls for). "According to the communitarian view, there is a necessary connection between the deliberative concept of democracy and the reference to a concrete, substantively integrated ethical community," writes Habermas, borrowing Hegel's language. While an ethical community (*sittlichkeit*) is concerned with what is good for itself, a moral order (*moralität*) is concerned with what is universally good for all (Habermas 1996b:24). Political philosophers term these concerns ethics versus morality (rather confusing, since usually the terms are barely distinguishable), as well as "the good" (what is good for us) versus "the right" (what is just or right for all). Habermas favors focusing on universal morality rather than particular notions of the good. His worry about communitarianism's use of deliberation is that it is focused on particular attachments, not universal justice. In Habermas's view, the communitarian focuses on the ethical community because "otherwise one could not explain . . . how the citizens' orientation to the common good would be at all possible. . . . The individual can get a clear sense of commonalities and differences, and hence a sense of who she is and who she would like to be, only in the public exchange with others who owe their identities to the same traditions and similar formation processes" (ibid.). The communitarians' focus on "the clarification of collective self-understanding," says Habermas, "does not sit well with the function of the legislative processes they issue in" (ibid.). Insofar as collective deliberations are about regulating our lives together, that is, about law, they should focus on universal principles of justice.

> To be sure, discourses aimed at achieving self-understanding—discourses in which the participants want to get a clear understanding of themselves as members of a specific nation, as members of a locale or a state, as inhabitants of a region, and so on; in which they want to determine which traditions they will continue; in which they strive to determine how they will treat one another, and how they will treat minorities and marginal groups; in short, discourses in which they want to get clear about the kind of society they want to live in—such discourses are also an important part of politics. *But these questions are subordinate to moral questions* . . . [emphasis added], questions of justice. The question having *priority* in legislative politics concerns how a matter can be regulated in the equal interest of all. (Habermas 1996b:24–25)

In Habermas's ideal politics, questions of universal moral validity, that is, justice, take precedence over questions of solidarity. Habermas subordinates deliberation aimed at choosing what kind of community we would like to be to deliberation aimed at questions of justice. The distinction itself is fine, at least for analytic purposes; but the notion that these can be engaged in independently of each other is wrong. Whenever people deliberate about what kind of community they want to be, they are addressing matters of justice. And whenever questions of justice are on the table, they are approached in the context of a particular community's concerns. A political community addressing an issue of immigration is simultaneously struggling to integrate its desire to stand for openness and freedom with the exigencies, whether real or felt, of limited resources. Communities that are deliberating about how to "treat minorities and marginal groups" are very much involved in questions of justice while struggling to forge their own self-understanding. What I or we stand for is very much a part of who I or we are. In such cases, deliberations turn on how to forge a *particular* community that upholds values that all might be proud of upholding. Our own self-understanding is tempered by what we think others will think of us, and most of us want to be seen as member of a moral order. So deliberation aimed at forging collective purposes is always already wrapped up with questions of more universal morality.

Moreover, it is these very deliberations aimed at deciding what kind of community we want to be that turn a people into a public that might also take up questions of justice. Unless a public makes itself in the work of deciding what it ought to do on matters of common concern, there will be no public to adjudicate questions of justice.

Michael Sandel makes a similar point in his rejoinder to John Rawls's *Theory of Justice*. Like Habermas, and also following Kant, Rawls prioritizes the right over the good, universal principles of justice over particular concerns of a given community. Sandel argues that questions of justice are posed *somewhere*, in some particular context, among some particular people. The public work that makes a people a public is as vital as the public work of deciding matters of justice, and probably prior to it as well.

I asked earlier about this work that makes people a public; what kind of work is it? Derrida in his writing on public judgment said it was a judgment, a yes or no, not a knowledge. Likewise, Aristotle long ago noted that choice and deliberation in politics are about matters that have no certain answer. We deliberate about what we should do. We deliberate well when we have a sense of what good ends are, and that can only be arrived at through practical deliberation, not scientific knowledge. Yet Habermas's political questions take a form more akin to questions of knowledge than questions of purpose. He is quite explicit about this. Normative questions can be answered formally and cognitively, and their answers are either universally valid or not. The answers are found through the process of reason-giving in conversation when all who are potentially affected have an opportunity to weigh in on whether the proposed policy would be best for all. Ultimately, in this round robin conversation, the force of the better argument will prevail.

Note how different this is from the "engaged evaluation" that Derrida says is called for in forming public opinion (Derrida 1992:90). Recall: "this judgment is not some knowledge, but an engaged evaluation, a voluntary act. It always takes the form of a 'judgment' (yes or no)." Habermas also sees the end result of deliberation as forming a kind of public opinion—public will—that, normatively, should exercise control of sorts over parliamentary politics. But where Derrida's public judgment is formed through engagement, decision, a yes or no, Habermas's is formed through a cognitive appraisal of which policy is right, which will lead to unanimity on which policy meets the test of universalizability. The less tainted by parochial concerns, by matters of solidarity and self-understanding, the better.

Does a public form itself in a Habermasian deliberation? No—in the volley of argumentation, there is little room for the sharing of perspectives that can be integrated into a better understanding of the whole. In fact, coming to deliberation with partial perspectives is detrimental, Habermas thinks, to reaching understanding and agreement. His model of the deliberative forum is more like a logic class, while the Derridean, and I'd add Deweyan, one is more like a literature class. English professor Peggy Prenshaw described her own experiment in bringing deliberation to literary studies in an article she wrote for the 1998 issue of the *Higher Education Exchange*. In a project on the humanities and public deliberation, she thought through the relationship between understanding literature and deliberating on public policy:

> The comparison I am pursuing here is that of the empirical undecidability of the questions raised by the text and a similar undecidability of public policy questions raised in citizens' forums. Resolution is reached by persuasion, by enlisting empathetic agreement, by noting facts, recalling historical precedents, reporting relevant personal experience, raising questions about the language and actions manifest in the text. An interpretation of a literary text, like a group's response to discussion of a public issue, is an act of judgment, an act that is language-bound,

culture-bound. It is contingent on the disposition of a group of individuals in a given place at a given moment. (Prenshaw 2004:67)

In both deliberative forums and literature classes, the conversation can
ramble; it will tarry on particular cases and focus on odd details. But most
important in both kinds of conversation is a kind of "work of ascertaining
the *meaning* of the data and texts" (ibid.)

Prenshaw's observation is vital to understanding the gulf between
deliberations aimed at universal answers and deliberations that can give
rise to a public and public judgment. Like the broken limb that is healed
in returning to its function, in bearing weight, the public is formed by
connecting disparate people through a process of forging common meanings and delineating possible courses of action. Any course of action will
continue the process of public formation, so with trepidation and anything
but universal certitude, we make our choices.

DELIBERATIVE FORUMS

All this discussion of how a public makes itself through deliberation may
sound very abstract. But in fact it takes place in all kinds of venues, formal
and informal. To close this chapter, I describe the venue with which I am
most familiar, the National Issues Forums.

In the late 1980s I was doing some research and writing for the Kettering Foundation, which had, beginning around 1980, been helping to foster
a national informal network of grassroots deliberative forums called the
National Issues Forums.[2] The foundation, along with a group in New York
called Public Agenda, produced three books a year that would each address
a political issue and lay out three or four possible policy options, using non-
technical, "public" language. Issues (such as immigration, poverty, health
care, violence, and foreign policy) and policy choices were laid out in a way
that most any reader would find something palatable, as well as something
problematic, in each option, so that by the end he or she would have difficulty choosing any one simple proposal; and in a room full of people deliberating on an issue, participants would likely hear points of view they hadn't
considered before. In the process they would likely find that they were each
as torn individually as much as they all might be collectively. Their deliberations, as Aristotle noted, would be about matters that had no definite
answer, no right or wrong solution waiting to be discovered. They were
to decide, to judge, which course of action would be best for the political

community, but "best" had no ground other than their own estimations of which policy might fare best and best satisfy the values of the community, values always in the making, even being made in such deliberations.

From the outside, an NIF meeting looks like a simple public discussion, but one of its architects set up the process to aim at coming to public judgment. This was one of Public Agenda's founders, the opinion researcher Daniel Yankelovich, who had long been studying how public opinion can move over time into a stable, coherent public judgment. In the 1970s he had been a colleague of Hannah Arendt at the New School for Social Research and he was very taken by her idea of representative thinking. He was also interested in Freud, whose work led him to think that public opinion cannot become public judgment unless people have an opportunity to consider choices, grieve what they will lose when they choose one path over another, and work toward making a choice and resolution. The other force behind NIF, the president of the Kettering Foundation, David Mathews, received his doctorate from Columbia University, where he had pursued his interests in American pragmatism as well as ancient Greek democracy. He then became the youngest president of the University of Alabama and served for a few years as Gerald Ford's Secretary of Health, Education and Welfare, where he became much chagrined with electoral, bureaucratic, and top-down politics. For many pressing reasons, Mathews and Yankelovich thought it was important to put the public back into the policy-making process, to resurrect the old "town meeting" model, which might result in what Habermas would separately call "public will formation," public will that might make its way into law, for the benefit of the political community. So they brought together community leaders from around the country and started the National Issues Forums.

NIF got going before the heyday of democratic theory in academic circles, before deliberation got defined as a process of the give-and-take of reasons aimed toward mutual understanding. The thinkers behind it were more influenced by Aristotle, Dewey, Mary Parker Follett, and Arendt than they were by Habermas or Rawls. At various meetings to discuss these ideas, they were joined by Jane Mansbridge, Ben Barber, Harry Boyte, and other democratic theorists, and a broader circle of political philosophers (Michael Walzer, Michael Sandel, Dan Kemmis, Paul Starr) lent articles to their publications and students to their summer research programs. At the grass-roots level, the people who convened and moderated local NIF forums had little if any background in theory, but they were keenly aware of the need to create public spaces for tending to matters that affected their communities. These moderators included community college teachers, extension agents, local officials, labor organizers, adult literacy teachers, and other volunteers. They focused on developing ways of talking with fellow citizens that would elicit comfort, openness, and freedom. With a little help from the Kettering Foundation, but mostly of their own accord, they developed principles and practices that would guide public deliberations: making sure that everyone had an opportunity to talk; defusing dogmatic assertions with requests for stories that explained points of view, personal history, experience, and context, stories that might bring forth people's underlying values and hopes.[3]

This storytelling feature of NIF is the most noticeable difference from the way most deliberative theorists envision deliberations. Rather than the back-and-forth argumentation one might witness in a seminar room, in a forum people take turns telling stories, giving their own perspectives on problems and on the possible consequences of proposed solutions. Most importantly, each two-hour public forum is designed to culminate with some kind of choice. Toward the end of the session, moderators ask, on this issue that affects us all, what are we going to do? The answer says as much about participants' thoughts on the issue as it says about who they are—or hope to be—as a community. In fact, the way they respond is a way of performatively choosing what kind of community they will be.

In the 1990s, having returned to graduate school, I lived a kind of double life. I helped write training manuals for NIF moderators and convenors, edited a journal on deliberative politics, and helped direct a national deliberative opinion poll with the political theorist James Fishkin. At the same time, I was writing a dissertation on politics and subjectivity in Kristeva and Habermas. It seemed that my studies of Habermas's discourse ethics and deliberative politics should have been more intertwined, but the truth was that they seemed to be operating in different universes. For many years I thought that something was amiss, that perhaps the practice wasn't living up to the theory, and then it finally occurred to me that the theorists were missing a human, real, and vital part of what happens when people deliberate and engage in politics together. Since then I have been integrating insights from continental and pragmatist theory, including psychoanalytic and semiotic research, into understanding actual politics. Having seen how people in actual political communities deliberate and decide together about matters of common concern, I have developed a certain sensibility about political theories. In the next chapter, I show how that sensibility reads feminist theory and what kinds of ideas in feminist thought are most productive for democratic life.

CHAPTER 7

Feminist Theory, Politics, and Freedom

In this chapter I use feminist theory and politics as a case study for showing how a deliberative approach can help move people through trauma and repetition. In the span of recorded history, as far as we can tell, fully half of the human race has undergone some kind of repeated trauma. Women nearly universally are considered second-class citizens, if citizens at all. Still today, they are victims of degradation and violence. Much of the feminist consciousness that has risen to counter this history itself bears the marks of this trauma, visible through its language of oppression. Here I unpack a suspicion that much feminist thought about politics flows out of a misconception about the nature of the problems that women face, ultimately a misconception about the nature of politics and the public sphere. I suspect that the more conventional feminist approaches have a rather flat or narrow idea of politics as primarily a one-way transmission of power, flowing from the oppressors to the oppressed. In this view, little if anything is done to conceptualize or problematize the media through which this supposed transmission passes; the media disappear, and all that is visible are actors with either sinister or innocent intentions. Just recall Catherine MacKinnon's claim that on day one men oppressed women and then on day two they set up the stereotypes of femininity and so forth that would uphold and conceal the oppression. I want to draw out another feminism that sees how actors or subjects are situated in a matrix of signs and symbols, of meaning making (semiosis), of perspectival interpretation and perception.

To do this, I use the resources in various semiotic and pragmatist traditions, which have a much richer view of politics and the public sphere as discursive and semiotic processes and arenas. My initial suppositions coincide with those of John Dewey, that the public finds itself communicatively. From there I have turned to semiotics, developing my own synthesis of Peirce's and Kristeva's views, to see how the public sphere is a discursive space in which subjectivity, identity, and meaning are created, dispersed, and interpreted. In this second picture of the public world, feminist thought has a different task than in the first one: instead of simply "fighting power," feminist practice calls for rethinking how meanings and identities are created in discursive and communicative processes and matrices. In this second perspective, political thought moves from an agonistic toward a more deliberative view of the political public sphere. In short, the model of fighting oppression gives way to thinking about discursively and deliberatively reconstituting the public sphere, claiming freedom, and building new worlds.

When feminists identify the problem as that of an oppression that can be peeled away, as the effect of an other that can be excommunicated, what we get is a politics of exclusion and another repetition compulsion. This might take the form of separatism, as championed by radical feminists such as Mary Daly. Or it might take the shape of agonistic politics—a politics of struggle—with adherents ranging from Chantal Mouffe to Bonnie Honig and, some argue, Hannah Arendt (though she can be read otherwise as well). By "agonistic" I mean the view that politics is a struggle over resources, over who gets what, where, and when, a competitive, aggregative process driven by self-interest. Feminist theorists and practitioners have long taken this position, engaging in the *agon* in order to garner a more just and equitable distribution of power and resources for women.

ONE FEMINISM

Many of the current generation of political theorists grew up in a world where freedom or resources for one group came at the expense of the liberty and goods of another, and even as gains are being made, many of these theorists, feminists included, are on the side still struggling. An agonistic lens shows the continuity between first-wave feminists who fought for equal rights and second-wave feminists who have been fighting for sexual and cultural freedom. Tying them together is the notion that patriarchy, the fathers in power, have found it in their own interests to deny women basic rights and resources. Feminist political struggle, in this view, is a battle to increase women's portion of the political pie. We can see this common orientation across the spectrum of feminist approaches: liberal feminists seek more rights; cultural feminists seek greater validation of historically female practices and institutions; socialist feminists seek more access to economic power; and radical feminists want to attack the root of the problem, to undermine patriarchy's project of oppressing women.

All of these approaches, in one way or another, divide the world between female friend and male foe. Seeing the problem as one of oppression, they see men's and women's interests as antithetical;therefore, any triumph for women will be at men's expense. They share the notion, flowing out of this analysis, that politics is agonal (that is, a matter of struggle) and is democratic when previously excluded or marginalized people, namely women, get entrée into the public arena. This feminist politics sees political struggle as a means to create a more democratic society. One French "radical democrat," Chantal Mouffe, writes that "far from jeopardizing democracy, agonistic confrontation is its very condition of existence" (Mouffe 2000:103). She traces the word "politics" back to the Greek *polemos*, struggle and war. (In my own etymological sleuthing, I have found no such connection.) She uses this etymology to support the common notion that politics is war by other means. For Mouffe and her early coauthor Ernesto Laclau, political success, following Antonio Gramsci, is the creation of a new cultural hegemony, in which the values and aims of the previously marginalized groups come to dominate and appear transparently as what is right and good (Laclau and Mouffe 1985). Under this new hegemony, the needs of the majority of people will move to the fore, becoming the new public policy. In the sense that this new politics will meet the needs of the majority, this view considers itself to be democratic. The means, though, are not democratic: they might include propaganda, manipulation, ways of creating a new hegemony of those who have been excluded over those who held power beforehand. In other words, Mouffe's radical democracy arguably has a more democratic end in mind—a public sphere that includes all who have previously been denied the prerogatives of citizenship—but the politics itself is not necessarily democratic. Agonal feminist political theory is democratic only in the majoritarian sense, wanting to create a new hegemony of the previously silenced majority.

Because of my own peculiar biography and set of experiences, this approach never sits right with me. The closest I have been able to accept is that something we might call the sociosymbolic system oppresses us. Iris Young's analysis in her classic book, *Justice and the Politics of Difference*, moves a bit closer, seeing oppression largely as an effect of social structures. From this point of view, men and women are all implicated together, for there is no *other* that foists the system upon us. We are all a part of it, simultaneously its victims and its perpetrators. And sometimes freedom from one oppression leads to a wholly new one (just as my ability to be a mother and a philosophy professor rests upon my economic privilege to pay others much less than I make per hour to care for my children).

Nonetheless, the notion of a sociosymbolic system can be even more powerful than Young's notion of structures. If we bring in Lacanian conceptions of the symbolic, we can see even more thorough and pervasive ways in which sociosymbolic systems "oppress" women. These systems are not something we can sanely reject, though, for they are the very systems that allow us to differentiate and judge, think symbolically and speak with our fellows, write books and present at conferences. If this is an "oppression," it is a very assiduous one indeed. It cannot be peeled away like a dirty garment. Perhaps it can be reworked or reformed by replacing bad structures or dichotomies with more liberatory ones. As I'll discuss shortly, this may be a fruitful approach, but if we pursue it then we may find that the language of "oppression" is no help at all, for such language presumes flat flows of power and ignores the multidimensional trajectories of meaning and intervention that occur in a communicative public space.

TOWARD ANOTHER POLITICS

But before I turn there, let me take one more pass at how feminists define "the problem." When the problem is seen as the product of an external oppressor—that is, when one is still in the throes of an unworked-through trauma and its concomitant repetition compulsion—it is natural to look for a politics that seeks to banish, triumph over, or even annihilate the other. There are strands within feminist theory itself that call this approach into question and hence undercut the very ideas that underlie agonistic politics of repetition compulsion. (These strands can be found in feminist critiques of liberal theory. See Mansbridge 1998, Jaggar 1983, and Frazer 2002.) And theorists such as Nancy Fraser, Jane Mansbridge, Carole Pateman, Iris Young, Seyla Benhabib, Anne Phillips, and many others have provided powerful critiques of the view of politics inaugurated by Joseph Schumpeter and played out through much of the twentieth century.[1] They take issue with the idea that self-interest is formed prepolitically. Both agonistic and liberal political theory seem to presuppose that one's interests precede one's entrance into politics, which is the arena where one acts to maximize one's own given set of interests. But for these other feminists I am now alluding to, and for pragmatists and others who have read Hegel seriously, there is no self prior to its formation in a sociohistorical world. So it does not make sense to think of politics merely as an arena in which one barters (the liberal view) or struggles (the agonal view) to become better off than others. Self-interests or, to put it better, our conceptions of the good—of meaning, value, and purpose—are formed in the thick of politics, in and through our relations in a sociohistorical world. In short, as I have indicated in the preceding chapters, subjectivity and its concomitant desires are formed socially and experientially in a world with others. There is no exclusion of the other without some dissolution of oneself. Hence, agonistic politics is a serious misadventure.

So how might the problem be conceived otherwise? Perhaps the fault lies not in oppression from without but in the way that sociosymbolic systems constitute us through and through. Various theoretical frameworks try to get at these systems. Both psychoanalysis and semiotics consider how the self is constituted through language and relations with others. Certain approaches to linguistics, history, economics, and other social sciences consider how the social world, in time and through time, constitutes the self. American pragmatism and German critical theory dispute old concepts of fixed identity in favor of historical views of how the self performatively announces itself in a field with others. Heirs of Marx look at how the economy and its structures help shape our possibilities. Philosophers from Bergson to Royce consider the way that our understanding of time, extending backward through memory and forward through hope, connects us to a world of others, helping to create an identity in community. All these theoretical lenses open up aspects of our sociosymbolic world as a matrix through which we are constituted and positioned. We are not the holders of signs and symbols; they hold us. We can interact back, with the sort of techniques and probes Robert Innis discusses in his work; but these actions are always within a field that interacts back again.

A promising feminist project follows along the lines that Charles S. Peirce drew: an examination of the signs that make up our world and, with it, our selves. Instead of seeing politics as a flat field in which power flows from oppressor to oppressed, a semiotic approach sees a multidimensional world permeated by signs, with meaning and identity being produced as subjects (or at least those positioned as subjects) actively produce, interpret, and reinterpret meaning. The realm of signs, the semiotic public sphere or sociosymbolic order, is a dynamic repository of subjects' sublimations, their transformations of energy and desire into a publicly accessible space of language, art, and culture. We make, transform, and find ourselves in and through these cultural representations. Looking pragmatically and semiotically, we can see how the world is permeated by these "signs" of ourselves—or sometimes our selves are occluded by their exclusions from the public sphere—and how signs demand interpretation. And we see that any active, novel interpretation, offered perhaps as a political act, produces new meanings and signs that in turn demand interpretation.

I think it is a step forward to move from a flat model of oppression to a multidimensional semiotic model, but then we see the magnitude of the task at hand. We live in a world in which signs and symbols, in multiple and overdetermined ways, constitute deep structures that continually keep women as second-class citizens, if citizens at all. These structures have positioned women as beings less able to engage in meaning making, semiosis, and civilization. But feminists attuned to this symbolic framework understand that the systems at hand cannot simply be tossed away and replaced. The task is to find ways to reconfigure the signs, along with their semiotic processes and structures, that produce negative conceptions of the feminine, conceptions that disappear from view and become "natural" insofar as they operate at the level of metaphysical thinking, suppositions about what is "really real." The feminist project, then, is huge: to raise to consciousness the fundamental myths at work in the dichotomies of real/apparent, natural/cultural, active/passive, one/many. It is also to intervene in the way that signs are deployed, to transform the structures that have heretofore served to exclude women from semiotic engagement.

Theorists who take signs at face value, as tools wielded by oppressors, fail to appreciate the ways that signs can be played with and turned on their head. Even with theory lagging, though, feminist and other activists have been able to intervene. Think of the way Madonna inverted the trappings of femininity, how the group the Guerrilla Girls unmasked the masculine bias of the art world, how the gay liberation movement used the derogatory term "queer" to gain power. These activists understood the power of signs, the kind of autonomy they have, and the ways they can be redeployed for political ends.

ANOTHER FEMINISM

A constellation of feminist theories take up this challenge. Over the past two decades, some feminists have begun to approach politics in a way that can be recognized as pragmatic, democratic, and deliberative. As opposed to those who see it as a contest, I think they understand that the fundamental task is to understand politics as a symbolic field in which the meaning of what it is to be a woman is discursively or semiotically constituted. The forces at work are not exactly anonymous, but neither are they the forces of particular agents, e.g., oppressive men, misogynists, or patriarchs. Nefarious actors do not run the scene. Rather, we are all, men and women, born into a world in which symbolic structures always already constitute us as feminine or masculine with all the supposed affiliated attributes; that is, our subjectivity is formed through these semiotic processes and structures. We learn to speak and to think in and through them, and then we in turn raise or inculcate other generations into and through them. This does not mean that we are passive victims of patriarchal structures, but it does mean that feminists are in the funny position of having to use the tools of a patriarchal structure or symbolic field in order to try to transform it. From a semiotic point of view, the hope of a political activist, feminist or otherwise, is to intervene in the way that signs are deployed. Such interventions do not come from outside these semiotic processes, but in and through them; in other words, discursively and semiotically. We refashion language and symbols by *using* language and symbols, by discursively highlighting and questioning the ways semiotic processes function. There is no *outside* the system, no we/they dichotomy that the oppression model supposes. Instead of a politics of one party trying to overcome another, this alternative model understands the need to use language to work through these traumas, to come out the other side as related members of a common sociosymbolic field. Rather than pointing to *agon,* this model moves toward interventions into what we all share.

Of course, feminists understand that this common public sphere situates members differently, with women nearly universally positioned at the negative poles of binary thinking. In a symbolic field that sets at odds and hierarchizes concepts such as active and passive, mind and body, culture and nature, the feminine is positioned on the lower end. Situated at the negative poles of the symbolic field, women who intervene can come at them from the margins. The French feminist philosopher Luce Irigaray does this famously well, though I won't go into how. Suffice it to say that her interventions use the language of the sociosymbolic field, but in a way that shows its weaknesses and blind spots. Hence, such interventions are critical without being oppositional. Likewise, other feminist theorists who focus on sociosymbolic fields part company with agonistic feminism.[2] I have in mind some thinkers loosely known as continental feminists, though they also have strong affinities with pragmatist thought: Julia Kristeva and some continental feminist theorists based in the United States such as Judith Butler, Drucilla Cornell, Kelly Oliver, Linda Zerilli, Cynthia Willett, and the late Teresa Brennan.

It might be a stretch, but I think I can safely say that their ultimate interest is the commonweal and not the partisan interests of one segment of humanity. Then their approach is open to what Sheldon Wolin describes as the political, "the idea that a free society composed of diversities can nonetheless enjoy moments of commonality when, through public deliberations, collective power is used to promote or protect the well-being of the collectivity" (Wolin 1996:31). While none of them directly addresses democratic theory, their views point toward democratic feminist politics in the same way that Peirce's semiotics paved the way for Dewey to argue that the public "finds itself" *communicatively*. Attending to sociosymbolic structures and processes and the ways these formulate "the feminine" is the fundamental political task for feminists. Only after such work has begun can we take on more tangible tasks, such as legal reforms and economic measures. In a real sense, these other problems or symptoms are superstructural effects of fundamental maladies in the communicative public sphere.

As I discussed earlier, the poststructural, semiotic term "the sociosymbolic field" is ultimately another way of talking about the central category in democratic thought today: the public sphere. Drawing on Habermas's notion that this is a communicative arena in which lifeworld questions— questions of solidarity, kinship, meaning, purpose, love, and justice—are addressed, we can see from another angle the ways such matters of the commonweal—fundamentally political questions—are attended to discursively. They are constituted symbolically from and by the multitude of public actors, citizens, and subjects. The political public sphere is not a place but an ongoing semiotic happening, the grids and flows of communication: the mass media, dinner table conversation, Web logs, cable access television, the local paper, the art world, PTA meetings, letters to the editor, chattering on the playground and in the classroom. All of these are intersecting communicative fields in which meaning, identity, and purpose are created.

Feminists who understand "the problem" as how this sociosymbolic field or discursive public sphere is structured tend to work directly on various ways the field structures subjectivity and experience. Many see subjectivity as a process, not a static entity, as do many process philosophers. Radically departing from the Cartesian picture of the self as mind, a glassy essence that is indivisible and fully transparent to itself, pragmatically inclined feminist thinkers understand that the self is continuously constituted via dynamic processes. They argue that it emerges through a particular culture, language, history, time, and place. This does not mean that subjectivity is constituted groundlessly, but that it is always a product of some particular sociohistorical symbolic framework.[3]

Along with much of the rest of philosophy in the twentieth century, continental thinkers took the linguistic turn. Continentally inspired feminists did so in especially productive ways. Kristeva, for example, develops the conception of *le sujet en procès* or the subject in process and on trial (Kristeva 1984). She points to the ways we constitute ourselves through our signifying practice. In short, the signifying process includes not only our straightforward attempts to be meaningful but also the subterranean effects of our affects and drives. These make their way into language, not directly but through a kind of channeling or sublimation, as Kelly Oliver has argued. To put it simply, our "animal" or libidinal energy and desire are transformed into "human" meaning, the signs and symbols of a sociosymbolic sphere. We take part in human community, or what Aristotle called the *polis*, at least to the extent that we are able to join in this quintessentially human, political activity. The public sphere is an effect of sublimation, a repository of past identity formations; those who have been othered are foreclosed from speaking.

Attempts to silence someone, through torture or other dehumanizing activities, deprive them of membership in the sociosymbolic field. This is the evil of sexism, racism, and colonization. Changing and recovering from these systems require that those who have been silenced begin to speak. Kelly Oliver argues that survivors of political brutality reconstitute their own subjectivity by bearing witness, publicly, to the wrongs they endured. Thus they performatively re-create their sense of being a self worth heeding.

To this point I have sketched out two feminisms. With strokes that might seem too broad, I have painted one as an agonistic view that sees the self standing outside of politics, which is an arena one enters to battle for one's own given interests. The other I have found in the traditions that take Hegel seriously, that see the subject as always emerging *in* history. Adopting the second view necessitates working through the trauma of sexism that still imprisons the first one. It calls for a political mourning that might free up the imagination. In this way, feminists working within post–Hegelian traditions—pragmatism and continental philosophy—might imagine the self otherwise; they can decide not to take "the self" at face value, as some given subject with given attributes, something prior to history that can be *restored* to purity, freedom, and autonomy once the vicissitudes of history have been corrected. This other feminism begins with an understanding that subjects come to be in time, in a socio-symbolic field, a semiotic public sphere that structures our sentiments, identities, ideals. Theorists who take this semiosis, this public production of meaning, seriously focus on the field, not on the hapless patriarchs, bigots, and misogynist policies its structures produce. Instead of fighting power in a friend/foe schema, they attend to the semiotic workings of the public sphere itself. By differentiating between agonistic politics and the politics of the public sphere, I do not mean to exclude the ways contestation enters into politics. The making of the public sphere always involves difference, struggle, discord, and tension; but this agonistic dimension is not the meaning of politics per se. Central to politics, central to the motivation of anyone who cares to enter into the fray, is the hope that some kind of agreement might be reached. Without such hope, there would be no will to enter.

ARENDT, ZERILLI, AND WORLD-BUILDING FREEDOM

One of the most important figures in political thought in the twentieth century was Hannah Arendt, a woman who had little, if anything to say about feminism. Yet feminist theory inspired by her work can be very productive for both feminism and politics. In this vein, Linda Zerilli's *Feminism and the Abyss of Freedom*, while decidedly a feminist book, has much to say about politics as well, even about deliberative democracy. The book argues for a feminism that is freedom-centered rather than mired in the question of sexual difference. This question, Zerilli argues, has consumed feminist theoretical energy regardless of which way it has been answered—whether for sameness or difference or even for a radical skepticism about the possibility of categorizing woman and hence about a feminist politic. The question itself is misguided for at least two related reasons: it sees feminist politics as a matter of finding the right concept of "woman" as a base, when it is mistaken to think that any politics can be grounded on or guided by a concept; and it occludes a better goal for feminist theory, which is to orient feminist politics around issues of freedom.

Feminists would be better oriented toward political freedom, Zerilli argues, though not the freedom of liberal sovereignty but rather a political freedom of collective participation in world building. Political freedom breaks with the realm of causality. Following Arendt, Zerilli argues that this is the freedom to create something new without needing any ground, cause, or determining antecedent. People postulate new concepts, figures, and possibilities by putting them forward, by holding them, by claiming them to be so. Whether these claims succeed is a matter of whether they are taken up by others (closure) or continue to circulate, contested, in a political back-and-forth (openness). The question "What is a woman?" for example, is a question whose answer will not be *found*; the answer is to be created politically, built with others. The intersubjective validity of a claim arises in a collective world-building politics.

What becomes truly interesting politically is not just whether some group or category of things *exists* but what these things *mean*. Their meaning is to be created in world-building political practices. Zerilli argues that feminists have for too long searched backward and underneath their theorizing to find a ground or a concept that can guide feminist politics. But any ground they have found has quickly been undone by other feminists. There is nothing to stand on, but it is wrong to think that something cannot stand. Feminists should take a leap, create, and lay claim to a world and identities and possibilities that they want. The frightening and exhilarating thing about freedom is that by taking it up we claim the power to create the kind of world we'd like to live in. It is not created willy-nilly, because it has to pass the muster and judgment of a community of others likewise striving.

Feminism and the Abyss of Freedom is certainly oriented toward feminists and feminist theory. But the very same theoretical resources, including those developed in the chapters on Monique Wittig's *Les Guerilleres* and the Milan Women's Bookstore Collective, could easily be marshaled toward other kinds of politics, not just of other identity groups but also of democratic and republican traditions. What Zerilli says about feminism and freedom we can also say about democracy and freedom. Her work helps explain some otherwise inexplicable features of deliberative democracy. These are features that I have noted, in one way or another, for years; but the way that I will state and inflect them here is already inflected by my reading of Zerilli.

Public deliberation does not require impartiality; it can use the plurality of perspectives on an issue to develop a better sense of the whole.[4] Unlike a Habermasian model of deliberation, which seeks rational agreement, NIF and other integrative approaches to deliberation are more forgiving of disagreement; in fact, they realistically accept that political problems become political problems in large part because of disagreement. Where some think the solution is unanimity, whether found through the force of the better argument or through a common identity, Arendt, Zerilli, and most people who have participated in or observed deliberative forums know the value of multiple and even clashing views. The task of deliberation is to be able to understand other perspectives, to be able to see what others see, even if one doesn't share the same view; Zerilli quotes Arendt on how public speech, as the Greeks found, opens to the door to seeing from multiple viewpoints:

> In [their] incessant talk the Greeks discovered that the world we have in common is usually regarded from an infinite number of standpoints, to which correspond the most diverse points of view. In a sheer inexhaustible flow of arguments, as the Sophists presented them to the citizenry of Athens, the Greek learned to exchange his own viewpoint, his own "opinion"—the way the world appeared and opened up to him—with those of his fellow citizens. Greeks learned to *understand*—not to understand one another as individual persons, but to look upon the same world from one another's standpoint, to see the same in very different and frequently opposing aspects. (quoted in Zerilli 2005:139)

Zerilli points to the continuing political importance of this ability to understand how the world looks from many different positions at once. "Arguments are valuable," she writes, "not when they produce agreement—though they well may do so—but when they enable us to see from standpoints other than our own and deepen our sense of what is shared or real" (Zerilli 2005:140). In an increasingly polarized world, this skill is more endangered than ever. One of the striking things people have said about their experience in deliberative forums is that while it might not have changed their own views on issues, it changed their views of other people and their views. By beginning to see how a problem appears to others, participants begin to appreciate its complexity. The problem takes on new meanings, suggesting new ideas about what will need to be done to address it best for all involved.

In integrative deliberations, participants are motivated to fashion a new *public* world, which is like putting together a puzzle, trying to see what all the pieces are, especially the pieces held by other participants, and then seeing how they might fit together, however imperfectly and provisionally. In order to come up with a practical way to solve a problem, participants in deliberative public forums need to be able to integrate the multiple perspectives in the room into one larger whole. Zerilli calls this the practice of judgment. The resulting more comprehensive picture might ultimately show us a direction that might work.

Public deliberation is a kind of politics that calls for and helps cultivate certain political skills, which add up to political judgment. One such skill is listening to others without presuming that they are just like oneself or radically different, finding commonality with someone from a different social and economic space without collapsing into uniformity. In her chapter on the Milan Women's Bookstore Collective, Zerilli traces the collective's development of the political skill of using plural and unequal points of view. At the start they learned the pitfalls of a feminist ideology that supposed that the members of the collective were all the same. A major insight came when one member made the startling pronouncement that "we are not all equals here" (108), voicing the obvious but unspoken differences of class, social standing, and abilities. Yet it was not enough for there to be plurality without assessing and judging differences. They needed to create ways for the collective to start making judgments through and even about their differences. Until they had a space "for strong conflicts or disagreements," the Milanese had "no space for strong desires and no possibility of genuine politics" (109).

The space of the forum can also be a political one. In "political" we need to understand a difference that Zerilli and Arendt, as well as Sheldon Wolin, identify. Recall Wolin's observation that unlike the politics of contesting and bartering for resources, the political is "an expression of the idea that a free society composed of diversities can nonetheless enjoy moments of commonality when, through public deliberations, collective power is used to promote or protect the well-being of the collectivity" (in Benhabib 1996:31). What makes this collective power palatable is that it can be of the sort that Arendt says arises when people "gather together and 'act in concert'" (Arendt, *The Human Condition*, 244, quoted in Zerilli 2005:21)—not power over but power with. Using Arendt's idea, Zerilli gives an account that could, word for word, apply to the kind of politics at work when regular folks enter into a deliberative forum to talk about what their political communities should do. They come with their plural interests and predilections, but they expect to act or work together to try to develop a coherent public judgment. Or, as Zerilli puts it:

> Foregrounded in Arendt's account is politics . . . as a world-building activity, for which the pursuit of interests may be enabling or corrupting but is, either way, certainly secondary to the practice of freedom. In contrast with the idea, central to liberalism and to most forms of feminism, that the function of politics is to pursue individual and group interests (that is, people come to the table with certain interests already in hand, which then need to be articulated as claims and adjudicated in terms of their validity), we have the idea that interests serve as the occasion, a catalyst of sorts, to engage in politics. The instrumentalist or adjudicative approach to politics sees the pursuit of interests not only as the motor but also the raison d'etre of politics itself, for which speech and action are a means. . . . Arendt, by contrast, holds that speech and action can themselves be political, regardless of the interests we pursue or the ends we may realize when we come together politically. In a very specific sense, then, politics may involve the articulation of interests but is not driven by the questions of expediency; it is not a means toward an end. Political are not the interests as such but the world-building practice of publicly articulating matters of common concern. (Zerilli 2005:22)

How does one build a world through talking with others about matters of common concern?

With Zerilli's conceptual tools, we can observe that *deliberative politics pushes toward a public judgment that is not grounded on logical proof but on the* sensus communis *that arises in the political practice of taking in other points of view.* To those steeped in more conventional deliberative theory, this seems almost heretical, for as Habermas argues, the force of the better (read, most logically compelling) argument will prevail in deliberations. Others worry that letting the views of others influence their own is tantamount to heteronomy or illegitimately coercive. But as I have observed over the years, people in deliberations welcome other views and make their collective choices not on the basis of logical proof, but according to a new picture of the whole that emerges in deliberation. As Zerilli puts it,

> [The] ability to persuade others of one's views does not depend on facility in logic. One may well have the so-called force of the better argument and fail to convince one's interlocutors (and not because they lack competence, that is, fail to understand what a good argument is). The ability to persuade depends upon the capacity to elicit criteria that speak to the particular case at hand in relation to particular interlocutors. (144)

Deliberative politics allows participants to see something new, to imagine new possibilities. They begin to connect ideas in ways they hadn't before, to see each other in a new light, and through their collective imagining, to point out new directions for their political community.[5]

In the course of their deliberations, participants may make assertoric claims, but the force of their claims is performative. On this point, Zerilli writes, "political claims have a fundamentally anticipatory structure: we posit the agreement of others, that is, we perform an act of closure. Whether others do agree, however, is another matter and part of the openness of democratic politics itself" (171). Political claims are not knowledge claims, she successfully argues. They anticipate a world that those making the claim think should be. And in making the claim, sometimes, if it is taken up successfully by others, they help bring that world into being.

Public deliberation creates something new; deliberative public forums alter and open up the world. This is really an act of imagination, of creating possibilities that had hitherto not existed. The possibilities are not built on some ground or by some kind of deductive, logical process. They are built when old ideas are put into relationship. Zerilli describes imagination as the "faculty that allows us to bring particulars into an unexpected and potentially critical relation with each other—critical because we are able to see something new, something not given in the object itself" and to note "the context in which we engage other points of view in forming a judgment" (61). For example, years ago I helped organize a series of deliberative polls on public utility issues in Texas. All the stakeholders who helped write up the materials and oversee the process thought they had listed all the possibilities, and most anticipated that Texans would rank renewable power last in preference, since it is so expensive and only able to supply a fraction of energy needs.

But the participants in those forums put in relation things that no one had expected, and they came up with an option to let ratepayers choose to have a portion of their electricity supplied by renewable energy, at a slightly higher rate than most could afford. This novel idea occurred when people had the space, opportunity, and freedom to imaginatively build something together. Subsequently, the state legislature and the utilities turned this notion into real policy—a real-world, world-building example.

Unlike the kind of politics that simply aggregates personal preferences, discourages choice and judgment, leaves people in their own private cocoon of opinions, public deliberation pushes participants to judgment, to a new understanding of the whole. Zerilli quotes Arendt on this point: "If the world, as Arendt argues, 'is the space in which things become public,' then judging is a practice that alters that world. In this space, the objects of judgment appear. She writes, 'The judgment of the spectator creates the space without which no such objects could appear at all'" (160).

"Politics," Zerilli states near the end of the book, "is about making claims and judgments—and having the courage to do so—in the absence of the objective criteria or rules" that could provide certainty and guarantees. Political freedom calls on us to be courageous.

CHAPTER 8

Public Knowledge

In chapter 5 I discussed the role of narrative in working through trauma. I noted that the "truth" that emerges from witnessing to trauma, from the stories that are told, lies somewhere between *phronesis* and *sophia*. It folds what happened into a scheme of what should not have happened and what might possibly happen, if we are fortunate enough, in the communities we are trying to create anew.

In this chapter I focus on the idea of public knowledge in the broader context of democratic practice. My hope is to show the quality of publicly generated knowledge and the ways democratic deliberation is about much more than legitimating governments and policies. A heterogeneous public engaged in talking across differences is able to generate a kind of knowledge otherwise unavailable.

From here on, I draw out the practical ways in which public talk can address oppressive sociosymbolic structures. When people deliberate on political problems, their collective deliberations circulate in the sociosymbolic/public sphere. If they are deliberating about how to keep black folks from voting (as they did in the South in the 1950s) then the result is an oppressive public sphere. If people start deliberating about how to overthrow Jim Crow (as they did in the civil rights movement) then the result is something else. As I discussed in chapter 1, the public sphere is an overlapping field of collective and individual sublimations, some successful, some misfired and failed attempts to work through trauma. As societies become more democratic, we need to listen more carefully to discern the ways the public can begin to generate a more open and inclusive public sphere.

∎ ∎ ∎

Political philosophers have argued for democracy on radically different grounds. The primary justification is that of legitimacy, the view that laws and governments are legitimate if and only if they are authorized by the public and that the people should not be subject to laws they have not made. A quite different justification is epistemic, that under the right conditions the people can make the best decisions, or at least decisions that are as good as any made by experts. The epistemic case can be made in two distinct ways: by recourse to a rationalist, Enlightenment understanding of knowledge or by theorizing a pragmatic, situated kind of public knowledge. The first way of thinking about epistemic capacity holds that knowledge should be disinterested, impartial, and objective; the pragmatic approach recognizes that people know things from their situated, partial, and interested perspectives.

In this chapter I argue for the latter conception. With the pragmatists and other kindred spirits, such as Gadamer, I believe that public knowledge is best created from this situated perspective. The public knows where the shoe pinches and so can best decide in what direction the shoe (public policy) should be moved. This view has to answer critics of democracy (from Plato to Schumpeter) who worry that the public has too little objectivity and impartiality to know what is best. These critics have a point: taken one by one, people have little knowledge of the whole. If they presume that they have "the whole truth," they may well turn into bigots like Archie Bunker. For this reason, people need to escape the cloisters of kith and kin and enter a world of unlike others. They need to be open to other perspectives and concerns. They need to deliberate with others in public. In other words, an inchoate plurality of people needs to become public in order to develop a more comprehensive picture of the whole and to define "where the shoe pinches." Democracy requires that the multitude deliberate publicly in order to create shared knowledge by which sound public policy can be formed.

THE ARGUMENT FROM LEGITIMACY

Much democratic theory rests on the view that self rule is best because it is the most just and legitimate form of rule. This is a kind of moral justification, the idea being that it would be wrong to force people to live by rules that they did not authorize themselves. The view has a definite Kantian overtone. Kant borrowed the idea of consent from Locke and gave it a powerful moral-political form: he wrote in "Perpetual Peace," "as regards my freedom, I am not under any obligation even to divine laws (which I can recognize by reason alone), except in so far as I have been able to give my own consent to them" (Kant 1970:99). Kant bases this thought, like so much of his theory, on the notion that people ought to be understood as autonomous, as giving ends to themselves, and so should never be treated as mere pawns in someone else's game. To be politically autonomous agents, citizens should make the laws themselves—or at least authorize others to make them.

With this last caveat, that people can delegate the task of decision making, room arises for a representative form of government. The people need not make the actual laws and policies; they can deputize representatives to do that. In a representative scheme, a government is legitimate to the extent that it is revocable by the public. Every two, four, or six years, the people can take away a political official's mandate (i.e., vote her out of office). A government's policies are legitimate if they are ones that the people would have authored themselves *if* given the opportunity, time, and inclination—a big if that need never be invoked.[1] Presumably, then, even in representative democracy, the people are the ultimate authority.

This set of ideas is what I will refer to as the legitimacy thesis or legitimacy argument.[2] It goes roughly as follows: for a government or policy to be democratically legitimate, it needs to be one to which the people (or at least a majority of the people) would consent. If the people withhold their consent but the policy or government continues, then it is illegitimate. In this view, the people need not be the direct authors of a policy (their own judgment may veer considerably from it); they merely need to be willing to let it be. As for forming governments, legitimacy calls for even less: the people only need to have voted for their representatives—for any reason whatsoever. (Maybe voting isn't even necessary, as the lack of an uproar after George W. Bush's 2000 "election" seems to suggest.) The legitimacy thesis demands little of the people. Though they need to at least tacitly consent, to *have* authority in a thin sense, they do not need to *be* any kind of authority. The legitimacy thesis certainly does not need a public with any substantive ability to produce sound public policies.

The nice thing about representative democracy, some would say, is that it allows for the possibility of electing representatives who might have the time, inclination, ability, etc. to give careful thought to political matters, deliberate with other representatives, bargain with other parties, and, one would hope, make sound political decisions. How much better (we are told) this is than direct democracy, where a very busy, ill-informed public would surely falter in deciding complex matters. Here we hear an echo of

Plato's *Republic*: the masses are often too taken in by images, propaganda, manipulation, whims to know what is good for them.[3] Better to leave things to an elite, well-educated class of rulers. Representative democracy, some might think, combines the best of two seemingly incompatible schemes: the Kantian claim that political authority rests with the public and the Platonic idea that most people cannot rule themselves very well. How convenient: we can assuage any moral concerns by allowing people to have ultimate, if thin, authority even as (or if) we think they lack the wherewithal to decide matters of substance. This reconciliation of opposing views gives rise to the cult of expertise, to professionalism, progressivism, and the ability to say with a straight face that America is a democracy. I think it explains how some of the biggest defenders of democracy have low opinions of the public's ability. (I recall a cocktail-party conversation with a well-meaning liberal philanthropist: the very mention of any kind of direct democracy evoked a gasp and visible shudder.)

Certainly democratic legitimacy is important in its own right. I for one am very persuaded by Kant's formulation of the argument.[4] I think he makes a powerful and moving case that all people should be guided by ends they choose themselves, that anything less is a kind of slavery and denial of their intrinsic dignity. One of the major strengths of a robust view of democracy is that it takes this Kantian ideal seriously. I am not arguing against an argument from legitimacy. Nonetheless, we should be aware that one can sustain that argument (in the form presumed in representative schemes) while also holding a deep disdain for the people's ability to deliberate and choose. I want to suggest that being a real democrat calls for more than upholding the legitimacy thesis. A democrat should also believe that on matters of public concern the people not only *have* authority but can *be* authorities.

JUSTIFYING DEMOCRACY

Under the epistemic models I will consider here, it is not enough that the people consent to a policy or government; they should also contribute to making sure that it is sound. By "sound" I mean solid or ample, able to withstand trouble and tribulation, just as a sound ship can negotiate treacherous waters. A sound public policy is one that will work in the long run, that accounts for multiple constraints, purposes, values, and consequences. A democratic, epistemic model will hold that the public has the capacity to judge whether a policy is sound.[5] How can it do this?

"Pure" Proceduralism

Some theorists argue that deeply democratic procedures will produce democratic outcomes. (By "democratic" they usually mean authored or consented to by the people in some kind of deliberative procedure—not merely by representatives.) These proceduralists will say that a decision is right (or sound or just, depending on their vocabulary) if the right procedures were followed, for example, if all parties were fully informed, had full access to the process, were equal participants, and had an opportunity to share their views.[6] Pure proceduralists do not discuss democratic outcomes, only democratic procedures. The proceduralist is wary of any attempts to second-guess the outcome itself and will remain silent on the question of its content. We could say that the proceduralist rests his view on the legitimacy argument, though probably in a more robust form than the one outlined above. A democratic outcome is right (notice I do not say "correct") to the extent that the process that produced it is democratic. Of course, this formulation is deeply tautological and skirts the question of why a democratic outcome is better than, say, a benign expert one. The implicit answer is that it does not matter. All that matters is that the decisions are derived from the people.

But despite this seeming agnosticism about the public's epistemic capacities, democratic proceduralists often seem to presuppose that a democratic procedure will produce policies that *are better* than those produced by alternative procedures. This could be due to the fact that democratic procedures embody (in the procedure) and so perhaps reproduce (in the chosen policy) certain values that most anyone would agree are intrinsically better than other values: fairness over injustice, equality over hierarchy, full information over secrecy. Many deliberative proceduralists will say that freedom and equality are necessary preconditions for democratic procedures to take place, so democracy cannot even get off the ground unless certain values are respected.[7] (Whether this argument works is a matter of debate.)

Epistemic Proceduralism

The language of some other democratic proceduralists suggests something more: that democratic conditions allow for people's *reason* to flourish and thus, presumably, will result in more rational (read better) policies.[8] This rational deliberative view appears in Habermas's discourse ethics: if certain democratic conditions prevail in public deliberations, then presumably the better argument will prevail as well. It is also in Seyla Benhabib's formulation: "It is not the sheer numbers which support the rationality of the conclusion [under majority rule], but the presumption that if a large number of people see certain matters a certain way as a result of following certain kinds of rational procedures of deliberation and decision-making, then such a conclusion has a presumptive claim to being rational until shown to be otherwise" (Benhabib 1996:72). Habermas, Benhabib, Joshua Cohen, and others we might, following David Estlund,[9] call "rational deliberative proceduralists" implicitly suggest that democratic deliberations can produce sound outcomes because public knowledge is created rationally. In Habermas's famous formulation, the "unforced force" of the better argument will prevail, meaning that our reason will compel us to assent when faced with the more rational argument. For Habermas, the operative form of reason in this democratic setting is communicative, internal to discursive practices. His theory of communicative action draws heavily on American pragmatist conceptions of self, truth, and action (certainly more so than the ideas of those deliberative theorists who began as rational choice political scientists). But (as I have argued elsewhere) in the end, it looks very much like Enlightenment rationality with its claims to universality, impartiality, and, in Benhabib's hands, reversibility of perspectives.[10] Habermas's theory of communicative action and allied theories of public reason giving are put to use in deliberative theory, laying out the limits of the kind of talking (that is, reasoning out loud) that ought to occur in a deliberative forum. For example, Joshua Cohen writes,

> In an idealized deliberative setting, it will not do simply to advance reasons that one takes to be true or compelling: such considerations may be rejected by others who are themselves reasonable. One must instead find reasons that are compelling to others, acknowledging those others as equals, aware that they have alternative reasonable commitments, and knowing something about the kinds of commitments that they are likely to have. (Bohman and Rehg 1997b:414)

To be sure, these limits on reasoning are understandable and even admirable. But they presume that public deliberations will revolve around making assertions, that the discussion will be about whether or not any given moral, political, or empirical claim is true. They ignore other forms and aims of discourse. In presuming that deliberation is a matter of adjudicating the truth of assertoric statements, Cohen and company focus on the ability to reason in a universal fashion, unmarred by particular interests or perspectives.

The Problem of Partiality

The rational deliberative proceduralist view has to contend with a criticism that may not be in vogue in philosophical circles but is certainly at work in larger intellectual venues: the concern that "the people" (i.e., the unschooled masses) are not very smart. The provenance of this criticism is eminent: Plato. In the twentieth century, certain neo-Platonists, such as Walter Lippmann and Joseph Schumpeter,[11] pointed out how *irrationally* the public always seems to behave.[12] One reason Plato opposed democracy was that he thought the people patently unable to rationally ascertain what would be for the public good. Hence, it would be folly to let them rule. Other pessimists could share this view, noting the high standards that the rationalist model holds and arguing that the people could never meet them. Can the people obey the dictates of rational deliberative proceduralism? Can citizens adopt the universalist perspective of the general other? Would people aim in their deliberations to be disinterested—when in fact their interests are often the motivating force of their political engagements? If not, the argument goes, then democracy could never work. Oddly, the heirs of Plato and the rational proceduralists share a fundamental view: so long as the people remain mired in their perspectives, biases, situations, deeply felt values, and ephemeral impressions, they will be unable to contribute epistemically to public life. Both groups reject the possibility that anything short of pure disinterestedness and full rationality can lead to sound policy or, in other words, that any view that is not universalizable and objective can contribute to democratic deliberation. Plato's solution was to abandon democracy altogether. Habermas's solution, at least in his work in discourse theory, is to articulate the conditions under which people can become more rational.[13]

To turn to the second epistemic model, I suggest a line of inquiry: What if, instead of going Habermas's route, we accepted much of Plato's? What if we were to agree with Plato that people do see only a portion of the whole—that they are not always terribly objective or disinterested? What if we agreed with Nietzsche that "the truth" is a matter of perspective? Or with William James's assertion that the truth is what works? At first such statements may seem dire. But imagine that Gadamer is right and, while we begin our conversation from our own vantage points, we are able to bring in the perspectives of others, to broaden our own horizons, through talk. Consider the likely possibility that we are not first or foremost isolated individuals but beings always in relation or community with others, that our "reasoning" is really no more than the art of conversation we learned from others and carry on with ourselves.[14] Suppose that we are passionate beings who are not always terribly clear about our own motivations and desires, that we might be more transparent to others than we are to ourselves. Very quickly here, I am trying to sketch a picture of plural, situated, interested, partial, finite, and complicated human beings, the kinds of beings I think we are.

A democrat might despair. If this picture of humanity is true, then how could citizens ever be anything like an authority on what should be public policy? Some of these are the very features that make some people bigots, racists, even sociopaths. This is a legitimate worry, but I think it only arises in a world in which people are under the false impression that they need to go it alone, that the unit of living is as an individual. What made Archie Bunker a bigot was that he mistook his partial understanding of other people to be "the whole truth." He never invited in other perspectives. What transforms a bigot into a humanitarian is a willingness to converse with unlike others. In short, partiality and situatedness cease to be problems for democracy when citizens recognize that they need the perspectives of unlike others. Partial perspectives can complement other partial perspectives, creating a better picture of the whole.[15]

BECOMING PUBLIC

The view that I am outlining calls for people to leave their enclaves and join with unlike others. In addition to talking across class, race, and religious lines, they need to become open to the many kinds of outlooks that proliferate beyond these categories. In other words, the multitude needs to take up a public way of being, which is not that of a realm of friends but of an arena of strangers who must try to see what these others see. We are often among strangers—in a shopping mall, on a street corner, at an airport—but not with the political imperative of comprehending how consequences of common life affect each other. This is a major challenge in contemporary politics: finding ways for, as Dewey said in *The Public and Its Problems*, the inchoate public to become choate.

In Dewey's day, other political theorists, namely Walter Lippmann, pointed out the absence of a public in a political system that paid so much lip service to "the will of the people." Lippmann's solution, outlined in his books of the 1920s, was for an elite group of decision makers and social scientists to do the work of governing. The people themselves were too diffuse and preoccupied. What we call a public, Lippmann famously observed, is merely a phantom. Where he and other progressives called for developing a class of guardians to solve public problems, Dewey focused on understanding and reconstituting the public, which he defined simply as all "those indirectly and seriously affected for good or evil" by the "human collective action" of some particular group of people (Dewey 1954:27, 34–35). Whenever any group's actions have consequences for a community as a whole, that community is a political public. Some people's actions have consequences for the whole of society, but a problem arises when this public cannot find itself, when it is bombarded but inchoate. Writing in the early twentieth century, Dewey noted how complex and difficult to fathom were the kinds of issues facing this public. When problems become immense and their consequences difficult to perceive, the problems begin to eclipse the public. In Dewey's day, as in ours, observers lamented the public's indifference to social problems, its apathy. But apathy, Dewey noted, is best understood as "testimony to the fact that the public is so bewildered that it cannot find itself" (Dewey 1954:123). "At present, many consequences are felt rather than perceived; they are suffered, but they cannot be said to be known, for they are not, by those who experience them, referred to their origins. . . . Hence the publics are amorphous and unarticulated" (ibid. 131).

The way Dewey poses the dilemma is odd: widespread consequences of some human actions call a public into being (i.e., a public is a group affected by human actions), but when its problems become immense, this public cannot find itself: "The machine age has so enormously expanded, multiplied, intensified and complicated the scope of the indirect consequences, has formed such immense and consolidated unions in action, on an impersonal rather than a community basis, that the resultant public cannot identify and distinguish itself" (ibid. 126). Yet he also points to a solution: "An inchoate public is capable of organization only when indirect consequences are perceived, and when it is possible to project agencies which order their occurrence" (ibid. 131). If Dewey is right, then the challenge we face today, when actions have global, interconnected, and highly complex consequences, is even more formidable. What was his solution in his own time—and will it help us today?

Dewey's solution is three-pronged and interconnected. First, to find itself, the public needs to be able to fully fathom the consequences and the origins of human actions. An example today might be accepting that there is in fact global warming that is upsetting the climate, ecosystems, and habitats, and that this is the result of our unprecedented use of fossil fuels, of policies and geopolitics that promote this use, and of the practices of industries that profit from it. As I believe, and I think Dewey would agree, one does not discover such consequences of human action alone but by engaging others, inquiring how they are affected by events.

Second, Dewey argues, to be able to make such connections and to make good political judgments thereafter, the public needs increased intelligence—not on the minutiae of geology and meteorology, but the kind of intelligence able to "judge of the bearing of knowledge" that geologists and meteorologists produce (ibid. 208–209). In my view, to the extent that public deliberation is about ends, about deciding what kind of political communities the participants want to produce, deliberators decide "what to make of" particular facts in light of their broader purposes and aims. They need knowledge of where they want and are willing to move as a political community given all the constraints, consequences, trade-offs, competing values, aims, and necessary sacrifices they discover in their deliberations. Such intelligence is not an attribute of experts or individual citizens but something possessed by a community: what I call public knowledge.

This brings me to the third prong of Dewey's solution. To create this kind of intelligence or public knowledge, Dewey calls for a "practical reformation of social conditions," namely people's reconnection to their local communities, where face-to-face intercourse can occur (ibid. 211). His impetus is not a nostalgic longing for an Aristotelian *polis* or for communitarian virtue but a pragmatic observation that any individual's ideas are "broken and imperfect" unless they are "communicated, shared, and reborn in expression" (ibid. 218).

> Signs and symbols, language, are the means of communication by which a fraternally shared experience is ushered in and sustained. But

the winged words of conversation in immediate intercourse have a vital import lacking in the fixed and frozen words of written speech. Systematic and continuous inquiry into all the conditions which affect association and their dissemination in print is a precondition of the creation of a true public. But it and its results are but tools after all. Their final actuality is accomplished in face-to-face relationships by means of direct give and take. Logic in its fulfillment recurs to the primitive sense of the word: dialogue. (ibid. 218)

In this passage, Dewey points to the importance of verbal communication, which political theorists might refer to today as public deliberation. Such public talk makes possible a "fraternally shared experience" or understanding of political phenomena *as* phenomena that are perceived and felt by a public. Dewey observes that when people inquire together about political matters, they create more knowledge of these matters and of themselves as a public. This is not merely the result of aggregating their bits of knowledge. Rather, it is the result of being able to weave together the interconnections, dispersed consequences, multiple and sometimes clashing aims that the public can conceive only when it talks together. As people begin to fathom the roots and effects of public problems, they begin to form and identify themselves as a public, as actors who might be able to channel and direct public action.

Dewey's emphasis on publicness is—remarkably—absent from most contemporary discussions of democratic theory. Even theories that invoke the public sphere and civil society treat the public as simply an aggregation of individuals or groups of individuals. (Even "the group" becomes an individual.) Equating the public with an aggregation of individuals might fly when one is under the impression that an individual is capable of knowing the whole. But as soon as one supposes otherwise (that people are situated, partial, etc.) then an aggregation goes nowhere. We just multiply our ignorance. An integrative model calls for beginning with the fact that participants in public discourse have their own biases, partial perspectives, historical contexts, and other particularities. Each is differentially affected by public policies. Their goal in public discourse is not necessarily (though it might at times be) to offer reasons for why their favored policy would be better for all; rather, it is to explain how a given policy would or would not satisfy their own concerns, values, and ends—including the value they place on the welfare of the community itself. (I do not see these participants as purely self-interested, utility-maximizing individuals!) In turn, they listen to others with different perspectives and concerns and often come to appreciate why others see the world the way they do. When people deliberate in this public fashion, they complement one another's understanding instead of just aggregating them. They fill in the gaps, share how policies would affect those differently situated, and tell one another how they came to hold their views. In the end, they might not agree, but they often come to see the need for a policy that will take into account multiple concerns and aims.

In a speech on democracy being a way of life, Dewey pointed out how the kind of public I am describing could serve an epistemic function, pulling together the knowledge needed for public problems to be addressed.[16] "The foundation of democracy is faith in the capacities of human nature; faith in human intelligence, and in the power of pooled and cooperative experience. It is not belief that these things are complete but that if given a show they will grow and be able to generate progressively the knowledge and wisdom needed to guide collective action" (Dewey 1986:vol. 11). Because the people know where the shoe pinches, they can point to what problems need to be addressed.

Dewey makes room for the expert only once the public has gathered and begun to carry on its inquiries. The expert is at the service of the public, providing information needed to make wise decisions. Acknowledging that contemporary social problems involve complexities that the average person may not know, Dewey sees a need for expert knowledge. To the extent that contemporary problems include technical matters, "they are to be settled by inquiry into facts; and as the inquiry can be carried on only by those especially equipped, so the results of inquiry can be utilized only by trained technicians" (Dewey 1954:125). But solving problems is not just a matter of fact but also a matter of interest, value, and purpose, and "a class of experts is inevitably so removed from common interests as to become a class with private interests and private knowledge, which in social matters is not knowledge at all" (Dewey 1954:207). Social or public matters require public knowledge, which includes an understanding of how policies affect what people need and care about. "No government by experts in which the masses do not have the chance to inform the experts as to their needs can be anything but an oligarchy managed by the interests of the few" (ibid. 208).

For these reasons, for there to be any sound public policy, a public needs to come into being and deliberate together. Some might dismiss this as a utopian or communitarian longing for a public that is of one mind, is geared toward agreement and consensus, and puts the public good over self-interest. But what I am arguing for does not call for unanimity, homogeneity, agreement, consensus, altruism, or even much virtue. Neither does it mean that politics is necessarily a divisive affair always marked by contention and struggle.

To the contrary, politics begins as a radically pluralist endeavor, with participants coming from heterogeneous, partial, situated perspectives. In itself, partiality is not a problem. Problems arise when only a portion of perspectives is present, when all those affected do not have a voice in deliberative proceedings.[17] Rationalist proceduralists try to achieve universality of perspectives by having participants mentally strip themselves of affective associations and particular views, by being the "public man" who can mentally represent all. As others have noted (especially Young 1997), this claim to universality is deeply presumptuous and misguided. No one can possibly fully represent the perspectives of all others. Moreover, I would add, it is unnecessary. Rather than have participants pretend to mentally represent others, they should invite those others into the room. When the invitation is extended, and if it is accepted, then participants in a public political forum need not leave their interests and perspectives at the door. Rather, they should bring and voice their particularities. They need not restrict themselves to the language of universal reasons; they should also employ the language of felt concerns.

Recall how the rational deliberative proceduralists focused solely on the need to offer reasons in public deliberation. These theorists do not seem to recognize or appreciate another form of talk that occurs in such settings. I recall attending a public deliberative forum several years ago on the topic of hate speech. Many of the participants were carrying on the kind of talk Cohen describes, discussing the civil liberties merits and demerits of various approaches. If hate speech were banned, wouldn't that restrict people's rights? Or did hate speech violate the rights of those subjected to it? This discussion proceeded as Cohen suggests above, in the give and take of reasons for various claims. But then one African American woman stood up and told a story: walking to her car one day with her two small children, she heard taunting, racist derogations from a man standing near the car. She described her terror and pain: fear because she did not know what this man might do, pain because her children had to hear such humiliating and harmful words. In our deliberative forum, she didn't make a claim, and certainly not any universal ones; she didn't offer any reasons in support of a stated position. She just told a story. In this sense, quite likely, she failed to offer the kind of "reasons" that Cohen and Habermas would call for. But her example shows why such a call is misguided. After this woman sat down, the deliberation changed considerably. Instead of operating at the abstract level of principle, it moved to a deeper level and began to plumb the values, concerns, and hopes of the people in the room. To take the woman's story as an oblique set of reasons in support of an unstated claim would miss the point. Her story gave all who listened a keenly felt sense of what it might be like to experience hate speech. She imparted to people like me, who had always focused on the "better" reasons hate speech should be permitted, an understanding of the kind of harm such speech produces. Her narrative made it possible for the deliberation to proceed at a level that would have to contend with the ways participants (and those they love) are *affected* by policies. On the whole, the forum increased the store of knowledge that could go into developing a sound policy on hate speech. As I am arguing, deliberation can be much more than a contest of reasons aimed at allowing the unforced force of the better argument to prevail. More importantly, public deliberation can explore the ways various policies might shape political communities and might or might not further the various, and often competing, things that people value.

Many critics have faulted Habermas's discourse model for its universalistic and highly rationalist features. Some feminist critics, such as Iris Young, point out the extent to which most communicative settings operate under conventions very different from the expectations inherent in deliberative theories.[18] Young rejects those ideals in favor of the norms at work in most communicative settings, where discussion proceeds through what she calls greeting, rhetoric, and storytelling. She would point to the hate speech story above as an example of how actual communicative discussions happen. She argues that any theory that excludes such discourse from a model of "true" deliberation also excludes all those people (namely those who have been relegated to the margins of political societies) who prefer these modes of discourse. I agree, but I think more can be said about why these other kinds of talk are vital in creating public knowledge and about how difference helps. Where Young argues that difference poses a serious challenge to deliberative theory, the theory I develop here and in the next chapter shows how multiple perspectives are essential to productive deliberation.

In a deliberative forum, participants can contribute their various perspectives on an issue. They can show how any policy will differentially affect them and their loved ones, point out consequences and promises that others might not have noticed. Not only can they increase the store of public knowledge, they can work through, in the Freudian sense, what they might be willing to give up in order to make progress in light of the broader public knowledge they have gained. In short, plurality and difference, partiality and even bias, can help deliberation and democracy flourish.

Policy processes that try to circumvent such public deliberations often run into trouble. For example, at the end of the 1980s, the leadership of the American Association of Retired Persons met in closed-door sessions with leaders of Congress to hammer out a catastrophic health care act. Their long and thoughtful, but private, deliberations produced a policy that would call for wealthier seniors to pay more into the system. The act was passed shortly before Congress adjourned, with little if any public discussion. Immediately thereafter, seniors across the country decried its provisions. After all, it was going to force concessions onto people who had not had the opportunity to work through the costs and consequences, the trade-offs, in the issue and the proposed solution. In response, when Congress reconvened one of the first things it did was rescind the act. The problem was manifold: having been produced without consulting the public, the act did not allow those affected an opportunity to come to terms with the costs it might entail. Those who were being called on to sacrifice had not heard the stories of those who needed help. The closed-door deliberations did not draw on the multiple perspectives that this public might offer, and thus did not make use of any real public knowledge. Nor did the deliberations make possible the formation of a public will to solve the problem.

The public alternative I am sketching has its own costs. Someone might enter a forum with her own biases, but this person does open herself to other possibilities and perspectives. Her biases become vulnerable to the horizon-broadening influences of conversation. Her comfortable worldview might become discomfited! A participant in a public deliberation leaves like-minded allies to enter a world of unlike others.[19] To help develop a more comprehensive picture of the whole, she must first begin to understand the concerns of someone unlike herself, whom she may have preferred to demonize. If she retains an agonistic posture, she can never hear, much less appreciate, other perspectives. Yet if she pretends that all are, at bottom, really the same, she may fail to hear the truly different perspectives that others bring. She must abandon any presumption that she can fully fathom someone else's experience or that somewhere down the road all can agree.

Along these lines, it is my contention that politically engaged theorists do not have to choose between views that argue for community (like the communitarian view) and those that say politics is necessarily an agon (such as a Nietzschean or radical democratic view). Both are right. I think human beings have a desire (what Cynthia Willett calls social eros[20]) to be with others. But once we are with these others we will unavoidably, at times, disagree. As a citizen of an old New England town, I relished attending town meetings and being part of the often divisive discourse that ultimately becomes the voice of the town—even when it remains divided (just as any individual can remain torn about some question). Deliberative politics thrives even among differences in orientations and interests. Acknowledging the role of interests need not take us down the path to anything like a rational choice model of self-interested, preference-based, individualistic politics. It is pointless and wrong to conceive of members of a political community as purely self-interested. The model I am calling for holds, to the contrary, that deliberators have an interest in the community itself.

Social movements based on particular as well as broad interests have often served critical roles as catalysts for public knowledge creation. Inspired in part by Rachel Carson's book, *Silent Spring*, the ecology movement began as a seemingly fringe group worried about the ways that certain human actions, such as the use of pesticides, were harming the ecosystem. This movement acted, to use Habermas's term, as sensors (Habermas 1996a:358), alerting the larger public to something deeply amiss in the natural and political environment. Experts did not notify the public of the environmental crisis; it was citizens who came together as a public (by talking together about matters of mutual concern) who alerted others, all the while forming a new social movement, which began to hold the government under siege until it did at least a few productive things, such as form the Environmental Protection Agency and begin to enact environmental legislation. Moreover, the very conception of social movements is useful for thinking about publics. Rather than static or passive entities, we could think of them as forms of energy, made up of a multiplicity of diverse and finite people together seeking a path forward. If public is a way of being, then, to borrow the words of David Mathews, the public is not analogous to a light bulb but to electricity.[21]

In conclusion, an epistemic and pragmatic model of democracy can work if people turn away from isolation and toward a public way of being, open to the perspectives, concerns, and purposes of others. This means giving up any illusions that one can know the whole truth by oneself. It means making democracy a way of life and not just a rubber stamp.

CHAPTER 9

Three Models of
Democratic Deliberation

By now it should be clear that my ideas of deliberative democracy depart considerably from those of Habermas and company. What I am sketching is more compatible with poststructuralist notions of subjectivity and discourse. The thread that runs from that kind of continental philosophy to this kind of democratic theory is the practice we call talk, which political leaders and traumatized body politics shudder at engaging in. How are we to talk with the other who seems so unreasonable? How are we to talk when we still cannot fathom what has befallen us? In this chapter I aim to sharpen the difference between what I am calling an integrative theory of deliberative democracy and other versions. I want to show that this ideal is something toward which those hoping for a better democracy might aim.

I draw on my experience working at the intersection of three models of deliberative democracy: the preference-based model held by many deliberative theorists in the social sciences; the rational proceduralist model suggested by John Rawls's political philosophy and Jürgen Habermas's discourse ethics; and what I have been calling an integrative model, which has been overlooked in the literature but can be seen at work in most actual deliberative forums composed of members of a polity deliberating on that polity's direction. The latter includes the National Issues Forums (NIF), described earlier, a network of civic organizations that run deliberative forums consonant with a quasi-Deweyan approach to public deliberation. My aim in this chapter is to see the extent to which any or all of these models can be mapped onto actual deliberative forums, including deliberative polls, the method developed by James Fishkin (1991 and 1995). The three models are not mutually exclusive. A deliberator might see herself engaged in more than one at a time (perhaps testing out, as in the second model, whether a justification for a policy is acceptable to all, while hoping to find some integration even where participants cannot reach accord, as in the third model). Any combination could work, in practice, even though some of the methods may, in practice, work at cross-purposes. For example, focusing largely on the normative aims of the second model might minimize the empirical facts of people's actual, strategic aims, of which the third model is highly aware. I want to draw out the theoretical differences among these approaches and show how the differences matter in practice.

My own "intersection" among the three approaches is rather makeshift: I happened to begin working with Professor Fishkin on a deliberative poll we called the National Issues Convention (NIC) while I was a graduate student at the University of Texas (writing a dissertation, in part, on Jürgen Habermas). I was never Fishkin's student; our collaboration began because of my association with the Kettering Foundation, which is a major force behind NIF.[1] Fishkin became allied with NIF and the Kettering Foundation because of their shared interests in deliberation and because Kettering offered support in finding trained moderators and putting together issue briefing books. Most of the deliberative theory swirling in the air drew on the resurgence of political philosophy brought on by both Rawls's work and Habermas's notion of reasoning, that in moral, ethical, and political discourse participants should try to offer justifications for their favored policies that would be agreeable to all others affected by them.

The intersection of deliberative thought in deliberative polling, normative political theory, and actual deliberative practice is a more general phenomenon. All draw on the key term "deliberation," and observers expect a commonality because of this. But this intersection is not altogether seamless. Many who take part in deliberative experiments have rather different ideas of what "deliberation" means, but the term often gets used as if everyone agrees. The differences are not merely semantic; they are rooted in very different conceptions of politics. Because it operates at the intersection of these differences, deliberative polling, specifically the two National Issues Conventions held in the United States, offers a useful case study of how these approaches converge and diverge. In this chapter I describe the three models I see at work and offer some preliminary ideas of how they enter into deliberative polling. My goal is not to offer an encyclopedic account, but enough details to flesh out the key differences in their orientations and goals and to show the virtues of an integrative model of deliberation.

THE PREFERENCE-BASED MODEL OF DELIBERATION

The first model I consider comes out of the social sciences, primarily via political scientists' adoption of the language and theoretical structures of economics.[2] From the point of view of classical economics, a human is *homo economicus,* a being who sees the social world as a market in which he or she tries to maximize his or her own preferences. Political science takes this notion and makes it democratic by saying that a democracy would be rule by the people in a way that helps them maximize individuals' preferences as much as possible. But given that one person's aims will no doubt conflict with another's, democracy calls for some way to compromise or to aggregate preferences while treating every individual as an equal, respecting the preferences of all. Though aggregating, e.g., voting, seems to be a very democratic decision procedure, it has its problems, especially when individuals' rankings of options are somehow incoherent (for example, ranking a conservative option first, a liberal one second, and a moderate one third) or when a group of individuals' rankings show no clear winner (for example, when one person prefers A to B, another B to C, and a third C to A).

Social choice theorists have tried to solve such problems, attempting to discover how social or public policies that respect and preserve the preference rankings of the individuals within a polity can be devised. There are two sides of social choice theory: individuals ranking their preferences between two or more policy options and social planners devising ways to meld these numerous, individual rankings into one rank ordering of options. Yet social choice theorists have yet to find a nonproblematic way to do this (Elster and Hylland 1986:2). Most agree that people's individual, given preferences should be aggregated in some way. But how? What kind of voting system would ensure that "the will of the people" really does emerge, especially when there is no clear first choice? For example, what happens when the option that got the second highest number of votes is nearly everyone's last choice? Our winner-takes-all system leads to all kinds of counterintuitive inconsistencies and difficulties, and social choice theorists have taken it on themselves to try to solve these problems, often by mustering intricate formalisms and tackling logical minefields. Decades of failure have led to the view that there is no "will of the people" that can be objectively put forward. Any aggregation scheme introduces its own shape to what this will seems to be. Moreover, no scheme seems to do a good job of illuminating social preference without being vulnerable to individual voters manipulating the system to get their favorite candidate chosen. Perhaps the whole enterprise of trying to develop a public policy that is consistent with individual preferences is doomed, along with democracy in general.[3]

Certainly by the 1970s, the science of politics had led to the view that democracy is a vain hope, inconsistent and absurd. This was an odd place for a discipline to land, especially one that began in part as an attempt to understand the mostly American democratic project (Smith 1997). Perhaps in response, a more optimistic area of study has emerged in political science departments since about the mid-1980s: deliberative democratic theory.

Social scientists who have taken the deliberative turn reject the following views: that individual preferences are fixed prepolitically; that they are primarily self-regarding; that individuals are rational to be ignorant— meaning that they'd just as soon not bother to inform themselves since they think it wouldn't make any difference—and hence their preferences are ill informed; and that each individual set of preferences will likely remain incoherent. Jon Elster has argued that deliberation is a means for transforming individual preferences (Elster 1998:1). Fishkin and his colleagues argue that deliberation can help people develop opinions that are more informed, reflective, and considered (Luskin et al. 2002). Because they retain the social science focus on individual opinions and preferences, I call this model the preference-based view. Still, there are key differences between *deliberative* theories of preference and the old classical economists' notion. The latter holds that preferences are given in advance of the political process and that each individual's preferences are primarily self-regarding—that individuals tend to put their own desires before others. Hence politics is an arena for getting what one wanted before entering into that arena. From a deliberative standpoint, preferences are not fixed in advance; they can be informed with balanced briefing materials and expert knowledge and transformed through deliberations with others, making them other-regarding, not just self-regarding. In short, these deliberative theorists think that people can transform their preferences for the better during deliberative, informative discussions with others in the community, making them more reflective, informed, and cognizant of others' concerns.[4] Such preferences would not be so difficult to aggregate rationally and democratically. Hence democracy becomes a possibility, as a kind of governance in which preferences transformed through deliberation are the basis for public policy.

In this view, though, public policy is not formed in the deliberations.

Given that deliberators will rarely unanimously agree on what policy is best, a deliberative polity still needs some kind of external decision-making procedure (Miller 1992). This might be a direct vote or a matter of transmitting up the political ladder the new, improved set of individual preferences. Unlike conventional democratic politics, where policy makers make policy on the basis of unreflective preferences captured in standard public opinion polls, this model offers policy makers a snapshot of what a deliberative public thinks. That is how John Dryzek characterizes deliberative polling:

> From the point of view of deliberative democracy, ordinary opinion polls are pointless because they register only unreflective preferences. The idea of a deliberative poll is to assemble a random sample of members of the public, have them deliberate about the key issues of the election, poll them on their positions on the issue, and publicize the results. The intent here is to model the distribution of opinions that the general public would hold if they were able to engage in genuine deliberation, a far cry indeed from the unreflective preferences which ordinary opinion polls register. (Dryzek 2000:55)

Through deliberation, participants turn their unreflective preferences into what Fishkin calls "considered judgments" (Luskin et al. 2002), but ultimately these are still judgments that will be framed as a policy after the deliberations have concluded. As Dryzek notes,

> The opinion poll administered at the conclusion of deliberation requires the analyst to summarize and aggregate opinions, so it is not clear how this particular transmission mechanism solves the problems of aggregation as defined by social choice theory—except by handing them back to the institutions of government. (Dryzek 2000:55)

Without diminishing the importance and usefulness of deliberative polling, I want to highlight one of its self-imposed limitations (which others might take to be a benefit): it truncates the *political* task of trying to turn individual views into public judgments. The end product of a deliberative poll is not any kind of collective judgment about the nature of the problem and what ought to be done. Moderators are specifically instructed to avoid questions that might, to some, seem at all coercive, such as, "What do you think we [meaning the political community] should do?" or "Is there any common ground for action on this problem?" The result is not a public expression about what might be the best course of action, only an indication of the distribution of individual opinions. However considered these are, they do not equal an integrated policy. Even aggregating the results does not lead to a coherent, democratic policy or even to *the* will of the people, as social choice theorists well know. A legislature might take on the political task of trying to integrate the various needs, aims, and constraints into something like a coherent public policy. If it does so on the basis of individuals' considered judgments, so much the better. But we should be keenly aware that the political work occurs at this higher level, not at the level where deliberators work on transforming their own preferences. The preference-based view shows how individual opinions are transformed into superior opinions, but not into public policy.

Why do deliberative polls shun any deliberation aimed at developing a public voice on an issue? Like other deliberative theorists, preference-based adherents are committed to democracy. Their commitment is shaped by the view that democracy calls for respecting individual preferences and that anything that exerts any "untoward" (e.g., coercive) force on individual preferences is undemocratic. Such forces include factions, the "tyranny of the majority," social pressure, and the like. Hence, there is some tension inherent in an individualist, preference-based model of deliberation, for the more people deliberate in public with others, the more likely they are to be moved by these others in their midst. Therefore, preference-based deliberative theorists try to guard against public pressure on individual deliberations, a real problem in the setting of public deliberation. Their goal is for participants to use deliberative settings to transform their preferences without being unduly swayed by others. In their view, deliberations should be geared toward giving participants full information and a clearer picture of how each option on the table would or would not satisfy each participant's preferences;[5] they should supply expertise and an appreciation of others' concerns, not social suasion. These theorists tend to worry that deliberations might lead participants to conform to others' expectations rather than to refine their own preferences (Elster 1998:15; Sunstein 2003), which they think would result in a kind of "false consciousness" where participants are not fully aware of their own, true self-interests and opinions. For them, democracy means rule by fully informed individuals. *Autonomy equals not being unduly influenced by anyone else.*

The social scientists' approach to deliberative theory goes a long way toward turning *homo economicus* into an other-regarding democratic citizen. But at the end of their deliberations, there is no discernible *public* transformation. Each individual might transform his or her opinions, in light of more information and exposure to others' perspectives, but there's no expectation that the result might be public views; they will just be more rational and considered views. At the end of the deliberations, individuals' views still have to be transformed into some kind of social ordering. If everyone were to agree on the nature of a problem and what policy best addresses it, there would be no difficulty. But most anyone steeped in the facts of public life, Elster included, thinks this is unlikely (only the normatively oriented, to whom I turn in the next section, think this is a possibility). Given the fact of disagreement, some way needs to be found to make collective decisions. If the way is through voting, then the preference-based theorists have come full circle to the problem of articulating "the will of the people" out of a set of individual preferences. Bound to individualism, preference-based thinkers still face the challenge of social ordering.

THE RATIONAL PROCEDURALIST MODEL

The second model I want to lay out here comes from a different direction, not the supposedly empirical and normatively agnostic orientation of the social scientist but the normatively steeped orientation of the philosopher.[6] This model sets a very high bar for what kinds of reasons deliberators should offer and accept: participants should deliberate on the basis of reasons that are rational and acceptable to all. This view specifies what can count as a good reason and what kind of procedures should be in place to ensure a good outcome. Accordingly, I call it the rational proceduralist model of deliberation.

In this second model, citizens are guided by a will to come up with universalizable norms—or at least norms that are acceptable to all affected by any given policy. This view can be traced back to both the social contract tradition of consent theory and the Kantian normative claim that we, as rational individuals, can act morally by only acting on the basis of maxims (or policies) that can be rationally universalized, i.e., applied to all equally and without contradiction. Here we have an explicitly philosophical conception of autonomy: it means acting and choosing on the basis of universalizable norms; true self-rule is to live by rules that hold for all, not just for oneself. Rational deliberators offer arguments concerning justice and the public good. In this view, motivations of self-interest stand in the way of developing legitimate public policies, which should be good for all. This theory encourages deliberators to adopt an impartial, objective point of view and to offer reasons (not rhetoric) that all others would find compelling. Otherwise, a policy would not attract general consent—consent of all those rational agents affected by it. Irrational agents need not be heeded; in fact, according to Gutmann and Thompson (1996), they should not even be in the room.[7] Though this view sees deliberators as always already in community, it does tend to think of them as capable of imagining themselves stripped of affective and communal associations, roles, and conventions so that they might be able to deliberate objectively and impartially. They need to use their reason so as to imagine how a policy would affect anyone else. They are rational agents.

In this model, *deliberation is a way individuals collectively decide whether a policy is legitimate.* A policy or law is just only if all those affected by it have an opportunity to consider, collectively, whether or not it is just and if all those affected assent to it. Deliberation, then, is the process through which people decide whether a proposal is normatively or ethically right. It involves the back and forth of argumentation, with everyone having an equal opportunity to put forward his or her own case. Ultimately, the "unforced force of the better argument" will prevail; that is, all the participants should ultimately agree on which proposal is most rational and right. The rational procedural model considers deliberative democracy as a way to create legitimate public policy, that is, policies that all citizens would, under ideal conditions, have authored themselves.

Both Habermas and the political philosopher John Rawls contribute to this approach. As Elster writes, "the arguments advanced by Habermas and Rawls do seem to have a common core: political choice, to be legitimate, must be the outcome of *deliberation about ends among free, equal, and rational agents*" (Elster 1998:5). It is no wonder then that Habermasians like Seyla Benhabib and Rawlsians like Joshua Cohen arrive at roughly the same philosophical position on deliberation. Whether one adopts the Habermasian regulative ideal of the ideal speech situation or the Rawlsian regulative ideal of the original position, in democratic deliberations all those affected should recognize the outcome as in keeping with what they would have chosen had they had an opportunity to participate.

For Habermas, the operative form of reason in this democratic setting is communicative, internal to discursive practices. Though Habermas's theory of communicative action draws heavily on American pragmatist conceptions of self, truth, and action, ultimately it looks very much like Enlightenment rationality with its claims to universality, impartiality, and, in Benhabib's hands, reversibility of perspectives (see McAfee 2000:ch. 1). Habermas's theory and allied theories of public reason-giving are put to use in deliberative theory, laying out the limits of the kind of talking (that is, reasoning out loud) that ought to occur in a deliberative forum.

In this model, partiality is a serious fault. One should be able to see the whole picture, not just one's own arena. It seems that one need not actually consult others to find out what the world looks like from their perspective; each sovereign citizen should have a mental map of the whole. Accordingly, the ideal deliberator reasons publicly with others not to get more information about how policies would affect others, but to get their consent. This model holds out hope that decisions can be reached by consensus. If all agree on what policy is best, then there will be no need for social-choice type aggregation, bargaining, or voting.

In its search for unanimity, deliberation becomes a contest, a battle of arguments in which the best argument wins. To be a contender, a policy needs to get universal consent. This kind of deliberation does not try to piece together second-best alternatives into something with which most everyone could live. It looks for policies that are simply the best. As a result, it is possible that the participants in such deliberative ventures are more interested in winning a contest than in solving problems. This model seems to lose sight of the reasons people enter into public deliberations—to work through traumas or other difficulties that have jammed public politics or because their communities are wracked by problems that politicians seem unable to solve. In actual community deliberations, participants are not looking for which claim is normatively right, but for which picture of the problem is most telling and which courses of action have promise.

Yet even though universality may be the guiding ideal, most deliberative proceduralists realize that consensus is rarely reached and some kind of vote will be needed. As a result, this view runs into the very same problems that social choice theory does: finding the best way, short of consensus, to articulate the will of the people (see Dryzek 2000:38–41).

THE INTEGRATIVE MODEL

Anyone familiar with deliberative theory probably recognizes the above two models readily, especially with the little bit of detail that I have provided.

The third model has not been discussed in the literature, or certainly not to any great extent. It is the model that I came to know firsthand through observing the deliberative forums that are part of the National Issues Forums network. As mentioned earlier, some of the intellectual founders of this approach include Kettering's president, David Mathews; the survey researcher Daniel Yankelovich; and the political theorists Benjamin Barber and Harry Boyte. Also instrumental have been the works of Hannah Arendt and John Dewey.

While NIF now has many sister organizations around the world, I trace the intellectual roots of this model to an American pragmatist tradition that is concerned more with "what works" than "what is true." The model has some roots in the civic republican tradition as well, though its normative conceptions are not as strong as those criticized in Habermas (Habermas 1998:244–249). It sees the public as heterogeneous, not the collective actor of a Rousseauean model. This model is empirically observable, but participants have normative concerns: when people deliberate together about public matters they develop an interest in the public welfare (in solving public problems) that may override their particular preferences.

Even with all these theoretical resources, the National Issues Forums are primarily driven by the way people actually deliberate and what their aims and concerns seem to be when they sit down together and try to solve problems that resist solution. The deliberators are motivated by the need to find a way forward on problems that affect them and their communities. Here the reader might recall E. J. Dionne's book, aptly titled *Why Americans Hate Politics.* Its main point is that Americans do not care about ideology, which seems to be the currency of conventional politics; rather, they want solutions to problems. This is an insight that has long steered NIF. David Mathews and I spent a few years writing guides for deliberation to be used by NIF convenors and moderators. We oriented the texts according to a framework we called "choice work." The aim was for citizens to consider an array of policy options and, on each one, to spell out the costs and consequences as well as the trade-offs that would have to be made if the approach were adopted. Only by "working through" the various choices, grappling with what must be abandoned in order to proceed in a particular direction, do deliberators begin to develop a public judgment about what policy might be best. Though it often evokes the language of "finding common ground for action," this approach does not aim for happy consensus. Rather, choice work engages deliberators in the pragmatic task of delineating what courses of action might work given polity members' many aims and constraints.

According to the integrative model, *deliberation is a process through which people grapple with the consequences of various public problems and proposals.* Participants focus on solving public problems in ways that are consistent with their publicly formed understandings and ends. Instead of narrowly focusing on autonomy, this model sees democratic choice and action as practices that involve people considering how various options would affect their communities. The public dimension of deliberation is indispensable to the task of fathoming problems and forming a public that can respond. Instead of seeing politics as bargaining about preferences, people see it as a difficult matter of deciding what kinds of communities they are making for themselves. Instead of merely *preferring,* deliberators *choose.*

At the outset, I called this model "quasi-Deweyan." By this I do not mean that Dewey spawned the integrative model but rather that his observations mesh with it uncannily well. I noted in the previous chapter that Dewey's work in *The Public and Its Problems* intersects with the understanding of deliberation that I am laying out here. Both Dewey and NIF hold that public communication can be a way citizens simultaneously develop an understanding of public problems and of themselves as a public that can and should create sound and effective public policies. Having defined the public as all "those indirectly and seriously affected for good or evil" by the "human collective action" of some particular group (Dewey 1954:27, 34–35), Dewey understood the centrality of deliberating to define both public matters and the public: "An inchoate public is capable of organization only when indirect consequences are perceived, and when it is possible to project agencies which order their occurrence" (ibid. 131). In keeping with Dewey's insight, actual public deliberations usually spend a great deal of time developing a public picture of what a problem is and how it affects those in the room and others throughout the political community. As deliberators gain an understanding of the nature and the many aspects of the problem at hand, they also begin to see themselves as a public.

Unlike the second model, which expects deliberators to act according to the Enlightenment, universalizing ideal, this model aims for integration of multiple, heterogeneous views, accepting and making use of citizens' particular perspectives. Because each participant starts out with a limited picture of how a policy under consideration might affect others, they deliberate in order to learn. They seek information, not so much about facts but about the consequences of various policies. In this model, citizens' partial perspectives can be *integrated* into a viable, sound policy choice that is always provisional and subject to change.

When people come together to deliberate on matters that affect their polities, they seem to transform personal concerns and interests into public ones. To understand this phenomenon, observers and political theorists need to move beyond the tired dichotomy between egoism and altruism. It is not that public deliberations turn participants into altruists. Rather, the deliberations help forge an immediate interest in public matters, conjuring up the history of the term "interest" itself, *inter-esse,* a way of being between and with others. Participants develop an interest in the welfare of their political communities.

Moreover, this model attends to the problem over which both the first and the second models stumble: how to set policy direction when there is not full, or even much, agreement. Participants use their disagreements as productive constraints that help them identify in which possible directions, albeit few, the polity might move. In the many deliberations that my colleagues at the Kettering Foundation and I have observed, participants left saying that even when they did not agree with other participants, they came to see why the others held the views they did and changed their views of others' views. Even in the face of trenchant disagreement, participants would focus on coming up with a direction that would accommodate the plural concerns in the room. Unlike the first model, which leaves the aggregation problem to social planners, this integrative model understands that deliberators want to have a hand in shaping policy, that indeed, this shaping is central to deliberation itself. People do not want to just be preference inputs into some social utility function. They want to help decide what the policy should be in the very process of trying to understand what the problem is, how it affects all concerned, and what kind of polity they want to forge.

Of the three, this view is the least idealistic. It has the most "communal" understanding of human psychology, seeing people and publics as constituted through their common language, customs, norms, relationships, and communities. It does not call on participants to imagine themselves stripped of affective and social associations in order to deliberate well. People do, and should, bring their particular concerns to the table when they deliberate with others. This model of deliberation shares the same kind of philosophical frame as social and material theories of history and community as well as Gadamer's hermeneutics and poststructural accounts of meaning making.

In practice, moderators try to ensure that all participants have an equal opportunity to speak, that no speakers dominate the deliberations, and that other factors in keeping with Habermasian speech-setting ideals are in place. But moderators also try to elicit stories from deliberators, using prompts such as "Tell us how you came to hold the view that you have." (This usually brings forth a story that helps explain why someone would hold a view that others might find objectionable or unreasonable, in the process showing another aspect of an issue that others might not have considered.) As stories emerge, participants begin to weave them together into a larger narrative of the meaning of events, in a way not unlike what occurs in the process of testifying to traumatic pasts. Working through is evidenced by new shared accounts of what the circumstances are and what is politically possible.

This model aims at getting participants to take into consideration other participants' concerns, aiming for a choice that reflects a considered, public judgment on the issue. Through their discussions, deliberators come to see possible outlines for public action. And they come to see themselves as part of a public, as public actors with considered judgments and purposes who can help shape public policy. The goal is not *rationality* per se, but the possibility of understanding the public dimensions of problems and identifying what, if any, sound and sustainable directions toward which the public might move. At the very least, it sets the boundaries of what Yankelovich calls public permission.

THEORIES IN PRACTICE

These three definitions certainly do not exhaust the alternatives, but they do capture what seem to be the three most prevalent views. All have their virtues. But unless the different emphases among these views are made clear—and unless their tensions are addressed—deliberative practice can falter. With this in mind, I close this chapter with some thoughts on how these themes manifested themselves in the National Issues Convention, sometimes undercutting the potential of the event. Deliberative polling and National Issues Conventions are tremendously valuable political events. I simply want to show why the proponents should move closer to an integrative model instead.

The role of experts: Drawing primarily on the preference-based model of social choice, Jim Fishkin and his colleagues take one of the central tasks of deliberation to be informing participants' discretion, giving them the means and the opportunity to develop opinions "worth" listening to. As Luskin, Fishkin, and Jowell write, "The scientific value of the Deliberative Poll is that it provides a way of addressing the effects of information (and thought and involvement) on policy preferences" (2002). To this end, deliberative polling relies heavily on panels of experts and policy makers to answer questions that arise during deliberations. During the last NIC, participants worked through two policy choices and then stopped to select questions for experts. They then went into plenary sessions to listen to how the experts answered. Afterward, they returned to their small groups, deliberated a bit more, and worked on developing more questions. They ended the afternoon with another plenary session with the experts. Before dinner, they met again to come up with questions for policy makers. The Sunday morning session was devoted to policy makers taking citizens' questions. By the end of the weekend, much more time had been devoted to formulating questions or putting them to experts, and listening to the responses, than to deliberating. Observers noted that participants took much care in how they worded the questions, more, it seemed, to get the panelists' attention than to get information. Despite the organizers' intentions, the experts did not seem to be there in service to the deliberators, and the participants felt frustrated when their own questions could not be posed due to limited time.

Expertise plays a much smaller role in the NIF or integrative style of deliberation. NIF does use "issue books," balanced, informative guides that offer three or four policy choices, discussions of pros and cons, trade-offs, and other data. Deliberations tend to focus more on how various proposals will affect participants' and their communities' ends and purposes. Questions of fact arise far less often than questions of value and consequence. In my observations, deliberations proceed quite differently depending on whether they see expertise as a resource for (as NIF tends to do) or as something to aim for (which deliberative polling inadvertently does). Deliberative polls could improve by lowering the profile of "the experts," treating them as interested parties (which they usually are) who have some knowledge of how proposed policies fit into the larger political picture. Instead of speaking on panels that take up large portions of the program, these parties could be available in the background to answer any questions that spontaneously arise.

The meaning of politics: The three models I have described here have radically different conceptions of politics. The first holds that politics is the practice, exogenous to public deliberation, of turning deliberative preferences into public policy. Politics is the province of government. The second and third models expand the arena of politics beyond government to include the deliberations that go on within civil society (see Dryzek 2000). The second hopes that the deliberative public can engage in policy making, to the extent that it is able to reach rational agreement. The third is more forgiving of disagreement, recognizing that politics begins because there is disagreement, and it puts what is obvious first: that people enter into politics to solve problems. Of course, the first two models might want to lay claim to that purpose as well. But they limit public problem solving to, respectively, the use of individual preferences and rationality. In the integrative model, participants are motivated by their sociality to meet with others they may neither like nor understand in order to find solutions to problems concerning what they care about dearly—the public world that they inhabit, the world they will leave for their children and future generations. They are motivated to fashion a new *public* world, which is like putting together a puzzle: trying to see what all the pieces are, especially those held by other participants, and then seeing how they might fit together, however imperfectly and provisionally.

None of the above is meant to suggest that there is anything intrinsically wrong with deliberative polling. To the contrary, I think it is a tremendously important advance in democratic practice. My concern is that deliberative polling has been too informed by a preference-based model of democratic deliberation and not informed (nor, as a result, formed) enough by an integrative model. In its concern to help individuals deliberate and refine their opinions, it has overlooked the public task of politics. Yet while many of the theorists behind the scenes might think they are culling well-formed individual preferences, deliberators steadily set about integrating their many perspectives, experiences, and purposes into potential policies that are decidedly public. Each deliberative polling experiment ends with a survey of individual views. Participants each retreat to a secluded spot in the room to take the "after" survey, without consulting anyone else. The survey researchers gather and compare the pre- and postdeliberation responses. Then they hold a press conference—and public television airs a program—revealing the extent to which individual opinions changed. It is thought that the results, when aggregated, will point to what public opinion would look like if people were to think about the issues. But back in that same room, at the end of the deliberative poll, just before the surveys are distributed, there is another public voice to be heard. It is the voice of the people comparing notes, trying to piece together all the moving and conflicting and unsettling matters they have deliberated on together; it is the voice of people trying to take account of and integrate their own and their fellow deliberators' perspectives, concerns, and desires. The question they return to is, on this matter at hand now, what shall we do? In these rooms the people know that in politics, at the end of the day, our task is not to decide what each of us wants, but to decide what we as a polity should do.

CHAPTER 10

The Limits of Deliberation, Democratic Myths, New Frontiers

As the previous chapters have explored, public talk can accomplish much. In the truth and reconciliation commissions that serve to help nations recover from brutal pasts, it can help survivors of trauma reclaim their title as citizens; help the people of a nation fathom the depths of the wrongs that were committed; and help past perpetrators, at least those who mourn their deeds, find reconciliation in a new society. In the deliberative forums of more developed democracies, it can "de-colonize" the public sphere (Habermas 1987), giving the public a way to help develop a public will that can guide public policy (Habermas 1996a). This public will is vital not only because democratic legitimacy calls for public consent but also because, as I argued in chapter 8, a deliberative public is ultimately, cognitively, the best judge of what policies are best.

Throughout this book I have referred to public talk—from the testimonies of truth commissions to the deliberations of public forums—as a sort of analogue to the "talking cure" of psychoanalysis. Just as a traumatized individual needs to work through his or her troubles in order to move ahead in life constructively rather than continuously reenact, revisit, and repeat the scenes and sources of trauma, a political community needs means for working through its troubles. Otherwise it is doomed to its own repetition compulsions, most recently evidenced by the American "war on terror" that has inflicted its own terror, directly and indirectly, on thousands of innocents in the Middle East and beyond. The best means for working through trauma may well be discursive ones, a thought anathema to those who insist that we should never "negotiate" with terrorists. If we cannot talk with those who want to annihilate us, the only means left are coercive (even sanctions are coercive), not good recipes for peace.

Public deliberations and other forms of public talk are powerful, but if they are to be enduring phenomena, they need to be rooted in public institutions. These might be the kind of institutions that Robert Putnam observed in Italy that gave rise to habits and norms of cooperation, social capital that made northern Italy a flourishing region (Putnam et al. 1994). They could be choral societies, garden clubs, bowling leagues. Others might be the spaces of social movements focused on shared problems: environmental degradation, community health, education. As much as deliberation matters, the informal and formal institutions that host the deliberations matter even more. Otherwise deliberation can appear one moment and disappear the next. This chapter pushes toward understanding the importance of mediating public institutions, by examining the way the public has been treated via a myth that is not terribly different from Plato's antidemocratic myth of the metals. Overcoming this modern myth of democracy led innovators toward creating the National Issues Forums, study circles, and the like; but so far it has stopped short of supporting the kind of enduring public institutions that can sustain this work.

THE MYTH OF DEMOCRACY

Plato's *Republic* begins with a question, "What is justice?" and ends with an answer, harmony of the soul. A rather odd answer arrived at in a rather circuitous manner. The detour is by way of an analogy: perhaps a soul can be compared to a city, and if we find the ideal, just society then we might have a formula for an ideal soul. The ideal city, as it unfolds in the book, is one in which each part minds its own business and leaves others' business alone: rulers rule; soldiers protect; and the mass of people produce goods and obey whatever the rulers dictate. To keep each part doing its own thing, the city needs an overarching myth, "the myth of the metals," which explains that people are born with certain metals in their blood, which suit them to different kinds of work: those destined to rule have gold; to be soldiers, silver; and to be productive workers, bronze. Someone with gold blood is unsuited for making money, and someone with bronze could hardly rule. That this was called a myth indicates that, in fact, the framers of this ideal republic knew it wasn't true; people are not born with blood that determines their station in life, and the mass of people are not compelled to defer to the wisdom and judgment of the few. But the framers knew that it was vital to pass off the myth as truth if there were to be any harmony in the city.

Students who read the *Republic* today scoff at this myth, but in a sense they and their fellows, parents, and teachers generally subscribe to a modern equivalent: the myth of democracy. It goes like this: we live in a democracy that is so large that the people rule by electing representatives who decide matters of public policy in the public's interest. The representatives should heed public will in order to make sure the policies they enact are democratically legitimate. If there's any doubt, opinion polls can be conducted or hearings held so that the public's will can exert influence over public policy. The myth is that self-rule can be had without any serious work on the part of the people; that representatives can somehow "grok" what the public will might be in the absence of any serious public deliberation, or that public deliberation need not extend beyond deciding whom to elect. We hear so often that so-and-so winning an election equals a "mandate" to do x, y, and z, as if the thinking that led to choosing a representative was also a thinking through of policies. This might be true to a point, but after the election, politics continues while attention to public thinking and will wanes.

While this democratic myth isn't as blatantly elitist as the myth of the metals, it has much the same effect: so long as things run properly, leaders can lead and the mass of people can go about their business, ever so occasionally interrupted by a trip to the ballot box or a knock on the door from a pollster. Elected officials and leaders of institutions can say they consult the public, but for the most part they are interested in managing the public and manufacturing public opinion that suits their own interests. We say we live in a democracy, but everyday behavior belies this. This is not to say that representative democracy is a bad thing. Having representatives deal with the day-to-day business of lawmaking makes good sense; but having things so in the absence of ongoing public deliberation does not.

The myth and how it is used are quite seductive. We can pay homage to the will of the people without bothering to heed it, much less cultivate it. Instead of the trouble (and uncertainty) of getting a public to think long and hard about matters of common concern, we can make a kind of Singaporean pact with our leaders: lead us well, keep us happy and prosperous, and you can have your power and we will give up ours. If you don't lead us properly, you will get in trouble. We might boot one of you out of office or call for term limits, campaign reform, and clean living. But on the whole, we'll leave the pact in place as we search for another candidate to lead. The people of Singapore seem to have made this pact with their eyes wide open, but in America we have made it while wearing the blinders of a *faux* democracy. We pretend that we can have our "democracy" without having to go to any meetings or seriously to try to rule ourselves.

THE PROBLEM WITH DIRECT DEMOCRACY

What, then, is a real alternative to mythical democracy? Not direct democracy, especially if all that means is that an unreflective public decides matters by referendum rather than through the mediating office of a somewhat deliberative body. In the current scheme, even with all the corruptions of money and politics, at least *some* people are deliberating, albeit without the benefit of a deliberative public's judgment. Certainly people deliberate informally in their daily lives, but the issue here is whether and how we deliberate publicly, on political matters, with other members of our communities, especially with those who bring in new perspectives from different experiences. A major obstacle to nonmythical democracy—and the reason many reflective people worry about supplanting the myth—is that many do not trust "the people's" judgment. In fact, to say that a large group of people can have anything like *judgment* seems bizarre. The general public, after all, too often advocates policies that are short-sighted, inconsistent, and detrimental to the public weal. It is hard to believe they might be wise.

This concern may be precisely what heralded the past quarter-century's experiments in deliberative democracy. A resounding case of the public weighing in directly came in 1978, when voters in California passed Proposition 13, the so-called "People's Initiative to Limit Property Taxation." It was a test case for direct democracy, led by an antitax advocate who understood that a change as big as this one would not get passed at the legislative level, so he took it to the people. Proposition 13 brought down property taxes an average of 57 percent. It was a relief for property owners, especially corporations, but a blow to school districts, mental health providers, towns, cities, and potential homeowners. The goal was to rein in taxes, no matter the cost. But more than 25 years later, the costs are hard to miss: a chronic education problem and holes in the safety net of one of the most prosperous states in the country.[1] Whether it was a victory for democracy depends on one's definition of the term; for those who wanted direct self-rule, it was certainly a boon. The referendum movement took hold and took off after Proposition 13. It led to direct ballot initiatives in states from coast to coast; a recent one did away with bilingual education in Massachusetts and another dealt a blow to California's "terminator" governor.

Shortly after Proposition 13 passed, the dean of public opinion research, Daniel Yankelovich, and a former Health, Education, and Welfare Secretary, David Mathews, began to talk with each other about this development and what it meant for democracy. Back in 1978, they, along with many others in the country, had seen the problem lurking: Mathews worried about finding ways for a democratic public to understand the complexity of public problems; Yankelovich worried about how to hasten the public's move from its initial knee-jerk opinions to more reflective judgments (Yankelovich 1991). The passage of Proposition 13 revealed the depth of the problem. This referendum not only presaged a disaster for the economy of California but also cast a pall over democracy itself. And it indicated the troubles facing a nation whose public did not have opportunities together to learn, reflect, deliberate on, and decide matters of huge concern. Who could trust people to rule themselves when they made such poor choices?

A DELIBERATIVE ALTERNATIVE

What was needed was an alternative to this direct, unreflective democracy, settings for people to reflect, discuss, and deliberate together on matters of common concern. Just as the framers of the Constitution understood, legislatures work best as deliberative bodies; so too, a public works best when it deliberates. Out of this insight and some profoundly argued kindred ones (like those of philosophers John Rawls and Jürgen Habermas) grew the National Issues Forums, then study circles, eventually the National Coalition for Dialogue and Deliberation, the National Issues Conventions, the Deliberative Democracy Consortium, a host of other initiatives in deliberative democracy, and an academic cottage industry in deliberative democratic theory. The results—from the "scientific" findings of deliberative polls to the carefully analyzed but anecdotal video records presented in *A Public Voice*—are impressive. It is evident that a deliberative people, what we might even reverently call a public, can make sound choices when it deliberates.

The amount and quality of attention, research, and public work that went into addressing the worry that public judgment was unlikely—that went into deliberative theory—is impressive too. It has occupied the careers of faculty members in philosophy, sociology, urban planning, political science, and even architecture. It has led to academic conferences and special issues of journals. There have been national deliberative polls throughout the world, concerted research and grant making in the foundation world, and conventions of leagues of deliberative practitioners. It has transformed one field, conflict and negotiation, into another, dialogue and deliberation. It has gone hand in hand with a related development: the focus on civil society, the space between private and governmental life, as a major locus of political change. Hence, it has even been connected to the end of the Cold War, the fall of the Berlin Wall, and the rise of a global civil society. Deliberative politics has been heralded as an alternative to conventional partisan politics, and it has come under attack for the very same reasons. Those who think politics will always have an agonistic dimension deride deliberative theory as a mistaken and maybe even dangerous search for unity and consensus. Deliberative theory holds out the hope that another kind of politics might supplant the usual partisan, interest-driven, money-fed, public-ignoring kind that dominated the twentieth century.

At present, the most innovative and robust political forces seem to be deliberative forums, especially those that are intent on bringing together different parts of a community, the unlike-minded. Even better are those that also try to engage policy makers, so that representatives can directly brush up against public judgment. And even better are those that partner with the media, so that journalists might begin to frame issues in public terms and make room for public involvement. But even after twenty-five years, these public deliberations are barely discernible features of our political landscape.

THE TOLL OF POLITICS AS USUAL: ALIENATION

The usual politics, undergirded by the myth of democracy, is a tenacious creature, and even as hopes for deliberation have brightened, it has taken its deleterious toll. As the twentieth century ended and the twenty-first began, researchers started noticing new and serious problems in the body politic. One of the main researchers, Rich Harwood, beginning in 1992, started noticing disturbing kinds of alienation. First, people are seriously alienated from the political process itself. David Mathews described Harwood's picture as one of people locked out of their own house, peering in the kitchen window to see strangers sitting at the table. Deciding matters of common concern seems to have become the province of an elected class, while those who are directly affected seem to have little ability to steer the course of events.

People feel themselves alienated from the news media too—a disconcerting finding for those in journalism, who have seen themselves as soldiers for the public interest, the little guy's voice in the face of power and money. But the people Rich Harwood interviewed saw the news media as a source of their problem, a force that framed issues and laid out the news in a way that exacerbated the polarization in politics and left no room for the public.

A third kind of alienation that Harwood has found most recently is perhaps the most troubling: people are alienated from each other. We burrow deeper and deeper into our own homes, enclaves, and circles of kin. We keep to people like ourselves and increasingly disdain people with different views and backgrounds. We have become a country deeply polarized and privatized, a disturbing phenomenon in a world of ethnic division and religious wars that attempt to annihilate anyone different.

What is most troubling about these kinds of alienation is that they run so counter to what human beings seem to want: to be connected, to share a world with others, and to have a hand in shaping the contours of that world. It may be that the appeal of public deliberation is that it offers the possibility, if not the promise, of some relief from a world that is increasingly alienating. It offers a way to talk and connect with strangers, and that may be, just maybe, a means to make things right. But this last hope is the most remote. How might the deliberating and choosing that goes on in a roomful of citizens make any difference in a world dominated by the democratic myth of representative government that makes public deliberation unnecessary? While deliberative theory and experience have begun to quiet the worry that public judgment is impossible, the machinery of politics as usual has evolved to the point where it has already completely sidelined citizens.

OBSTACLES TO CHANGE

The central problem keeping us, the people, from loosening the democratic myth's hold remains the worry that the public lacks the ability to make sound choices. Twenty-five years of deliberative experimentation should have laid this worry to rest. What keeps it from a proper burial, however, is the related worry that no amount of public deliberation will make a damned bit of difference to how politics as usual runs. Until there is a way to link public deliberation to public and governmental action, the myth will survive.

The true believers hold that there is in fact a connection, though it might only be seen in retrospect, over the course of years or decades. Certainly over time, the public has moved from reactionary positions to more thoughtful and reflective judgments on matters of the environment, race, and, still too slowly, our place in the world. Both Daniel Yankelovich and Seyla Benhabib have a point when they say that deliberation occurs in all sorts of informal venues, shot through all kinds of sectors of society. Over the long run, these informal deliberations do result in more thoughtful public judgment that may, as Yankelovich maintains, profoundly influence public policy.

Nonetheless, after a quarter century of deliberative forums, the myth of democracy is still alive and present, whereas deliberative forums seem to occur only here and there, with little discernible effect. Even when they are a robust part of the life of a given community, their effects are minimal as long as elected representatives for the most part pay them little mind. This may be due to a number of causes. Maybe there just are not yet enough deliberative forums. Maybe there isn't enough incentive, still, for people to attend. Maybe deliberative theorists and practitioners haven't done enough yet to turn the tide. Clearly there are many who love such meetings, devout convenors of National Issues Forums, study circles, and the like. But in reality, only a very small percentage of people attend public deliberative forums. For a pragmatic people, the overarching question is: What good will it do? What difference is it going to make?

Maybe money and politics and the power of the state will continue to overshadow and ignore public will. Maybe this is at bottom a matter of power structures, the corruptions of capitalism, and the genuine inability of public will to steer a system in fact steered by the bottom line. Marxists have argued over this question for years, wondering whether the "super-structure" of politics and culture can have any autonomy from and influence over the economic and power structures of society. Yet history seems to be on the side of those who think there is some "relative autonomy of the superstructure." Meliorist attempts at transforming societies have resulted in fewer injustices than radical attempts to overthrow bad societies, which too often lead to further injustices. Falling back on a critique of capitalism leaves little room to move.

Finally, then, perhaps deliberative public meetings alone are not durable enough to link public will to public policy. When one deliberative theorist told an NIF convenor that in running forums she was aiming to change the politics of her city, the NIF convenor understandably responded with some incredulity. The link between holding deliberative public meetings and the politics of a city is tenuous indeed. Seeing it probably requires special equipment or theoretical edifices or special, well-designed retreats. It is indeed hard to connect what some roomfuls of people decide and what representatives in a mythically democratic society legislate.

Observers have long noted the deep disconnect between public deliberation and politics. For the many years I have been associated with this work, it has been an ongoing concern. There have been various attempts to bridge the gap, from meetings in presidential libraries and the White House to programs taped at the National Press Club. My worry is that these efforts won't do the trick, really, or not alone, as special occasions. Our real challenge is to find a way to connect public deliberation to public policy making, to find some way that public judgment can make its way into law. Something is still missing.

THE NEED FOR MEDIATING, PUBLIC INSTITUTIONS

All the good work on public *deliberation* tends to ignore a vital element of a more public *politics*. I'm reminded of a moment more than a decade ago when I was one of three guests on a public affairs show on public television in Austin, Texas. The other two guests were James Fishkin, who has adapted deliberative theory to the work of public opinion polling, developing a more deliberative, public means to gauge what a reflective and deliberative polity might believe about issues; and Ernesto Cortes Jr., the southwest regional director of the Industrial Areas Foundation, one of the most thoughtful and effective organizations involved in community politics. I was sitting between them, and at one point Ernie leaned over and around me and said to Jim, "Deliberative polls just drop down into communities, but what communities need are long-standing institutions through which they can become politically engaged over the long run."

The public institutions Cortes was talking about are not formal ones, NGOs, public interest groups, and the like. They are the informal ones people put together and run on their own. IAF usually begins with some institutions that already exist—churches or schools—and draws out and connects people from them into something like, for example, an interfaith group. Such new "institutions" are mediating bodies, places that bring together people in a community and thereafter provide a way for them to engage elected officials and formal institutions. The three kinds of alienation that I mentioned a moment ago all result from an absence of mediating forces. There is little to mediate between people and their elected officials, the public and the news media, or different parts of communities. The kind of public institutions through which IAF and other community organizers work redress these alienations, but they still represent a tiny fraction of America and function primarily in less-affluent communities. In most communities today, disconnected political life prevails.

This absence is felt as a kind of loss. There is a nostalgia for the time when such institutions did exist, but it is a nostalgia that has been present hundreds of years. Each generation thinks that the previous generation had it better: tighter communities, safer neighborhoods, more mindful adults, more effective organizations, stronger communal bonds. To go back to that would probably mean going back to a time that, from a modern perspective, would be unpalatable in many other ways. The tight-knit societies of yesteryear were also the authoritarian and conservative ones that we moderns shun. "Effective" organizations practiced and professed a kind of absolutism of belief or class. Perhaps freedom and self-rule necessitate a trade-off, fewer connections and less solidarity; if so, it is probably fruitless to look backward to and for "community." Rather, we need to figure out what kind of mediating institutions we can create for the twenty-first century.

We need mediating institutions that can help *translate* public will into law, that can take what emerges in public deliberations and other social movements—public will—and give it political efficacy. This question of translation was central to Jürgen Habermas's last, major book, *Between Facts and Norms*. It picked up where his previous huge, two-volume book left off: with a dismal sight of "colonization" of the public sphere by administrative, economic, and bureaucratic systems whose instrumental languages were putting a stranglehold on the public's ability to find and cultivate its own voice. The *public's* language, importantly, is one of solidarity, meaning, purpose, value; other languages are about bottom lines, means and ends, power. Even if the public should manage to hang on to its own way of reasoning and speaking, the systems had no way to fathom what on earth it was saying. *Between Facts and Norms* takes up the question of translating public will into law. It paints a picture of arrays of informal citizen organizations that are sensitive to the public weal and, when alerted to problems, deliberate on them, developing public will. When public policies are at odds with this public will, the organizations begin to put pressure on legislative bodies—or any governing entities that seem vulnerable to what the public thinks. Such bodies pass laws that translate public will into language that other systems can hear. So the environmental movement, for example, puts pressure on Congress, which then creates an Environmental Protection Agency that fines polluting corporations. The corporations can "hear" what a fine says, even as they may be impervious to public outcries and dead fish floating down the river.

Now, as I recount this explanation from Habermas, I can anticipate a reaction from those who think deliberative public politics should be shorn of the antagonistic trappings of conventional politics: the Habermasian picture of how public will is translated into law is simply politics as usual: purveyors of public will become formal public interest groups adept in matters of factionalism and power brokering.

The lure of conventional pressure politics is that, in the short run anyway, it promises results. If you make enough noise, join the right interest group, you can make a difference. Hence, thousands of people ante up to their favorite group, or write letters to Congress or for Amnesty International. A little effort, a little money, and a "public citizen" is born (at least in Ralph Nader's view of citizenship). But I think what differentiates Habermas's view from conventional politics is the role it sees for citizen groups as incubators of legitimate public will. This isn't an image of protesters on the street, of determined "greens" or "neocons." It's the image of people in a room, sorting things out together in the course of developing considered and collective judgment. Habermas goes beyond deliberative theory alone by offering an understanding of the role of social movements or informal public institutions that carry public will up the ladder, that hold formal political institutions accountable. Even if this view is antagonistic and conventional, we can nonetheless begin to imagine active institutions that behave more deliberatively. We don't even need imagination; we can see principles at work in successful models. Mark Warren describes in his book, *Dry Bones Rattling*, one successful IAF initiative, a job training program called Project QUEST, as follows:

> The existence of IAF organizations as mediating institutions, their abil-
> ity to implement community development policy without losing their
> participatory character, lies at the heart of Project QUEST's success.
> In that role, IAF organizations have an effect both on the social capital
> of communities and on the politics and policies of the urban environ-
> ment. By turning community building toward politics, the IAF creates
> effective power for local communities, so they generate the capacity to
> implement their visions. . . . The IAF strategy puts community build-
> ing and political power in symbiotic relationship.

IAF's focus on strengthening communities draws its attention to the range
of elements of successful politics: from building citizen organizations to
building the mechanisms, capacities, and relationships that make those
organizations' plans possible. The plans are arrived at deliberatively, but
the deliberations are not ends in themselves.

Perhaps the problem with focusing first on deliberation is that it tends
to lead into a corner, focusing primarily on how deliberation creates public will and then hoping against hope that public will might catalyze
people into taking seriously the office of citizen. This pitfall seems most
prevalent in middle-class communities where public problems seem a
bit removed from everyday life. Deliberation might seem to be a good
pastime but not necessarily something urgently needed to solve pressing
problems. Even as they engage in deliberating about what ought to be
done on matters of common concern, the participants can retain the conventional view of politics as matters of government with citizens peripheral to the process.

Contrast this to what happens when communities dealing with
crises turn to public talk. In his book *Politics Is About Relationships: A
Blueprint for the Citizens' Century*, Harold Saunders documents how a
citizens' peace process has worked in South Africa and in the poorest
of the former Soviet republics, Tajikistan. Here there can be nothing
idle about deliberation; it is part of a larger frame of public work. As
Saunders and his colleague Randa Slim put it, this work is part of a
larger effort. "We call it the relational paradigm: *Politics is a cumulative,
multi-level, open-ended process of continuous interaction over time engaging
significant clusters of citizens in and out of government and the relationships
they form to solve public problems in whole bodies politic across permeable
borders, either within or between communities or countries*" (Saunders and

Slim 2006 document, "A Democratic Strategy for Change"). Through this process, there are things that governments need to do, but also things that only citizens can do. Only citizens can transform conflictual relationships, modify human behavior, and change political culture. The greatest untapped resources in meeting the challenges of the twenty-first century are the energies and capacities of citizens outside government. A paradigm that leaves them on the margins by focusing primarily on political institutions is both ineffectual because it fails to take advantage of those resources and immoral because it marginalizes most of the world's people (ibid.).

As I discussed in chapter 6, the citizens' peace process that Saunders and Slim have nurtured involves what they call "Sustained Dialogue," a series of meetings between and among various sectors of society that might even be engaged in civil war (as they were in Tajikistan). These conversations develop over time. The first step is finding suitable places where all the parties can meet and talk together (which may mean finding ways to bring in people who had previously been marginalized or excluded from the public sphere). Next is identifying the problem and eventually steps toward change, and then working on moving back into the larger community, tapping already existing NGOs or setting up new ones. The key is that these dialogues are part of a larger political process and are integrated in and through mediating institutions.

Such a larger framework is needed to develop ways public will can affect public policy in countries that are not suffering from civil war or brutality. Deliberation needs to be part of a larger public politics. There are many kinds of public institutions that can convene a public and channel will into policy: community leadership organizations, convening or "boundary spanning" organizations, community development corporations, and many more outlined in recent literature, including both Mark Warren's book mentioned above and Carmen Sirianni and Lewis Friedland's book, *The Civic Renewal Movement*.

For democratic communities to work, there need to be these kinds of long-standing public institutions through which people can come together, institutions that are not shy about standing up for what citizens are coming to believe or shy about building relationships with officials. These institutions could convene public deliberations *and* serve as venues for public action, meeting with officials and even advocating for what the public wills.

Any community that has such organizations will have much public power in its midst, the kind of "power with" that is formidable and even more awesome than coercive or administrative "power over." It will catalyze new relationships between policy makers and the public. It will even make a connection between public will and public policy. In such a community, a pragmatic citizen will think efforts for deliberation and public action wise and well spent. The connection will be strong, maybe even obvious.

CHAPTER 11

Media and the Public Sphere

This final chapter describes opportunities for sublimation in a world of new media technologies that allow people to speak for themselves and far-flung people to speak with each other. Effective sublimation may make it possible for people to "find themselves" in a public sphere, as members of larger political projects, in a way that only the ancients could have hoped for. I go here cautiously, somewhere between technological determinists who think that all new media are liberating and skeptics who worry about the loss of face-to-face communication and the ironic isolation that occurs when everyone is a blogger and no one is listening to anyone else. The determinists are wrong to think that just because citizens can now have their own media, they won't use it poorly. The skeptics may be harder to convince, and that is much of what I will try to do in this chapter.

I start by quoting from an e-mail that a dear colleague, Bob Kingston, sent me in response to a post I had written on my own Weblog, or "blog," which he had learned about after his secretary printed it out and faxed it to him at home. The post had concerned the issue of time collapse in Iraq, a topic he did in fact find interesting (and that begins this book). But he was also interested in the whole process of blogging and what it might mean for politics. So he got out his recorder and dictated a long memo that his assistant later typed out and e-mailed back to me. Here is part of it:

> As I think you already know, I'm just a little skeptical about the util-
> ity and the morality of everyone "blogging merrily along." I remem-
> ber, when I was still a small boy, a hundred years ago, I used to linger
> around elderly gentlemen, sitting in groups of two or three on benches
> in the park, talking with conviction, camaraderie and high seriousness
> about the world today—in which they obviously played very little part.
> To a degree, I was always impressed by them: by their conviction, their
> experience, even their wisdom. Yet at the same time, my dominant

thought was scornful, in the way that only young can be to old: silly old fools, they could sit around talking because they have nothing else to do, and nobody was going to listen to them anyway! Something of that latter attitude prevails every time I hear of a blog, nowadays: why would anybody assume that somebody else had the time or patience to listen to whatever trivial preoccupation is on his or her mind? That's what friends are for; and people who might reasonably be relied upon to do something; but why the hell should anybody else want to listen to me! As one who is committed to, genuinely committed to, the continued and extended generation of a deliberative culture, I recognize that, ideally, everybody should be ready to talk and listen to serious commentary, by anybody, about the matters that affect us all. And this kind of freedom to express is ultimately much more important than the freedom to wear a tie or a hair-do that will attract others' interest. So I should welcome the habit of blog. Perhaps what I ultimately fear is that it might have a kind of inverse effect—not without some kind of kinship to the a-temporal difficulty that you cite in the blog itself: a kind of encouragement towards—and easy acceptance of—a group self-indulgence that could paradoxically lead towards a world in which we ultimately assume less responsibility, as individuals, for collective action. It may become, at worst, a kind of upscale version of the gripe: an easy way to justify the expression of personal disdain, instead of doing anything serious for collective improvement.

If it is true that blogging is akin to a few people idly talking to each other—or even worse, as I used to think, that it is like someone with a megaphone yelling in a desert—then there would indeed be little political value in it. Moreover, much blogging these days, especially in the United States, seems more like ranting than communicating. Despite such occasional use of blogs, I'd like to describe and discuss ways these new media can be—and are being—used in keeping with the aspirations of this book.

But first note something interesting about Kingston's reception of my blog post. His assistant printed it out and faxed it to him; he dictated a reply that he mailed to her; his assistant typed out and sent that reply to me by e-mail. There were many layers of mediation and separation between my post and his reply. Kingston did not encounter the blog on his computer. If he had, he would have seen that he could reply directly to the blog, and that others in turn could see and reply to his reply. In effect, our little conversation could grow larger and larger. Also, he would have seen that on my blog I have links to other people's blogs, and some of those have links back to mine. I can "tag" a post with key words that allow others interested in these topics to find it. As one Weblog hosting company puts it, "It's about the links, man." In other words, it's about creating relationships and larger circles of conversation. The elderly men on the park benches in Kingston's childhood might have attracted a few passersby; the virtual conversations online may attract exponentially more. But that is not the main difference or benefit of these new kinds of conversations. They leave signs that continue to circulate. And these new spaces allow all comers, not just the gentlemen.

Now I turn to exploring the democratic potential of these new media: not just blogs but wikis and podcasts and other digital media that invert or deconstruct older hierarchical relationships. First I look at how these new media do more than provide means for transmitting information; they help structure identity, experience, and relationships. Second, I take up a very promising example of an online global community and what it can teach us. And third, I look at how these new media provide for more democratic relationships between the professions and the public.

THE PUBLIC SPHERE AS A DISCURSIVE SPACE

As early as the 1960s, in my third-grade classroom, a novel idea was already becoming banal: massive strides in transportation and communication were making the world a smaller place. Well-worn textbooks trotted out the facts: step on a plane and in a few hours you could step off in another part of the world; go to the grocery store and you could find fruits from the tropics in your town in the dead of winter; pick up the phone and you could talk instantaneously with your Aunt Ema in Budapest. Other truths weren't mentioned: turn on the television and the bloodied jungles of Vietnam could be in your living room; hop in your car and you could be over the border into Canada in a matter of hours; drive to the darker parts of town and you could buy heroin from Afghanistan with the passing of palms.

In the 1980s Apple introduced the personal computer. When those computers arrived and roosted on desks in one home after another, they came with a curious software called hypertext. Few people knew what to do with this. If they learned it, they had an intriguing code for linking one bit of text with another, so for example, I could footnote a piece of writing ad infinitum with other text stored on my computer, even with drawings, later with pictures, video, music. But for must of the decade this hypertext program was an oddity. Then in 1989 Tim Berners-Lee dreamed up a way to use hypertext markup language (html) to link data in one computer to data in another, laying this technology over an earlier one that the military had devised to network computers across the country. Before Berners-Lee, in the early days, making a link from one computer to another was a matter of transferring data using a file transfer protocol (ftp) from one computer to another, a process that began with typing code after a white c: prompt on an otherwise black screen. I did my own venturing there, dutifully copying code from a manual in order to send a document across town in a mere twenty minutes. It would have been quicker to drive it over. By the early 1990s, light shone. A new form of software, a browser (Mosaic), used the hypertext transfer protocol (http) to link documents from one computer to another, displaying a colorful and light-filled way to access and link data across the world.

In the fifteen years since, the speed of connections and the amount of available information on the Web have increased beyond what anyone could imagine. I can not only look at most of the world's art from my own little computer but also retrieve information on practically anything, from the recipe for Ernest Hemingway's favorite cucumber soup to specifics on how to write my own will, tune my own car, sell my own house, or school my own children.

In the forty years since I read my third-grade textbook, the world has gotten even smaller and our mental topography of it has transformed radically. So now another banality has emerged: the Internet has radically changed communication, making it swifter but altering its trajectories. There are fewer hierarchical structures and more lateral connections; fewer ways for nation-states to censor public communication; more means for insurgent publics to organize themselves, raise funds, start movements, protect rain forests, or blow up trains; more self-authorizing and publicly acknowledged authorities running Weblogs. The public sphere proliferates and takes on new shapes. The Internet seems to be "up there" zinging information packets from one corner of the world to another: a new "blogosphere" produces reports on events large and small; distinctions between public and private disintegrate with the most intimate spaces and acts visually digitized and disseminated; a text message from Boston to Moscow asks a spouse to call home; the ding of "you've got mail" changes the space and time in which our relationships proceed.

The computer keyboard, hard drive, and screen become extensions of our own bodily limbs, brains, and organs, fundamentally altering perceptual abilities and fields.

In this context, Jürgen Habermas's notion of the public sphere as a discursive space resonates. Today the world seems more immediate not primarily because of high-speed travel, though that certainly makes a difference, but because no matter how remote our region, we can immediately and communicatively engage with others across the globe and take in the myriad images, symbols, and ideas that crisscross our perceptual field. Of course, this engagement is not at all im-mediate, that is, without mediation—it is highly mediated through high-speed cable, telephone, radio, and satellite infrastructures. Moreover, beyond these physical structures, communication is mediated through a vast array of signs and symbols through which we produce and negotiate meaning, identity, purpose.

But this is not exactly what Habermas had in mind when he described the public sphere as a discursive space. Habermas's fundamental model is of the speech-act communication between a sender and a receiver and the extent to which it is communicative rather than strategic. By "communicative" he means aimed toward reaching understanding, following the implicit, presupposed norms of validity, sincerity, and appropriateness that make conversation possible. In other words, we only bother to talk with each other because we presume that the other person will be, or at least ought to be, telling the truth, being sincere, and not trying to manipulate us. Speech acts that poach upon these presuppositions—for example, that take advantage of our assumption that the other is telling the truth—are strategic, not communicative. Understood so, advertising, political propaganda, lies, and other manipulations are strategic actions. Their aim is not to garner mutual understanding but to reach some other, often veiled, end: to get the other to buy, believe, succumb, or unwittingly obey.

In the same texts in which Habermas laid out this notion of communicative action, he also distinguished two modes of or perspectives on "where" actions take place: system and lifeworld. The latter, lifeworld, a term drawn from Edmund Husserl's phenomenological theory, is the realm of solidarity, kinship, love in which people try to orient their lives in a meaningful way. The former, system, comes out of the sociological work of Niklas Luhmann known as systems theory. From this perspective, actions in different spheres are coordinated according to different expectations and languages. The economic system is steered by the imperative to make money; the political system is steered by the media of power; the medical system (at least insofar as it is not another economic system) is steered by the need to cure illness. Different systems have different objectives, and it is often impossible to coordinate actions or make sense of the disparities among systems.

Where Luhmann would have called the family another system, Habermas exempts family from the logic of systems and refers to it and other kinship or community networks as the lifeworld. The lifeworld is best oriented by communicative action, through which people decide together how they want to live, what their communities should stand for, what is of value and importance. In contrast, systems operate by strategic action because they each have a certain function (to make money, to have power, to achieve health). Functional reason calls for strategic action. Habermas grants that such reasons may be appropriate in systems, but only to the extent that lifeworld considerations can prevail. The problem of our times, though, is that the system has begun to "colonize" the lifeworld. Its logic and modes of action have begun to infiltrate and take over lifeworld considerations, imperiling communicative action and the potentially liberatory reason that underlies it.

Habermas's notion of communication has come under attack, notably by Nicholas Garnham, Michael Warner, and Benjamin Lee. (See their essays in Craig Calhoun's *Habermas and the Public Sphere*.) As Lee puts it, there are textual functions of language not reducible to speech-act functions, and even speech acts themselves may be products of other aspects of signification (410–413). Moreover, communicative media that are not strictly linguistic do not operate according to the logic of sender-receiver models: "questions could also be raised about the applicability of a general theory of writing or textuality to mixed modes of semiosis, such as television and movies, which combine visual and oral modalities and whose production includes print-mediated processes as diverse as script writing and audience surveying" (414).

But matters are even more complex than Lee notes. There are many signifying media in the public sphere that do not necessarily aim to *communicate* any message, whether communicative or strategic, but simply to *structure* experience, desire, and identity. These signifiers do not try to tell us to agree, to obey, or to buy; they serve to shape our conceptions of who we are and how the world should be. Their semiotic function is not to transmit a packet of information or a normative claim, but to reconfigure our modes of being in the world, our comportments, attachments, self-conceptions, identities, abjections, and filiations.

Aesthetic media do shape experience; they carry out political tasks of forming identity, attachments, and a sense of possibility. Recall my discussion of Shannon Sullivan's reading of Fanon in chapter 2, of how racist habits are handed down from generation to generation as a collective unconscious. Borrowing from Abraham and Torok, Sullivan calls this collective unconscious a phantom, "an unspeakable secret from previous generations that will not die, that has a murky but very real presence among the living." The ways public media structure experience and our attachments with particular others have very real political effects.

Fanon found that the phantom of racism had slipped into his and his fellow Antilleans' experiences and attachments via the media he grew up with, history textbooks, songs, magazines, and movies. These media carried signs of a racist culture, the thwarted sublimations of those who denied others the ability to sublimate and participate in the sociosymbolic public sphere. These others then were subjected to images that denied them their own humanity.

Yet just as these and other media can carry racist messages, they can also carry others. And as new media break open the old monopoly that those in power had over media, people can begin to articulate new signs of themselves that in turn can begin to circulate in the sociosymbolic public sphere. To show how this has already begun to happen, I describe one such movement.

GLOBAL VOICES ONLINE

In December 2005, the blogosphere[1] touched down in a strange place: the new Reuters headquarters in the surreal urban space of Canary Wharf, a gleaming set of skyscrapers and shopping malls built upon what had once been known as the Isle of Dogs, a place on the outskirts of London so poor and bombed out that the shipping industry and then the poor left it behind. Today's brochures and maps of Canary Wharf studiously omit any mention of history. Its reason for being is business, banking, and information. It is quintessentially twenty-first century. No history is needed and any aura is manufactured. It is a place severed from context or roots, where the mostly rich go about the business of becoming richer.

Contrast that to the community that alighted there on Saturday, December 10, 2005: a community with a history then less than a year old, without any physical borders (though grappling with linguistic ones). This is a community spread across the globe of people who communicate virtually: Global Voices, a Web site that "rounds up" what's happening in the blogospheres of various parts of the mostly developing world.[2] It is a blog that takes visitors outward to other blogs, transports them to the conversation going on in the Middle East, sub-Saharan Africa, the Americas, Eurasia, Asia, and the Pacific.

Global Voices was conceived at a meeting in December 2004 at Harvard Law School's Berkman Center for Internet and Society. (Rebecca MacKinnon's report can be found at http://www.personaldemocracy.com/node/208.) That meeting brought together bloggers and scholars from around the world who began thinking about how to harness a nascent, decentralized movement as a forum for creating a truly global conversation. The conversation was going on already, in bits and pieces; the Web site of Global Voices made it possible to connect the pieces.

Many who came to the London summit were only now connecting names with faces, though one of the members had just recently compiled a "book" of participants, using digital images found on the Internet to piece together a Web page that would help people introduce themselves in person. But even though they were just now meeting in person and even though they'd been in virtual contact for a matter of months, this was a community much more connected and real than anything evident in the surrounding buildings. In less than a year it had become one of the top 100 most visited Web sites in the world. It had garnered a Google ranking of 8 out of 10 for its overall importance to other Web sites (Yahoo was a 9.) It had yet to employ a full-time staff person and was run mostly by volunteers. Though it had been conceived by some very bright folks at the Harvard meeting, its growth was due to the spontaneous and ingenious efforts of people throughout the world. Its intelligence is distributed and as a result probably more powerful and resilient than that of the brightest minds at any university.

The day's topics included these: how in the space of less than a year a new global conversation had emerged via the metablog, Global Voices; what kinds of relationships there might be between conventional journalists and citizen bloggers; how these conversations could occur across different languages. Some of the subjects were technical, others philosophical, with the day's conversation moving from translation engines to distributed networks. I took away from the meeting the following three insights.

Media That Can Create Public Life and Give the Public Voice

Global Voices has primarily used one form of "social software," the Weblog format, to start hearing and capturing a global conversation. The key, social factor of a blog is that it is usually a comment on someone else's comment—whether on an op-ed piece in the paper, a news broadcast, or someone else's blog post. As an utterance in the public sphere, the blog that comments on some other utterance becomes itself a subject for comment. And so begins a conversation. What we have then is a format for a public to begin speaking and listening together without the impediments of physically attending the public meeting (if there were one). One doesn't need a car or a babysitter, just access to a computer, something that is becoming more and more available even in the developing world.

Global Voices began with blogging as the quintessential social software, but other formats are emerging: the wiki format,[3] podcasting, video blogging, and no doubt more I haven't even heard of yet. Global Voices is one example—there are others—of how nonprofessional media users are using new media to create public space and public life. Unlike some enthusiasts of new media who see technology as a way to bring about more finely tuned consumer choice, these users see new media as tools for creating community and improving society.

Reporting on the 2004 meeting that spawned the Global Voices Web site, Rebecca MacKinnon writes,

> By the end of the day, most in the room agreed that we are indeed a movement: a movement not only of bloggers, but also of wiki-builders and users of other kinds of social or peer-produced media who want to build a better global conversation. People who believe in free speech, free access to information and a fear-free internet for all people on this earth. People who believe that conversations and peer-to-peer sharing of creative works between ordinary citizens in cyberspace isn't just "cool." It isn't just another business opp. It's vital to improving the state of the world.

These are not unusual sentiments in the West and other advanced regions of the world. But in the developing world, having easy access to information, freedom and opportunity to express oneself, and the right to talk and be heard, to tell one's own story, are still often not the norm. In Africa, especially, there has been little opportunity for people to speak in their own voice. Others have long defined them, and usually in terms of want, need, and deprivation. During the London summit meeting, Sokari Ekine, the Global Voices sub-Saharan Africa editor, said that one of the most important things about the African blogosphere it that it has been "presenting a new Africa"; it is "us speaking for ourselves." She described events that prompted "a conversation about the rights and wrongs" of public matters. In effect, the African blogosphere is providing a key element of democratic society: the freedom and space for members of a political community to deliberate together about matters of state and common concern.

Media That Can Create Public Knowledge

The Global Voices phenomenon is an example of collective-action theory in practice, a model of distributed organization.[4] It began with just Rebecca MacKinnon and Ethan Zuckerman of Harvard's Berkman Center on Internet and Society posting content to the site. It quickly grew to a larger and larger network of contributors. "We no longer own this thing," MacKinnon said to the group, "you do." While the server resides in Cambridge, Massachusetts, the network itself has no center: it is decentralized, distributed.

Dina Mehta, an Indian blogger, made a good point about the power of these new media (including blogs and wikis) as she experienced them following the 2004 Indian Ocean tsunami. Within hours of the event, she and her cohorts started a blog to which anyone could post. Within a few more hours, there were hundreds of posts, and the blog administrators switched to wiki formats so that the posts wouldn't get lost in archives. They did the same after Hurricane Katrina. Well-meaning observers urged them to form an NGO, but they resisted, wanting to keep the spontaneous dimension. Lesson: spontaneous, un-"organized" movements allow for more voluntary efforts, quicker reactions, more involvement, and wider ownership.

In a distributed network, change and innovation can and do come from any corner. For example, the summit organizers hadn't scheduled a group dinner the night before, but one was quickly planned when a participant, two weeks in advance, asked if anyone wanted to go to dinner.

Someone else started a wiki page so that anyone who wanted to could sign up. Another person found a venue and made reservations, and then someone else posted a map. The night before the summit, dozens of participants crowded the basement dining room of a Lebanese restaurant near Paddington, getting to know one another for the first time in person. It was a Global Voices event, but not organized by any central, "official" leader.

This decentralization is also what makes such networks vulnerable and perhaps a bit disconcerting for organizations accustomed to control: change and innovation can come from any corner. While blogging has been the main format, the new emerging technology in this network and others is the "wiki" method of making Web sites. The Web page allows multiple users to go into the document, edit it, and save the changes, so that the next person who comes along reads a new version. That next person might look up the early version and reverse the changes or might make more of her own. A truly wiki wiki can be edited by anyone. Entering into a wiki endeavor means giving up illusions of control and proprietary authorship. Advocates say that the result is much better and smarter than anything that one or two people might write; the more authors, the more authoritative it might be. Yet as the *L.A. Times* learned after briefly opening its online editorial page to the public via a wiki, the process can also turn things upside down.[5] This is a real challenge for media organizations that want to both harness public power and retain control over their site—and their reputation.

Media That Can Get Past the Blogging and Journalism Debates

At the London summit, the conversation moved beyond recent debates about whether bloggers were usurping journalists' roles without sufficient credibility or standards.[6] And no one argued for the other usual point of view: that bloggers were prima facie better at journalism than journalists. Both bloggers and journalists in the room discussed how the two groups needed each other. They noted that there is no one model of this relationship; much depends on the state of journalism and/or the state of blogging in a country. Where journalists are lazy, corrupt, and slipshod, bloggers end up doing their work. Where freedom of expression and robust journalism are under fire, bloggers defend journalistic freedom. Where blogging is strong, journalists sometimes crib from blogs without attribution. Still, all seemed to see the importance of strengthening both spheres and somehow relating them. One person talked about "fusing" the spheres. Another used the term "complementary" to describe an emerging relationship. Many other journalists turned bloggers said that bloggers were another form of first-person eyewitnesses; they didn't need to be objective—what journalists needed from them was their subjective experience and opinions. This was all a marked step beyond the recent worry that bloggers are being amateur journalists. But the meeting stopped short of looking further into what kind of relationship could be developed between the two spheres.

It's no accident that the meeting took place in the Reuters building and that numerous BBC journalists were in attendance. Both BBC and Reuters see the need for connecting with the blogosphere and learning from how it rounds up the public conversations that go on there. A Reuters officer said that Global Voices was doing this kind of coverage better than Reuters, even though Reuters might have one of the most extensive corps of reporters around the world.

In the past year, some broadcast media have been experimenting with ways to connect with these new blogging, podcasting, e-mailing publics. In the United States, Christopher Lydon's "Open Source" radio program is built around a Web site that invites public input. Beginning just six weeks before the London summit, the BBC started a new interactive program, "World Have Your Say," which uses the Web as its first source for bringing in global voices. The night before the London meeting, the program's producer, Mark Sandell, brought some of the main players in Global Voices into his studio, where they and the anchors were joined by the voices and e-mails of listeners across the globe. Sandell reports that he couldn't possibly do this program without the Web, that is, without a World Wide Web of regular people joining into a big conversation about their world together.

"Open Source" and "World Have Your Say" are young programs. Other media, notably public media and local newspapers, are experimenting with how traditional and new media can intersect in a way that fosters a bigger, more public conversation about current issues and how we in this diverse, contentious world are going to live together. The relationships between old and new media, between the broadcasters and the public are still in their infancy. Much is still to be learned about what kind of engagements work—both for making good television and radio and for fostering and strengthening democratic publics.

In sum, some citizen use of new media can create and is creating a more connected, intelligent, and robust public life. It is providing means for people in regions across the world to define who they are, to assess policies and problems, to hold power accountable, and to enter into the kind of conversations heretofore the province of elites. Social software programs such as blogging and wikis create a kind of power that is decentralized and resilient. They are a promising but not unproblematic resource for more conventional news media organizations. Much is still to be learned about how these spheres can complement each other. Innovative media organizations see the power and are already experimenting. Further inquiry is needed on how media can engage these "cyberpublics," how these conversations can be interpreted and used journalistically, and how blogospheres throughout the world can be nourished and strengthened.

EXPERTISE, PROFESSIONS, AND THE PUBLIC IN A DIGITAL AGE

Another, final worry I want to address in closing is that in a complex world, the public could hardly be capable of self-rule. In a world that is increasingly differentiated, as Niklas Luhmann described, with each sphere developing its own expert knowledge, we need experts and professionals to look after the common weal. The Internet seems to threaten that. Is this a dangerous development? Don't we need professions for more than their knowledge—knowledge that can be widely disseminated online—but also for their judgment?

The explosion of information on the World Wide Web is directly linked to the implosion of the boundaries of professional knowledge. I arrive at the doctor's office with a printout of the possible sources of my ailments. Now that I am armed with a little information, my relationship to her changes. Moreover, the connections that this new technology provides cut out the middleman. Why get a realtor when I can list my house online myself? Who needs a travel agent when you can book your own travel? Can a travel agent provide something that expedia.com and the sites that allow travelers to comment on hotels cannot? Perhaps a little, but not too much.

The questions arise: Is there something more to a profession than an exclusive hold on some expert knowledge or protocol? Is professionalism simply a product of preserving this exclusion? Does it fall apart when the public, through technology, busts down the door, ransacks the files, shares all the goodies? And what happens when knowledge is not only shared but the nonexpert starts producing her own? When the unschooled and uncredentialed start dabbling in these professional enterprises, becoming producers themselves? It is one thing to use a curriculum that an educator has put on the Web; it is another to produce your own. It is one thing to read the paper online and another to start your own blog. The digitization of information that allows for widespread distribution of professional knowledge also allows for nonprofessionals to produce their own information and then distribute it to all who might tune in.

These phenomena produce natural reactions in the professions: admonishments, defensiveness, outcries, and paternalism. Woe is the layperson who ventures into these domains without expert assistance. The expert has been her protector and agent. When the layperson stops deferring to the professional, she puts herself in danger.

One of the most upturned professions these days is journalism, where, not so long ago, the hierarchy of knowledge production was clear. Reporters gathered the news and wrote the stories; editors cleared them for publication. Standards were firm, making the news as construed safe and fit to print. But now others are gathering the news, writing the stories, and publishing them online without much, if any, reference to journalistic standards. Of course, this has always been the case with "underground" newspapers, missives run off on mimeograph machines with all the bylines pseudonymous. But due to the inability of most underground publishers to cover even the modest costs of such papers, their circulation was small and mostly inconsequential.

Now the logic of circulation and reach is quite different. In the blogosphere, one's reach depends not on one's pocketbook but on one's network, salience, and eloquence. Perhaps only one person reads my blog, but if that persons links to it in her blog, and another blog links to that one, then my reach expands exponentially. With this kind of interlinking of blogs, of comments posted to comments; with "track backs" and information "running up the long tail" from micro to macro media; with cell phone pictures of the London Underground bombing and Hurricane Katrina showing up on the evening news, these new digital uses of media are turning journalism on its head.

There are three recognizable patterns of reaction. One is to denounce citizen media use as unprincipled, unverified, and dangerous. Here are citizens posing as journalists, but they have none of the ethos that the profession has carefully cultivated. Another reaction is deference, bestowing on citizens the mantle of journalist, and then wondering what there is left for the old journalists to do. Maybe the credentialed now become editors, selecting and broadcasting citizen media. The *L.A. Times* had a brief and disastrous experiment in letting readers write editorials; it led to massive polarization, online slurs, an abrupt end to the experiment, and Michael Kinsley's departure from the paper. A third reaction is to co-opt, to turn reporters and columnists loose as bloggers, opining in a way contrary to all they've been taught.

Finding another response calls for rethinking what this thing called a profession is. Perhaps, as Michael Walzer grants, it is more than maintaining an artificial boundary. Professionalism is also "an ethical code, a social bond, a pattern of mutual regulation and self-discipline" (155). But Walzer barely gives such other possibilities any consideration. Certainly professions have ethical codes, some more robust than others. Codes for realtors are paltry at best, while those for doctors are quite powerful. But adopting a code doesn't make a profession. Neither does mutual regulation nor even self-discipline. It seems rather that there is something in this notion of a social bond, let's say a social *relationship* between professions and their publics, a kind of promise, a willingness to evolve, develop, and extend judgment. I go to a professional for more than expert knowledge; I go for a bit of wisdom, some judgment as to how, if I do this or that, things might work out.

This criterion seems to separate the professions that have a rightful and important place in a modern democratic society from those that are dispensable. We might be a bit worse off without travel agents, but we'd survive. But we would be much the worse without lawyers (never mind Shakespeare), doctors, educators, and even journalists. When I go to the doctor armed with information on symptoms and the possible causes (according to WebMD, I seem to have the ebola virus!), I go in search of this professional's discernment, the way her education cultivated by experience can lead her to ask the right questions, weigh possibilities (no, you don't have ebola) and courses of action. Even with all the information I now possess, even with the change of our relationship—now less hierarchical, more of a partnership—I still expect something important from her as a professional.

The relationship of journalism to a public is more complicated. What made journalism happen in the first place was the ability to publish.

Standards evolved over time, mostly as a way to purchase credibility, trust, and readers. Digital technology changes all that. Twenty percent of teenagers in the United States blog. Law professors blog, as do stay-at-home-moms, foodies, economists, gardeners, seniors, stand-up comics, activists, passivists, you name it. Mostly they carry on conversations about their own hobbies, proclivities, and interests. But occasionally, as the metablogger Rebecca MacKinnon puts it, they commit random acts of journalism. Laypeople, not journalists, digitally transmitted photos from the London Underground after the bombings. Laypeople, not journalists, reported on much of the crisis during and after Katrina. After the hurricane, at least one TV station broadcast images from a blog, effectively turning the news show over to bloggers.

But MacKinnon's larger point is that most of what goes on in the blogosphere is a conversation, large, interrelated but uncoordinated, by a public that is trying to make sense of its world. Some of this conversation takes place in small venues where those interested in something swap information, but at other times the topic in this one little place becomes of great interest to the body politic. Suddenly there are hordes at the door listening in and entering the conversation. This happened to MacKinnon's own little blog on North Korea, where traffic spiked after Bush named North Korea as part of the "axis of evil." What had been a small parlor became a stadium.

For all the ranters and cranks, there is something truly remarkable about the blogosphere. It is making the public audible. Earlier ways of hearing the public were rather crude: an opinion poll, the sampling of letters to the editor, the sounds emanating from the street protest, or the five-minute diatribe during a city council meeting. We knew what the people around us were saying, but we could only imagine what "the public" was saying, not that a public had much of a way to say anything together, anyway.

A public is not a passive body waiting in the wings. It is the effect of a diverse array of people coming together to work through past traumas, forge new identities, and try to understand and decide matters that affect them in common. We don't often hear that take on the public, but it is a much more useful way of thinking about what might make democracy possible. So if a public is like this, something that happens when unlike people, thrown together in the same place, try to understand and deliberate about their common challenges, then there needs to be a venue where they can converse. The age-old lament about democracy in a far-flung country, about the possibility of democracy in any community larger than, say, 10,000 people, was that this was simply impossible. But not now.

Now we can discern an audible public conversation bubbling up through the blogosphere, where people compare notes (hypertext!), disagree, rant, lament, champion their pet causes, rail against others, hype their own views, but a conversation nonetheless where, occasionally, random acts of deliberation and reflection occur. Even with its unevenness, we can discern in it a sense of how a public is forming, identifying and naming problems (usually in its own and not expert terms), and might be inclined to proceed.

And this is where journalism comes in and where it needs to rethink itself. For a long time now, the most mundane and safe journalism abided by its own standards of fairness and balance, which for the unadventurous meant reporting two sides of a story, interviewing officials from one political party and then from the other. These were two sides of a very narrow political spectrum, but only one side of a body politic: the world of officialdom, experts, professions, government, not the lifeworld of the public. This public world or public sphere is the space between the private lives of citizens and the official sphere of government. It is a space in which two or more people come together to discuss matters of common concern. These conversations have long taken place, in fits and starts, in the associations of civil society: churches, labor unions, schools, civic associations. Slowly their conclusions could enter public awareness, becoming a public sense of what was right and wrong; think of the civil rights movement and the environmental movement.

An adventurous journalist would try to capture this public sense of things in stories, but this was hard to do and harder still to assess or verify. It called for a great deal of judgment and discernment, an ability to gauge public sentiment and concern. But now all journalists are being called on to be adventurous, because the public's conversation, however unwieldy, is manifest on the Web. But being a professional journalist does not mean handing the paper or the station over to bloggers and podcasters; it means using that same judgment to discern what issues are really of concern to the public—and what journalists damn well ought to be covering.

Journalists have other resources that laypeople don't always have, the connections and the skill to connect the dots, to find out how a matter of concern over here is connected to the machinations of some entity over there. They have the training and the resources to verify their sources and get the story right. Now one of their biggest sources is the public, something that Minnesota Public Radio is rightly exploiting in its project called Insight Journalism, in which it is calling on all listeners to become sources.

The emergence of an audible public brings to the fore something that was always important: that professionals stand not above the public but in relation to them. The digital revolution is more than a media revolution; it is bringing about a major change in how we as a people relate to one another and how we see our own role and expertise in relation to the whole.

Epilogue

The times we are in are truly momentous. Not only are we still reeling from and acting out the traumas that accompanied the birth of modernity, we are in a time that allows for sublimation on a scale never before seen. We can work through our troubles. Even in a world where *realpolitik* still reigns, we have a new politics of deliberation and civil work emerging. Even as genocide still haunts the earth, we have a global movement for truth and reconciliation. Even as the cult of expertise still has its grasp, we have a world where people are beginning to voice and shape their lives for themselves, together and in the company of strangers. It is up to us to make something good of these times. That's the hard part.

NOTES

Introduction: The Sociosymbolic Public Sphere

1. Note that I use the word "citizen" to designate the functions that members of a political community ought to have in a democracy. I am not referring to legal status. So I would even consider illegal aliens to be citizens of a political community in the sense that they too have a stake in what happens in their community and have a good claim that they should be able to help shape its direction. Were I to use the more neutral term "people," I would lose the specifically political role that I think members of a political community ought to have.

1. The Political Unconscious

1. See Erik H. Erikson, *Childhood and Society* (New York: Norton, 1950); Lawrence Kohlberg, "The Development of Modes of Thinking and Choices in Years 10 to 16" (Ph.D. diss., University of Chicago, 1958) and *The Philosophy of Moral Development* (San Francisco: Harper and Row, 1981); Jürgen Habermas, *Postmetaphysical Thinking: Philosophical Essays*, trans. William Mark Hohengarten (Cambridge, MA: MIT Press, 1992).
2. In this book I use the adjective "semiotic" to describe the ways in which multiple signs and symbols, from linguistic to aesthetic and beyond, are *meaningful*.
3. Participation does allow for individuation, which is what many seem to mean by "independence." But there is a significant difference. The ideal of independence sees human connection as a liability, whereas individuation is the process of how we come to make ourselves *singular beings* in and through a world with others. George Herbert Mead's work on this point is instructive.
4. Cf. Julia Kristeva's use of the term in "Women's Time," in *New Maladies of the Soul*, trans. Ross Guberman (New York: Columbia University Press, 1995), 201–224.
5. John Rawls, *Political Liberalism* (New York: Columbia University Press, 1996), 243.
6. See ibid.; Jürgen Habermas, *Between Facts and Norms*, trans. William Rehg (Cambridge, MA: MIT Press, 1996); and Richard Rorty, *Objectivity, Relativism, and Truth: Philosophical Papers Volume I* (Cambridge, UK: Cambridge University Press, 1991) (especially "The Priority of Democracy to Philosophy," 175–196).

7. In his later work, Rawls made clear that his view was political, not metaphysical, meaning that it presupposed only actual agreements and did not presume that there were any larger, nonpolitical grounds for agreement:

> The aim of justice as fairness, then, is practical: it presents itself as a conception of justice that may be shared by citizens as a basis of a reasoned, informed, and willing political agreement. It expresses their shared and public political reason. But to attain such a shared reason, the conception of justice should be, as far as possible, independent of the opposing and conflicting philosophical and religious doctrines that citizens affirm. In formulating such a conception, political liberalism applies the principle of toleration to philosophy itself. The religious doctrines that in previous centuries were the professed basis of society have gradually given way to principles of constitutional government that all citizens, whatever their religious view, can endorse. (Rawls, *Political Liberalism*, 10–11)

Rawls presumes that modernity, as a movement that splits apart and compartmentalizes politics and religion, has spread across the globe. But as political movements based upon religious fundamentalism show, this is not the case.

2. Modernity's Traumas

1. See Kenneth Stikkers's unpublished paper, "Logics of Similutude and Logics of Difference in American and Contemporary Continental Philosophy," and Charles Mills's *The Racial Contract* (Ithaca: Cornell University Press, 1997).
2. See Niklas Luhmann, *The Differentiation of Society*, trans. Stephen Holmes and Charles Larmore (New York: Columbia University Press, 1982).

3. Targeting the Public Sphere

1. In Freud's work, the term "primary" generally refers to processes at work in the very early stages of development, prior to the differentiation of self and other. The term "secondary" refers to processes that occur later. Also, though, "primary" continues to refer to unconscious processes and "secondary" to conscious ones. Charles Rycroft notes, "Freud distinguished between *primary repression*, by which the initial emergence of an instinctual impulse is prevented, and *secondary repression*, by which derivatives and disguised manifestations of the impulse are kept unconscious. 'The return of the repressed' consists in the involuntary irruption into consciousness of unacceptable derivatives of the primary impulse, not the dissolution of the primary repression" (*A Critical Dictionary of Psychoanalysis, new edition* [London and New York: Penguin, 1995], 157). It is thanks to primary repression that the self/other differentiation is able to arise. Kristeva's addition to this literature is to note that there is an "other"

already at work in primary processes: the abject that the emerging self "spits out" on its way to becoming a subject. Thereafter the abject remains abject as a sort of safeguard of one's own "proper" self.

2. Secondary repression will be repression that allows becoming one in the realm of human beings.

3. I mean imaginary in the Lacanian sense, as a stage of development in which self-understanding is based upon internalized images of what is self and what is other. To say something is imaginary is not to say that it is fictive and inconsequential. The imaginary in Lacan's scheme is a powerful formative aspect or moment of development.

4. Paper presented at the 31st Society for the Advancement of American Philosophy meeting, March 2004.

5. I would not take this as far as civic humanism, the view that John Rawls disparages as specifying "the chief, if not the sole human good as our engaging in political life" (*Justice as Fairness: A Restatement* [Cambridge, Mass.: The Belknap Press of Harvard University Press, 2001], 143). I am not making a claim about what human good is, but about the ways human beings seem inclined to be.

6. For an alternative account of the humanity of *der Muselmann*, see Giorgio Agamben, *Remnants of Auschwitz* (New York: Zone Books, 1999) and Lissa Skittol's discussion of it in her unpublished paper, "*Der Muselmann* as the Specter of Holocaust Studies."

5. Recovering Community

1. See, for example, Robert I. Rotberg and Dennis Thompson, eds., *Truth v. Justice: the Morality of Truth Commissions* (Princeton: Princeton University Press, 2000) and Alex Boraine, *A Country Unmasked: Inside South Africa's Truth and Reconciliation Commission* (New York and Oxford: Oxford University Press, 2000).

2. The words "private" and "public" are useful and well worth keeping. In fact, in this chapter I will draw out some rich meanings of the term "public." The problem I see is with the polar opposition that has been set up between these terms. such that "public" is founded on the exclusion of what is deemed private. It may even be founded on the *abjection* of the private, to the extent that the private is equated with bodily necessity.

3. My thanks go to Harvey Cormier for bringing this issue to my attention.

4. The first volume of Kristeva's *Le génie féminin* (published by Fayard in 1999) is devoted to Arendt, as was an essay she published in *L'infini* in the spring of 1999, "Hannah Arendt, or Life Is a Narrative" (available in *Crisis of the European Subject* [New York: Other Press, 2000]). In my essay here, references to Kristeva's volume *Hannah Arendt* are to the volume published by Columbia

University Press in 2001, not to the volume of lectures by the same name published by the University of Toronto Press.

5. For an in-depth description of the "unmaking of a world" through torture, see Elaine Scarry's *The Body in Pain: The Making and Unmaking of the World* (New York and Oxford: Oxford University Press, 1985).

6. I thank Paul Christopher Smith for bringing this point in Gadamer's work to my attention. See Smith's *Hermeneutics of Original Argument* (Evanston, Ill.: Northwestern University Press, 1998).

6. Deliberative Democracy

1. The theory I develop is quite a departure from the other critiques of procedural democracy, different from, and I think more useful than, that of Iris Young and Chantal Mouffe. Though he doesn't work on deliberative theory per se, perhaps my closest intellectual colleague in thinking about democracy is John Stuhr, who draws on Dewey and poststructural theorists to develop a very compatible and helpful theory.

2. Further discussions of NIF can be found in John Gastil, *By Popular Demand* (Berkeley: University of California Press, 2000); David Schoem and Sylvia Hurtado, *Intergroup Dialogue* (Ann Arbor: University of Michigan Press, 2001); Carmen Sirianni and Lewis Friedland, *Civic Innovation in America* (Berkeley: University of California Press, 2001); and Daniel Yankelovich, *Coming to Public Judgment: Making Democracy Work in a Complex World* (Syracuse, N.Y.: Syracuse University Press, 1991).

3. In an interview in the *Higher Education Exchange* of 2004, I recalled learning "years ago from Joe Julian, who at the time was involved with the National Issues Forums while on the faculty at Syracuse University, that sometimes in a deliberative forum someone might make a flat-out dogmatic or ideological statement that can bring deliberation to a screeching halt, something like the pronouncement, 'Taxes are stealing.' Where does a moderator go from there? Joe Julian told me that at such moments he would say, 'Tell me how you came to hold that view.' This request would move the participant from making declarations to telling a story of his or her own experience. This move calls on deliberators to see how their views emerged from a particular history and context; it warns them away from making grand claims that everyone is supposed to accept universally—but hardly ever will—to grounding their views in their own experience. This approach is completely the opposite of what the Habermasians call for. But it's just what the feminist philosopher Iris Young applauds. Young likes storytelling because it is one of the practices of people who are too often excluded from the public sphere, perhaps people who aren't as schooled in the styles of speech of upper middle-class white America. That's a good reason, but

an even better one is that stories move deliberation forward, helping everyone in the room see how even the most foreign views can be the product of recognizable human experience. And it helps people see consequences of policies that they otherwise might not have anticipated. Storytelling is one of the ways deliberators come to have a fuller picture of an issue's political topography" ("Getting the Public's Intelligence," an interview with Noëlle McAfee, *Higher Education Exchange* [2004]: 44–54; quote on 51–52).

7. Feminist Theory, Politics, and Freedom

1. This is familiar ground, so I won't rehearse all the ways that feminists have found fault with agonistic politics, primarily as it is manifested in liberal (as opposed to deliberative) democratic theory. Alison Jaggar, Jane Mansbridge, and Elizabeth Frazer do a very good job of summarizing this critique. See, for example, Nancy Fraser, *Unruly Practices: Power, Discourse and Gender in Contemporary Social Theory* (Minneapolis: University of Minnesota Press, 1989); Carole Pateman, *The Sexual Contract* (Stanford: Stanford University Press, 1988); and Iris Young, *Justice and the Politics of Difference* (Princeton, N.J.: Princeton University Press, 1990) and *Intersecting Voices: Dilemmas of Gender, Political Philosophy, and Policy* (Princeton, N.J.: Princeton University Press, 1997).

2. Additionally, drawing on psychoanalytic theory, including Jacques Lacan's reformulation of Freudian theory, such feminist theorists understand that, as living, desiring beings, we are who we are as a result of the shape of our desires and attachments, which are forever shifting. We chase after things we think will satisfy us, but the real object of our desire (Lacan's *petit objet a*) is unattainable, so our search moves us from one object to another. As human beings grow and develop, their primary attachments change and transform, and so do their own identities. Moreover, our identities are socially constituted, even in the minimal sociality of a mirror image. Only by recognizing its image in a mirror, Lacan noted, does an infant develop an illusory yet delightful self-image as a unified being. The feminist legal theorist Drucilla Cornell uses Lacan to show how crucial it is for society to grant women reproductive rights, for these are ultimately about her bodily integrity and sense of self.

   By seeing subjectivity and individuation as social and even political processes, these feminist thinkers provide a way of thinking about people's involvement in common activities. Echoing the views of many American feminists (such as Virginia Held in her criticism of Thomas Hobbes's atomism), they argue that people do not spring into the world fully formed. They are here by virtue of their caregivers, attachments, and relationships. Continental thinkers add that these attachments (or what psychoanalysts call "cathexes") continue to shape subjectivity.

3. In one piece, reflecting on what seems to occur in deliberative forums, I noted that "the ancient view of reasoning as conversation holds that reasoning itself is a social event. We reason with others through our conversing, not merely in the presence of others. When I see people deliberate together about public issues I see this kind of reasoning occurring, in the back and forth of conversation, as people try to unfold a problem together, each offering a perspective, an anecdote, or concern. As this process goes on for a while, participants create an understanding of the topography of a political issue and they begin to see how various options would or would not be able to navigate that terrain. The more I watch this phenomenon proceed, the less and less relevant Habermas and Rawls become. I am not watching how a series of views fare in the tribunal of public reason; I am watching how a public develops an understanding that it could not create if everyone tried to reason alone" ("Getting the Public's Intelligence," an interview with Noëlle McAfee, *Higher Education Exchange* [2004]: 44–54; quote on 47).

8. Public Knowledge

1. Even in this weak formulation I may be granting too much democratic character to the representative scheme. Frank Michelman characterizes the liberal (which I take to be nearly synonymous with representative) position as follows: "Standing by itself, the liberal political deontology I have charted thus far does not—at least it does not directly and self-evidently—require deep democracy. It does not require authorship of the fundamental laws by everyone, not even in any remotely figurative, much less any 'nonfictively attributable,' sense. All it directly requires is consent in principle by everyone affected—that everyone should have, as I put it above, 'what are actually, for them as individuals (whether they appreciate this at the moment or not), good reasons to consent'" (James Bohman and William Rehg, *Deliberative Democracy: Essays on Reason and Politics* [Cambridge, Mass.: MIT Press, 1997], 154–155). Rawls's position is even weaker. In *Political Liberalism* he claims that a law is legitimate if it is made "in accordance with a constitution the essentials of which all citizens may reasonably be expected to endorse in the light of principles and ideals acceptable to them as reasonable and rational. This is the liberal principle of legitimacy" (*Political Liberalism* [New York: Columbia University Press, 1996], 217). In other words, the people do not need to consent to the law or even the government. If the provenance of a law is an acceptable constitution, then the law is deemed legitimate—no matter how much the majority of the people may abhor the law.

2. Deliberative democrats have a much more stringent conception of legitimacy than what I am outlining here. As the deliberative theorist Joshua Cohen writes, "Because the members of a democratic association regard deliberative proce-

dures as the source of *legitimacy*, it is important to them that the terms of their association not merely *be* the results of their deliberation, but also be *manifest* to them as such. They prefer institutions in which the connections between deliberation and outcomes are evident to ones in which the connections are less clear" ("Procedure and Substance in Deliberative Democracy," in *Deliberative Democracy: Essays on Reason and Politics*, ed. James Bohman and William Rehg, 73 [Cambridge, MA: MIT Press, 1997]).

3. Here's Plato's estimation of democratic man: "And so he lives on, yielding day by day to the desire at hand. Sometimes he drinks heavily while listening to the flute; at other times, he drinks only water and is on a diet; sometimes he goes in for physical training; at other times, he's idle and neglects everything; and sometimes he even occupies himself with what he takes to be philosophy. He often engages in politics, leaping up from his seat and saying and doing whatever comes into his mind. If he happens to admire soldiers, he's carried in that direction, if money-makers, in that one. There's neither order nor necessity in his life, but he calls it pleasant, free, and blessedly happy, and he follows it for as long as he lives" (Plato, *Republic*, trans. G.M.A. Grube [Cambridge: Hackett Publishing, 1992], 232) (561c–e).

4. Ultimately I think Kant's legitimacy thesis comes much closer to the deliberative one outlined by Cohen than the thin, representative one sketched above.

5. The temporality of this adjudication raises some questions. To the extent people are trying to ascertain what will work in the future, there is always immense uncertainty. What I am calling for, though, is that people decide whether a policy is sound based upon their present concerns, values, and aims.

6. In Seyla Benhabib's view, legitimacy arises only "from the free and unconstrained public deliberation of all about matters of common concern. Thus a public sphere of deliberation about matters of mutual concern is essential to the legitimacy of democratic institutions" (*Democracy and Difference* [Princeton, N.J.: Princeton University Press, 1996], 68).

7. See for example the articles by James Bohman, Jack Knight, and James Johnson in Bohman and Rehg, *Deliberative Democracy*. See also Jürgen Habermas, "Three Normative Models of Democracy," in *Democracy and Difference*, ed. Seyla Benhabib, 21–30 (Princeton: Princeton University Press, 1996) and *The Inclusion of the Other: Studies in Political Theory*, ed. Ciaran Cronin and Pablo de Greiff (Cambridge, Mass.: MIT Press, 1998) and, especially, Habermas's "Popular Sovereignty as Procedure" in Bohman and Rehg, *Deliberative Democracy*, 35–65.

8. We might call this epistemic proceduralism, to borrow David Estlund's term, if not his analysis, in "Beyond Fairness and Deliberation: The Epistemic Dimension of Democratic Authority" in Bohman and Rehg, *Deliberative Democracy*.

9. Ibid.

10. See chapter 1 of McAfee, *Habermas, Kristeva, and Citizenship* (Ithaca: Cornell University Press, 2000).

11. I say they are neo-Platonists only in their sense that the people do not have the wherewithal to rule themselves. In other respects, they certainly do not approach Plato's genius.

12. For a good account of this school of thought, see Daniel Yankelovich, *Coming to Public Judgment: Making Democracy Work in a Complex World* (Syracuse, N.Y.: Syracuse University Press, 1991), 17–21.

13. Habermas adopts a much more promising approach in his later work, especially in *Between Facts and Norms*, where he points to the way that new social movements have held the political system under siege (*Between Facts and Norms*, trans. William Rehg [Cambridge: MIT Press, 1996], 359).

14. This last point is spelled out beautifully in P. Christopher Smith's work on Aristotle and Gadamer, "Historical Perspectives on Contemporary Hermeneutics: The Uses of Aristotle in Gadamer's Recovery of Consultative Reasoning: *Sunesis, Sungnome, Epieikeia*, and *Sumbouleuesthai*," *Chicago–Kent Law Review* 76 (2000): 73.

15. I am indebted to David Mathews, who made this point more than a decade ago. It is evident in the work we have coauthored, published by the Kettering Foundation.

16. For a more sustained reading of Dewey's work on democracy being a way of life, see John J. Stuhr, *Pragmatism, Postmodernism, and the Future of Philosophy* (New York and London: Routledge, 2003), 45–74.

17. On this point, see Cass Sunstein's warning about the dangers of "enclave deliberation" of like-minded people. Sunstein notes that, no matter how diligently participants might restrict themselves to reason giving, their perspectives will skew the sorts of reasons and arguments they employ, leading participants to become more entrenched in their views. Sunstein enters "a plea for ensuring that deliberation occurs within a large and heterogeneous public sphere, and for guarding against a situation in which like-minded people are walling themselves off from alternative perspectives" ("The Law of Group Polarization," in James Fishkin and Peter Laslett, eds., *Debating Deliberative Democracy* [Malden, Mass.: Blackwell, 2003], 90).

18. See, for example, "Communication and the Other: Beyond Deliberative Democracy" in Iris Young, *Intersecting Voices: Dilemmas of Gender, Political Philosophy, and Policy* (Princeton, N.J.: Princeton University Press, 1997).

19. Of the various kinds of deliberative forums I have observed, James Fishkin's "deliberative polls" offer the greatest opportunity for people to deliberate with unlike others, for each small group session is itself a cross-section of a polity. For example, deliberative polls held in Great Britain in 1993 on the topic of crime included the gamut of citizens, criminals included. A deliberative poll

in the United States, in part on the topic of the family, included a so-called "welfare mother" from the projects in Chicago deliberating face to face with a wealthy matron from Westchester. These were very enlightening encounters for all involved. But of course, these "opportunities" for deliberating with unlike others are limited to those who have been randomly selected to participate. Fortunately there are other possibilities for public deliberation, with their diversity a matter of how much effort the convenors make to engage broadly. Some forums held through the National Issues Forums are quite diverse, especially citywide deliberative forums, which Grand Rapids, Michigan, has held for many years. Information about the National Issues Forums is available online at www.nifi.org.

20. See Cynthia Willett, *The Soul of Justice: Social Bonds and Racial Hubris* (Ithaca and London: Cornell University Press, 2001).

21. Unpublished remarks made at the annual meeting of the American Political Science Association, Boston, 2002.

9. Three Models of Democratic Deliberation

1. NIF and NIC refer to two different entities: the National Issues Forums (NIF) and the National Issues Convention (NIC). The former is a network of civic organizations in the United States (with sister networks in many countries throughout the world) that periodically holds deliberative forums in their own organizations and communities, using briefing materials produced by the Kettering Foundation and Public Agenda. These "issue books" lay out three or four possible courses of action on a given problem, drawing out the costs and consequences of each. For more information, consult their Web site at http://www.nifi.org/. The National Issues Convention is the name of two deliberative polls conducted by James Fishkin in the United States, the first in 1996 in Austin, Texas, and the second in 2003 in Philadelphia, Pennsylvania. To make matters a bit more confusing, both NIC events employed veteran moderators from the National Issues Forums, though they were explicitly briefed beforehand on the need to moderate according to the precepts of the first model of democratic deliberation, as I am laying it out here. Additionally, both NICs and many other deliberative polls have provided issue briefing materials drafted in line with the principles of the NIF issue books, though the NIC briefing materials avoid any language of working toward common ground.

2. I am a bit suspicious of the claim that social science research is primarily empirical, as opposed to work in the humanities, philosophy included. The social scientist's focus on the individuals and their preferences, as discussed here, does betray a strong philosophical commitment.

3. A more thorough overview of the social choice project can be found in Jon Elster and Aanund Hylland, eds., *Foundations of Social Choice Theory* (Cambridge: Cambridge University Press, 1986); K. J. Arrow, *Social Choice and Individual Values*, 2nd ed. (New York: Wiley, 1963); and John S. Dryzek, *Deliberative Democracy and Beyond: Liberals, Critics, Contestations* (Oxford: Oxford University Press, 2000).

4. In a public deliberation, the search to maximize one's own preference for X may entail offering generally acceptable reasons for others also to prefer X. If preferences are transformed to the point that individual preference disappears—when the deliberator's focus is on seeking agreement—then we are no longer in the realm of model 1 but into model 2. At a certain point, the line between the models has to do with perspective: the first focuses on individual preference, the second on individuals offering reasons they hope will be acceptable to all.

5. Some preference-based theorists have a very narrow view of how preferences are transformed. Adam Przeworski argues that deliberation informs participants about which kind of means will satisfy their given preferences or that their preferences might change to be in keeping with what they really wanted ("Deliberation and Ideological Domination," in Elster, ed., *Deliberative Democracy* [Cambridge, U.K.: Cambridge University Press, 1998]). There is little room in Przeworski's picture for Robert Luskin, James Fishkin, and Roger Jowell's ("Considered Opinions: Deliberative Polling in Britain," *British Journal of Political Science* 32, no. 3 [July 2002]: 455) broader notion that people change their individual preferences to more considered judgments that take into account the needs and concerns of others.

6. See note 3.

7. John Dryzek rebuts this view perfectly (*Deliberative Democracy and Beyond* 45–47). Usually in the course of deliberations, participants can unmask bigoted views and show how illegitimate they are. As I have observed first hand, exogenous constraints are rarely needed.

10. The Limits of Deliberation, Democratic Myths, New Frontiers

1. See James S. Catterall and Emily Brizendine, "Proposition 13: Effects on High School Curricula, 1978–1983," *American Journal of Education* 93, no. 3 (May 1985): 327–351 and the PBS program from the Merrow Report, *The Special Challenge of Proposition 13: How California's 1978 Tax Revolution Affected the Schools and What Legislators Are Doing About It*, http://www.pbs.org/merrow/tv/ftw/prop13.html.

11. Media and the Public Sphere

1. "Blogosphere (alternate: BlogSphere or BloggingSphere) is the collective term encompassing all weblogs or blogs as a community or social network. Many

weblogs are densely interconnected; bloggers read others' blogs, link to them, reference them in their own writing, and post comments on each others' blogs. Because of this, the interconnected blogs have grown their own culture" (Wikipedia, http://en.wikipedia.org/wiki/Blogophere).

2. http://www.globalvoicesonline.org.

3. "A wiki . . . is a type of website that allows users to add and edit content and is especially suited for collaborative authoring.

   "The term *wiki* also sometimes refers to the collaborative software itself (wiki engine) that facilitates the operation of such a website (*see wiki software*)" (Wikipedia, http://en.wikipedia.org/wiki/Wiki).

4. See Mancer Olson Jr., *The Logic of Collective Action: Public Goods and the Theory of Groups* (Cambridge: Harvard University Press, 1971) and Todd Sandler, *Collective Action: Theory and Applications* (Ann Arber: University of Michigan Press, 1992).

5. See http://en.wikipedia.org/wiki/Wikitorial and http://bayosphere.com/blog/dangillmor/072305/kinsley.

6. See http://cyber.law.harvard.edu/webcred.

WORKS CITED

Abraham, Nicolas and Maria Torok. 1994. *The Shell and the Kernel*. Chicago: University of Chicago Press.

Allison, David B. "Iconologies: Reading Simulations with Plato and Nietzsche." http://www.sunysb.edu/philosophy/research/allison_2.html.

Arendt, Hannah. 1958. *The Human Condition*. 2nd ed. Chicago: University of Chicago Press.

Armstrong, David. 2002. "Dick Cheney's Song of America: Drafting a Plan for Global Dominance." *Harper's* 305, no. 1829 (October): 76–83.

Armstrong, David and Joseph Trento. 2007. *America and the Islamic Bomb: The Deadly Compromise*. Hanover, NH: Steerforth Press.

Arrow, K. J. 1963. *Social Choice and Individual Values*. 2nd ed. New York: Wiley.

Bhargava, Rajeev. 2000. "Restoring Decency to Barbaric Societies." In *Truth v. Justice: The Morality of Truth Commissions*, ed. Robert I. Rotberg and Dennis Thompson, 45–67. Princeton and Oxford: Princeton University Press.

Benhabib, Seyla. 1996. *Democracy and Difference*. Princeton: Princeton University Press.

Bettelheim, Bruno. 1960. *The Informed Heart*. Glencoe, IL: Free Press.

Bohman, James and William Rehg. 1997. *Deliberative Democracy: Essays on Reason and Politics*. Cambridge, MA: MIT Press.

Bollas, Christopher. 1995. *Cracking Up: The Work of Unconscious Experience*. New York: Hill and Wang.

Boraine, Alex. 2000. "Truth and Reconciliation in South Africa: The Third Way." In *Truth v. Justice: The Morality of Truth Commissions*, ed. Robert I. Rotberg and Dennis Thompson, 141–157. Princeton and Oxford: Princeton University Press.

Borradori, Giovanna. 2003. *Philosophy in a Time of Terror: Dialogues with Jürgen Habermas and Jacques Derrida*. Chicago and London: University of Chicago Press.

Brennan, Teresa. 2004. *The Transmission of Affect*. Ithaca: Cornell University Press.

Butler, Judith. 2004. *Precarious Life: The Powers of Mourning and Violence*. London and New York: Verso.

Calhoun, Craig. 1992. *Habermas and the Public Sphere*. Cambridge, MA: MIT Press.

Carson, Rachel. 1962. *Silent Spring*. Boston: Houghton Mifflin.

Cohen, Joshua. 1997a. "Deliberation and Democratic Legitimacy." In *Deliberative*

Democracy: Essays on Reason and Politics, ed. James Bohman and William Rehg, 67–91. Cambridge, MA: MIT Press.

——. 1997b. "Procedure and Substance in Deliberative Democracy." In *Deliberative Democracy: Essays on Reason and Politics*, ed. James Bohman and William Rehg, 407–437. Cambridge, MA: MIT Press.

Cornell, Drucilla. 1995. *The Imaginary Domain: Abortion, Pornography, and Sexual Harassment*. New York and London: Routledge.

Crocker, David. 2000. "Truth Commissions, Transitional Justice, and Civil Society." In *Truth v. Justice: The Morality of Truth Commissions*, ed. Robert I. Rotberg and Dennis Thompson, 99–121. Princeton and Oxford: Princeton University Press..

Curtis, Kimberley. 1999. *Our Sense of the Real: Aesthetic Experience and Arendtian Politics*. Ithaca and London: Cornell University Press.

Derrida, Jacques. 1992. *The Other Heading: Reflections on Today's Europe*. Bloomington: Indiana University Press.

Des Pres, Terrence. 1976. *The Survivor: An Anatomy of Life in the Death Camps*. Oxford: Oxford University Press.

Dewey, John. 1954. *The Public and Its Problems*. Athens, OH: Swallow Press.

——. 1986. *The Collected Works of John Dewey, Later Works*. Carbondale, IL: Southern Illinois University Press.

Dionne, E. J., Jr. 1991. *Why Americans Hate Politics*. New York: Simon & Schuster.

Dryzek, John S. 2000. *Deliberative Democracy and Beyond: Liberals, Critics, Contestations*. Oxford: Oxford University Press.

du Toit, André. 2000. "The Moral Foundations of the South African TRC: Truth as Acknowledgment and Justice as Recognition." In *Truth v. Justice: The Morality of Truth Commissions*, ed. Robert I. Rotberg and Dennis Thompson, 122–140. Princeton and Oxford: Princeton University Press..

Elster, Jon. 1997. "The Market and the Forum: Three Varieties of Political Theory." In *Deliberative Democracy: Essays on Reason and Politics*, ed. James Bohman and William Rehg, 3–33. Cambridge, MA: MIT Press.

Elster, Jon, ed. 1998. *Deliberative Democracy*. Cambridge, UK: Cambridge University Press.

Elster, Jon and Aanund Hylland, eds. 1986. *Foundations of Social Choice Theory*. Cambridge, UK: Cambridge University Press.

Erikson, Erik H. 1950. *Childhood and Society*. New York: Norton.

Felman, Shoshana. 2002. *The Juridical Unconscious: Trials and Traumas in the Twentieth Century*. Cambridge, MA: Harvard University Press.

Fishkin, James. 1991. *Democracy and Deliberation: New Directions for Democratic Reform*. New Haven: Yale University Press.

——. 1995. *The Voice of the People: Public Opinion and Democracy*. New Haven: Yale University Press.

Fishkin, James and Peter Laslett, eds. 2003. *Debating Deliberative Democracy*. Malden, MA: Blackwell.

Fraser, Nancy. 1989. *Unruly Practices: Power, Discourse and Gender in Contemporary Social Theory*. Minneapolis: University of Minnesota Press.

Frazer, Elizabeth. 2002. "Democracy, Citizenship, and Gender." In *Democratic Theory Today*, ed. April Carter and Geoffrey Stokes, 73–96. Cambridge, UK: Polity.

Freud, Sigmund. 1961. *Civilization and Its Discontents*. New York: Norton.

Gastil, John. 2000. *By Popular Demand*. Berkeley: University of California Press.

Gevisser, Mark. 1997. "The Witnesses." *New York Times Magazine*, 27 June.

Grayling, A. C. 2001. "The Evil Banality of Ordinary People." *Financial Times* (London), October 20, Books Section, 6.

Gutmann, Amy and Dennis Thompson. 1996. *Democracy and Disagreement*. Cambridge, MA: Belknap Press.

Habermas, Jürgen. 1977. "Hannah Arendt's Communications Concept of Power." *Social Research* 44:3–24.

——. 1984. *The Theory of Communicative Action. Volume I. Reason and the Rationalization of Society*. Trans. Thomas McCarthy. Boston: Beacon Press.

——. 1987. *The Theory of Communicative Action. Volume II. Lifeworld and System: A Critique of Functionalist Reason*. Trans. Thomas McCarthy. Boston: Beacon Press.

——. 1989. *Jürgen Habermas on Society and Politics: A Reader*. Ed. Steven Seidman. Boston: Beacon Press.

——. 1990. *The Philosophical Discourse of Modernity*. Trans. Frederick G. Lawrence. Cambridge, MA: MIT Press.

——. 1992. *Postmetaphysical Thinking: Philosophical Essays*. Trans. William Mark Hohengarten. Cambridge, MA: MIT Press.

——. 1996a. *Between Facts and Norms*. Trans. William Rehg. Cambridge, MA: MIT Press.

——. 1996b. "Three Normative Models of Democracy." In *Democracy and Difference*, ed. Seyla Benhabib, 21–30. Princeton: Princeton University Press.

——. 1998. *The Inclusion of the Other: Studies in Political Theory*. Ed. Ciaran Cronin and Pablo de Greiff. Cambridge, MA: MIT Press.

Hedges, Chris. 2002. *War Is a Force That Gives Us Meaning*. New York: Anchor.

Heidegger, Martin. 1977. *The Question Concerning Technology and Other Essays*. Trans. William Lovitt. New York: Harper & Row.

Herman, Judith. 1997. *Trauma and Recovery*. New York: Basic Books.

Honig, Bonnie. 1993. *Political Theory and the Displacement of Politics*. Ithaca: Cornell University Press.

Jaggar, Alison. 1983. *Feminist Politics and Human Nature*. Lanham, MD: Rowman & Littlefield.

Kant, Immanuel. 1970. *Kant's Political Writings*. Ed. Hans Reiss. Trans. H. B. Nisbet. Cambridge, UK: Cambridge University Press.

Kohlberg, Lawrence. 1958. "The Development of Modes of Thinking and Choices in Years 10 to 16." Ph.D. diss., University of Chicago.

——. 1981. *The Philosophy of Moral Development*. San Francisco: Harper and Row.

Kristeva, Julia. 1980. *Desire in Language*. Trans. Thomas Gora, Alice Jardine, and Leon Roudiez. Ed. Leon Roudiez. New York: Columbia University Press.

——. 1982. *Powers of Horror: An Essay on Abjection*. Trans. Leon S. Roudiez. New York: Columbia University Press.

——. 1984. *Revolution in Poetic Language*. Trans. Margaret Waller. New York: Columbia University Press.

——. 1987. *Tales of Love*. Trans. Leon S. Roudiez. New York: Columbia University Press.

——. 1989. *Language: The Unknown*. Trans. Anne M. Menke. New York: Columbia University Press.

——. 1995. *New Maladies of the Soul*. Trans. Ross Guberman. New York: Columbia University Press.

——. 1996. *Sens et non-sens de la révolte: Pouvoirs et limites de la psychanalyse I*. Paris: Librairie Arthème Fayard.

——. 2000. *Crisis of the European Subject*. Trans. Susan Fairfield. New York: Other Press.

——. 2001a. *Hannah Arendt*. Trans. Ross Guberman. New York: Columbia University Press.

——. 2001b. *Hannah Arendt: Life Is a Narrative*. Trans. Frank Collins. Toronto: University of Toronto Press.

Laclau, Ernesto, and Chantal Mouffe. 1985. *Hegemony and Socialist Strategy: Towards a Radical Democratic Politics*. London: Verso.

Lippmann, Walter. 1925. *The Phantom Public*. New York: Macmillan.

——. 1965. *Public Opinion*. New York: Free Press.

Luhmann, Niklas. 1982. *The Differentiation of Society*. Trans. Stephen Holmes and Charles Larmore. New York: Columbia University Press.

Luskin, Robert, James Fishkin, and Roger Jowell. 2002. "Considered Opinions: Deliberative Polling in Britain." *British Journal of Political Science* 32, no. 3 (July): 455.

Mansbridge, Jane. 1998. "Feminism and Democracy." In Anne Phillips, ed., *Feminism and Politics*. Oxford: Oxford University Press.

Marx, Karl. 1934. *The Eighteenth Brumaire of Louis Bonaparte*. Moscow: Progress Publishers.

Mathews, David. 2004. "Afterword: 'What Public?'" *Higher Education Exchange*. Dayton, OH: Kettering Foundation Press.

McAfee, Noëlle. 2000. *Habermas, Kristeva, and Citizenship*. Ithaca: Cornell University Press.

———. 2004a. "Public Knowledge." *Philosophy and Social Criticism* 30, no. 2: 139–157.

———. 2004b. "Three Models of Democratic Deliberation." *Journal of Speculative Philosophy* 18, no. 1: 44–59.

Miller, David. 1992. "Deliberative Democracy and Social Choice." *Political Studies* 40 (Special Issue): 54–67.

Mills, Charles. 1997. *The Racial Contract*. Ithaca: Cornell University Press.

Minow, Martha. 1998. *Between Vengeance and Forgiveness: Facing History After Genocide and Mass Violence*. Boston: Beacon Press.

———. 2000. "The Hope for Healing: What Can Truth Commissions Do?" In *Truth v. Justice: The Morality of Truth Commissions*, ed. Robert I. Rotberg and Dennis Thompson, 235–260. Princeton and Oxford: Princeton University Press.

Morris, David. 2006. "The Body as the Institution of Temporality and as the Temporality of Institution." Unpublished paper read at the Merleau Ponty Circle, Washington, D.C., October 27.

Mouffe, Chantal. 2000. *The Democratic Paradox*. London and New York: Verso.

Nietzsche, Friedrich. 1956. *The Birth of Tragedy and the Genealogy of Morals*. Trans. Francis Golffing. Garden City, NY: Doubleday Anchor.

———. 1998. *Twilight of the Idols*. Trans. Duncan Large. Oxford: Oxford University Press.

Nino, Carlos. 1995. *Radical Evil on Trial*. New Haven: Yale University Press.

Oliver, Kelly. 2001. *Witnessing: Beyond Recognition*. Minneapolis: University of Minnesota Press.

———. 2003. "Forgiveness and Subjectivity." *Philosophy Today* 47, no. 3: 280–304.

———. 2004. *The Colonization of Psychic Space: A Psychoanalytic Social Theory of Oppression*. Minneapolis and London: University of Minnesota Press.

Pateman, Carole. 1988. *The Sexual Contract*. Stanford: Stanford University Press.

Plato. 1992. *Republic*. Trans. G.M.A. Grube. Cambridge, MA: Hackett.

Prenshaw, Peggy. 1998. "Humanities Study and Public Deliberation." *Higher Education Exchange*. Dayton, OH: Kettering Foundation Press.

Putnam, Robert, Robert Leonardi, and Raffaella Nanetti. 1994. *Making Democracy Work: Civic Traditions in Modern Italy*. Princeton: Princeton University Press.

Rawls, John. 1996. *Political Liberalism.* New York: Columbia University Press.

———. 1999. *The Law of Peoples*. Cambridge, MA: Harvard University Press.

———. 2001. *Justice as Fairness: A Restatement*. Cambridge, MA: The Belknap Press of Harvard University Press.

Rorty, Richard. 1991. *Objectivity, Relativism, and Truth: Philosophical Papers Volume I*. Cambridge, UK: Cambridge University Press.

Rotberg, Robert I. and Dennis Thompson, eds. 2000. *Truth v. Justice: The Morality of Truth Commissions*. Princeton and Oxford: Princeton University Press.

Roy, Olivier. 2004. *Globalized Islam: The Search for a New Ummah*. New York: Columbia University Press.

Rycroft, Charles. 1995. *A Critical Dictionary of Psychoanalysis, New Edition*. London and New York: Penguin.

Saunders, Harold H. 2005. *Politics Is About Relationship: A Blueprint for the Citizens' Century*. New York: Palgrave MacMillan.

Saunders, Harold and Randa Slim. 2006. "A Democratic Strategy for Change." Unpublished document.

Scarry, Elaine. 1985. *The Body in Pain: The Making and Unmaking of the World*. New York and Oxford: Oxford University Press.

Sen, Amartya. 1986. "Foundations of Social Choice Theory: An Epilogue." In *Foundations of Social Choice Theory*, ed. Jon Elster and Aanund Hylland, 213–238. Cambridge, UK: Cambridge University Press.

Sirianni, Carmen and Lewis Friedland. 2001. *Civic Innovation in America*. Berkeley: University of California Press.

——. 2005. *The Civic Renewal Movement: Community-Building and Democracy in the United States*. Dayton, OH: Kettering Foundation Press.

Slim, Randa. 2007. "Facing the Challenges of Emerging Democracies." *Kettering Review* 25, no. 1 (Winter): 27–38.

Smith, P. Christopher. 2000. "Historical Perspectives on Contemporary Hermeneutics: The Uses of Aristotle in Gadamer's Recovery of Consultative Reasoning: *Sunesis, Sungnome, Epieikeia*, and *Sumbouleuesthai*." *Chicago–Kent Law Review* 76:731.

Smith, Rogers M. 1997. "Still Blowing in the Wind: The American Quest for a Democratic, Scientific Political Science." In *American Academic Culture in Transformation: Fifty Years, Four Disciplines*, ed. Thomas Bender and Carl E. Schorske, 271–305. Princeton: Princeton University Press.

Stuhr, John J. 2003. *Pragmatism, Postmodernism, and the Future of Philosophy*. New York and London: Routledge.

Sullivan, Shannon. 2006. *Revealing Whiteness: The Unconscious Habits of Racial Privilege*. Bloomington: Indiana University Press.

Sunstein, Cass. 2003. "The Law of Group Polarization." In *Debating Deliberative Democracy*, ed. James Fishkin and Peter Laslett, 80–101. Malden, MA: Blackwell.

Taylor, Charles. 2004. *Modern Social Imaginaries*. Durham, NC: Duke University Press.

Truth and Reconciliation Commission [South Africa]. 1998. *Final Report*. Cape Town, 29 October.

Tutu, Desmond Mpilo. 1999. *No Future Without Forgiveness*. New York: Image Doubleday.

Viroli, Maurizio. 1999. *Republicanism*. Trans. Antony Shugaar. New York: Hill and Wang.

Volkan, Vamik. 1997. *Bloodlines: From Ethnic Pride to Ethnic Terrorism*. New York: Farrar, Straus & Giroux.

Walzer, Michael. 1983. *Spheres of Justice: A Defense of Pluralism and Equality*. New York: Basic Books.

Warren, Mark R. 2001. *Dry Bones Rattling: Community Building to Revitalize American Democracy*. Princeton: Princeton University Press.

Weber, Max. 1946. *Max Weber: Essays in Sociology*. Trans. and ed. H. H. Gerth and C. Wright Mills. New York: Oxford University Press.

Willett, Cynthia. 2001. *The Soul of Justice: Social Bonds and Racial Hubris*. Ithaca and London: Cornell University Press.

Wolin, Sheldon. 1996. "Fugitive Democracy." In *Democracy and Difference*, ed. Seyla Benhabib, 31–45. Princeton: Princeton University Press.

Yankelovich, Daniel. 1991. *Coming to Public Judgment: Making Democracy Work in a Complex World*. Syracuse, NY: Syracuse University Press.

Young, Iris. 1990. *Justice and the Politics of Difference*. Princeton: Princeton University Press.

———. 1997. *Intersecting Voices: Dilemmas of Gender, Political Philosophy, and Policy*. Princeton: Princeton University Press.

———. 2000. *Inclusion and Democracy*. Oxford: Oxford University Press.

Zaretsky, Eli. 2002. "Trauma and Dereification: September 11 and the Problem of Ontological Security." *Constellations* 9, no. 1 (March): 98–105.

Zerilli, Linda. 2005. *Feminism and the Abyss of Freedom*. Chicago: University of Chicago Press.

INDEX

AARP. *See* American Association of Retired Persons (AARP)
abjection, as defense mechanism, 50–53, 55–56
Abraham, Nicholas, 24–26, 43, 67
acting out, 4, 8, 79, 84. *See also* state violence; war; war on terror
Afghanistan, 77
Africa, 184; blogosphere, 196; genocide, 53, 56; truth and reconciliation commissions, 80, 85, 92, 103–4
African Americans, 41–46, 55, 153–54
After Virtue (McIntyre), 86
agonistic politics, 126–29, 178
agora, 98
Al Qaeda, 78
Allison, David, 36–37
American Association of Retired Persons (AARP), 155
The Antichrist (Nietzsche), 37
apathy of the public, 149–50
Arendt, Hannah: feminism and world-building freedom, 134–40; and Heidegger, 105–6; and the human condition, 97–99; and integrative deliberation, 166; Kristeva's analysis, 99–105; on modes of living, 98; on public sphere, 106; on public testimony, 93; on silencing the public sphere, 64; on "space of appearance," 59, 98
Aristotle, 18, 94, 106, 120
Armstrong, David, 71, 72, 77–78
authoritarian regimes, 19, 57–60, 64–66. *See also* state violence
autoimmunity, destructive, 75–78
autonomy: meaning in preference-based

model of deliberation, 162; meaning in rational proceduralist model of deliberation, 163–64; modern ideal of, 38–39, 207n3

Balkans, 53
Barber, Ben, 123, 166
Bartlettt, Dan, 88–89
battered wife syndrome, 62
BBC, 198
Benhabib, Seyla, 146, 164–65, 180, 213n6
Berkman Center for Internet and Society, 194, 196
Berners-Lee, Tim, 190
Bettelheim, Bruno, 66
Bhargava, Rajeev, 59–60, 70
bigotry, 148, 216n7
Black Panthers, 27
blogosphere, 83–84, 187–204; in Africa, 196; criticisms of, 187–90; defined, 216–17n1; and deliberative democracy, 202–3; Global Voices, 193–99; interlinking of, 200; and journalism, 197–204; and "talking cure," 8
Bloodlines: From Ethnic Pride to Ethnic Terrorism (Volkan), 2–3
The Body in Pain (Scarry), 61
Bollas, Christopher, 3–4, 112
Boyte, Harry, 116, 123, 166
Brazile, Donna, 88
Brennan, Teresa, 30
Brzezinki, Zbigniew, 77
Bunker, Archie, 148
Bush, George H. W., 71–72
Butler, Judith, 11, 50, 55, 91–92

sublimation (*continued*)
108; and the Internet (*see* media); Oliver on, 11, 14–15, 23–24; public sphere and failure to sublimate desires, 54–56; public sphere and the political unconscious, 11–15, 18, 23–24, 55; and silencing of public sphere, 65; and witnessing, 85
Sullivan, Shannon, 43–45
Sunni Muslims, 2, 4
Sustein, Cass, 214n17
systems theory, 191–92
Szmaglewska, Seweryna, 65

Tajikistan, 110, 184, 185
Tales of Love (Kristeva), 96
"talking cure," 7, 8, 32, 173. *See also* blogosphere; criminal tribunals; deliberative forums; truth and reconciliation commissions
Taylor, Charles, 38, 48
technology. *See* media
telos of human beings, 15–16
terror. *See* state violence
terrorism. *See* war on terror
Thompson, Dennis, 80, 86–89, 164
time: and identity formation, 129; time collapse, 2–4
Torok, Maria, 43
torture, purpose of, 61. *See also* state violence
"town meeting" model of deliberation, 123
transition to democracy, 109–10
transitional justice, 79–81
trauma, 28–47, 73–75; "chosen traumas," 111–12; and "collective raced unconscious," 43–46; and colonialism, 45–46; conflict fueled by religion and identity politics, 30; defense mechanisms, 31–32, 40–41, 48–50 (*see also* repetition compulsion); defined, 30–31; Derrida on, 74–76; disenchantment of the world, 38–41;

and fear of future trauma, 76–77; and fundamentalism, 39–41, 46–47; long-term effects, 62–63; media and transfer of trauma across generations, 46; modernity as product of traumas, 33–34; and narrative, 47; and nation-states, 48–50, 71–78; ordinary traumas, 32–34; and political identity of a people, 111–12; psychic effect as unconscious imprisonment, 3–4; and psychoanalysis, 30–32; psychological trauma inflicted for political purposes, 62–64; racial contract and the rise of modernity, 41–43; real world as fable and picture, 34–38; and repetition compulsion, 71–81; and "self-defense," 4; and sexism, 133–34; and time collapse, 2–4; war as "acting out" of trauma, 4, 50. *See also* recovery from traumatic events; September 11, 2001; state violence
Trauma and Recovery (Herman), 62–63
Trento, Joe, 77
truth and reconciliation commissions, 71; and countertransference, 103–4; and mourning, 92; narrative vs. forensic truths, 97; and psychoanalysis, 103; and reestablishment of public sphere, 9; and restoration of public being and public space, 85; in South Africa, 80; and "talking cure," 8; witnessing as a political act, 93–95, 97
Truth v. Justice (Rothberg and Thompson, eds.), 80
tsunami of 2004, 196
turning against the self, as defense mechanism, 31–32
Tutu, Desmond, Archbishop, 103–4
Twilight of the Idols (Nietzsche), 35

unconscious: Lacan's view of the unconscious as structured like a language, 7–8; peripheries of consciousness and the unconscious public sphere,